GUARDIAN OF SAVANNAH

Studies in Maritime History
William N. Still Jr., Series Editor

GUARDIAN
OF SAVANNAH

✳ ✳ ✳

Fort McAllister, Georgia, in the
Civil War and Beyond

ROGER S. DURHAM

The University of South Carolina Press

© 2008 University of South Carolina

Published by the University of South Carolina Press
Columbia, South Carolina 29208

www.sc.edu/uscpress

Manufactured in the United States of America

17 16 15 14 13 12 11 10 09 08   10 9 8 7 6 5 4 3 2 1

Library of Congress Cataloging-in-Publication Data

Durham, Roger S.
   Guardian of Savannah : Fort McAllister, Georgia, in the Civil War and beyond /
Roger S. Durham.
      p. cm. — (Studies in maritime history)
   Includes bibliographical references and index.
   ISBN 978-1-57003-742-9 (cloth : alk. paper)
   1. Fort McAllister (Ga. : Fort)—History. 2. Savannah (Ga.)—History—Siege, 1864.
3. Georgia—History—Civil War, 1861–1865. 4. Fortification—Conservation and
restoration—Georgia—Bryan County. 5. Historic preservation—Georgia—Bryan County.
I. Title.
   E477.41.D87 2008
   973.7'378—dc22
                                                                    2007051947

For my parents

CONTENTS

ILLUSTRATIONS

PREFACE

In the autumn of 1969, I visited Fort McAllister for the first time. I was a soldier serving at Hunter Army Airfield in Savannah, Georgia, and my interest in the Civil War had brought me to visit the site. Fascinated by the events that had occurred there, I found myself seeking to learn more. Ironically enough, nine years later I returned to Fort McAllister as superintendent of the historic site while employed by the Georgia Department of Natural Resources. During this time I became more aware of the complexity of the history that was there and how it had been overshadowed within the context of the conflict. I began seeking out the pieces of the puzzle. Although the basic story of the fort's history was well known, I found there was much more to be learned and set out to find the pieces and put them all together. That journey has led me across many years, and I have looked into many dark corners of archives and libraries to find those lost pieces. Many of the participants left an archival trail behind them through diaries, journals, letters, reports, photographs, service records, and pension records. In these documents they told their own stories in their own words, and by assembling them I gained insight into what it was like to have served there during those times. It is now time to put them all together.

The story of Fort McAllister has been narrated in magazine articles and books about the Civil War, but to date no comprehensive study has been made that focuses on the history of this facet of that great conflict. This book seeks to fill that void by exploring the story of Fort McAllister, its development, construction, and its adversaries and to place those events into their proper perspective and significance. My approach to this book is different than a mere recitation of facts, events, and dates. Where possible, rather than paraphrasing their words, I have made extensive use of quotes to allow the participants themselves to speak directly to the reader. In this way I have tried to put the reader in touch with the human element present in every historical event, as hearing the words of those who were there is as close to the actual event as the reader will ever get.

Fort McAllister's significance lies in three major points. First, it was used as a testing ground where the Confederates refined concepts of coastal-fortification design, and the Federals evaluated new warships and ordnance under combat conditions. Second, it was the final obstacle to Gen. William T. Sherman's March to the Sea and proved to be the key to his capture of Savannah. Gen. Sherman himself considered the success or failure of his march to hinge on Fort McAllister. And third, the physical survival of the fort to the present day is due to Henry Ford's interest and initial renovation in the mid-1930s. Thanks to Ford, this significant example of a Confederate coastal-defense earthwork fortification exists today while most have fallen victim to neglect or modern development.

I eventually left Fort McAllister to pursue other opportunities, but I was still connected to the fort and its history. In 1988 the staff at Fort McAllister brought to my attention the William Daniel Dixon journal and *Republican Blues Daybook* in the possession of Mrs. Caroline Thomas Bosbyshell of St. Petersburg, Florida. Mrs. Bosbyshell is a descendant of William Dixon and these documents had been handed down through their family. She provided photocopies of the original documents to the historic site, and I was allowed access to these photocopies in order to compile a transcript of each, for independent study credit for my master's degree. The Dixon journal provided special insight into Fort McAllister's history. His unit, Company C of the 1st Regiment, Georgia Volunteer Infantry, the Republican Blues, had been part of the garrison throughout the period of the naval attacks, and his journal is a day-by-day record of those events and the days of routine boredom and garrison duty. The excerpts from all sources are replicated with that author's spellings, constructions, and grammar, with some editorial additions within square brackets to help, it is hoped, in reading the excerpt; underlining has been retained.

Guardian of Savannah is the story of Fort McAllister, a massive sand fort that grew from a humble battery. It was one of many such defenses built to protect the city of Savannah, Georgia, against an attack from the sea. McAllister's role as the guardian of the Ogeechee River protected what was termed Savannah's backdoor. Located about twelve miles south of the Savannah River, it became the southernmost fortification upon which all of that city's eastern defenses were anchored.

As in every conflict, innovation in the technology of warfare allows the combatants to wage war with a more deadly efficiency. Two of the greatest developments of the Civil War were the rifled cannon and the ironclad warship. On the Georgia coast, these new weapons closed one chapter of military technology and opened a new one. The impact of the development of the rifled cannon was clearly illustrated against the masonry walls of Fort Pulaski, which protected the entrance to the Savannah River. The fort's fall to the rifled cannon sounded the end of the era of brick forts. But the humble sand parapets of Fort McAllister showed the way for future design and construction of static fortifications to defend against the rifled cannon.

The ironclad monitors of the U.S. Navy are hailed as the beginning of today's modern navy. Their baptism of fire in Hampton Roads, Virginia, against the Confederate ironclad *Virginia* pitted iron against iron, but they were also tested under the guns of Fort McAllister on the Ogeechee River where iron was pitted against earth. The lessons learned there by both sides had far-reaching consequences. In the end, Fort McAllister's final threat did not come from the sea but from beyond the western reaches of the state, and the sea itself was the goal the opponent sought to attain. Fort McAllister's final defense won the admiration and respect of friend and foe alike.

However, the history of Fort McAllister did not end with the conclusion of the Civil War. When the guns fell silent, and the soldiers returned to their homes, Fort McAllister was abandoned and forgotten. The story of its postwar history and how one man, Henry Ford, was instrumental in the fort being preserved is a chapter of its story that is as intriguing as any of its Civil War history. The complete story of Fort McAllister reaches well into the twenty-first century.

The story of Fort McAllister is like no other to come from the Civil War. The battles fought there did not cover large masses of land or involve tens of thousands of soldiers. The battlefield at Fort McAllister was compacted to a mere few acres of land; its garrison was a handful of men who stood defiantly against extreme odds. When machines of war failed, only overwhelming numbers of men succeeded in the end. The defenders of Georgia's soil fought with a sense of duty and honor for their homes and families. They fought for their land with guns and swords, lead and iron, and the land itself, for at Fort McAllister the very soil beneath their feet became a weapon of defense. This is the story of the hallowed ground of Fort McAllister, the guardian of the Ogeechee and Savannah.

ACKNOWLEDGMENTS

This book has been a long time in coming, and many people helped me and inspired me as I traveled through the years seeking the pieces of this puzzle. First would be Mary Jewett, director of the Georgia Historical Commission, who pointed me in the right direction. Alston C. Waylor, director of the Historic Sites Division of the Georgia Department of Natural Resources, gave me a chance when I needed one. Both he and Billy Townsend provided inspiration for me. Bill Marx of the Parks and Historic Sites Division of the Georgia Department of Natural Resources also provided me with support and realized that I was the one they needed at Fort McAllister at that point in time.

Bell Irwin Wiley was an unending source of inspiration and guidance for me as I tried to find my way to where I wanted to be. And he encouraged me to pursue my goals.

I can never fully express my gratitude to all those who deserve it, but here are a few of the principal people to whom I am indebted.

Lawrence E. Babits
Mary H. Bonaud
Caroline Thomas Bosbyshell
Danny Brown
Ford R. Bryan
Frank Chance
Paul Chance
Tom Dale
Tommy Darieng
Tom Dickey
John Duncan
Karl R. Eby
Robert C. Ellsworth
John Henry Harden
Col. Lindsey P. Henderson, Jr.
Robert Holcombe

Talley Kirkland
Walter W. Meeks, III
Ralph Reed
Tommy Ridley
Ralph Righton
David Roth
William Scaife
Greg Schmidl
Scott Smith
Henry Struble
Carolyn Clay Swiggart
Norman V. Turner
Alston Waylor
R. Martin Willett
Robert Willingham, Jr.

A special mention is due Danny Brown, superintendent at Fort McAllister State Historic Park, who has been a friend and colleague over the years through thick and thin regardless of the circumstances. Hiring him was one of the best things I ever did, and he has shared my vision of what Fort McAllister could be. He shouldered the burden of carrying forward when I had to put it down.

My wife, JoAnn, has faithfully followed me on this magical history tour that has been our lives since we left Fort McAllister, and she supported me in my affliction as I've researched and studied and sought the answers that are found in this book. Our children, Star and Lacy, have dutifully followed their Daddy and been a source of wonder and fascination for me over the years. I thank you all.

The following institutions are acknowledged for their assistance in this research.

Bentley Historical Library, Ann Arbor, Michigan
Civil War Naval Museum, Columbus, Georgia
Emory University Library, Decatur, Georgia
Fort McAllister State Historic Park, Georgia
Georgia Department of Archives and History, Atlanta, Georgia
Georgia Department of Natural Resources, Atlanta, Georgia
Georgia Historical Society, Savannah, Georgia
Hagley Museum and Library, Wilmington, Delaware
Henry Ford Library, Dearborn, Michigan
Indiana Historical Society, Indianapolis, Indiana
Library of Congress, Washington, D.C.
Midway Museum, Midway, Georgia
National Archives, Washington, D.C.
Ohio Historical Society, Columbus, Ohio
Savannah Public Library, Savannah, Georgia
U.S. Army Heritage and Education Center, Carlisle, Pennsylvania
U.S. Army Heritage Museum, Carlisle, Pennsylvania
U.S. Army Military History Institute, Carlisle, Pennsylvania
University of Georgia Library, Athens, Georgia
University of Toledo Library, Toledo, Ohio
Western Reserve Historical Society, Cleveland, Ohio

GUARDIAN OF SAVANNAH

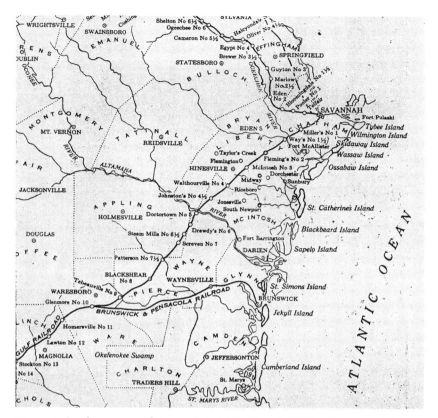

MAP 1. Southeast coast of Savannah in 1860. From J. T. Lloyd's topographical map of Georgia, drawn from state surveys, 1860

1

A Time of Change

The Georgia coast is an area of beauty and history. It vibrates with growth, industry, and vitality, and each year a multitude of visitors travel its highways, tour its points of interest, and seek its natural resources. But the beauty of Georgia's coast defies the fact that at one time, it was the stage upon which played the reality of war. That time was the 1860s, a decade of turbulent changes for the United States of America. Regional differences between the North and the South over issues such as states rights and slavery brought the nation to a crisis that split the country. The road that the union of states had followed since the founding of the nation became the road to war.

Abraham Lincoln was elected president in November 1860, and this precipitated a call for a convention of Southern states to discuss the idea of secession. By New Year's Day 1861, some Southern states had left the Union to form a Southern Confederacy they hoped could withstand Northern attempts to coerce their return to the Union. In January 1861 the crumbling nation faced an uncertain future. There was much activity in the North and the South as military preparations began, and volunteers rallied to their causes.

Secession fever ran high in Georgia that January 1861, and the state took measures to determine its own destiny. State troops seized and occupied Fort Pulaski at the mouth of the Savannah River in order to prevent Federal forces from sealing off maritime traffic as they had done in late December with Fort Sumter at Charleston harbor in South Carolina. A convention was called in the state capitol at Milledgeville to convene on 16 January to discuss the national situation and determine what action the state should take. On 19 January, Georgia followed its sister states of the South and signed an Ordinance of Secession.[1]

While the men of Georgia mustered for its defense in the event of war, the residents of the coast began to look to their own defenses. Everyone realized that if war came to the state, it would probably come from the sea because Georgia's coast was its most vulnerable point. Longtime residents of the low country vividly recalled the War of 1812 when British naval raiders had seized and burned American commerce vessels, many times within sight of their harbors. The memory of British naval activity during the Revolutionary War and the War of 1812 brought conjecture about what role the U.S. Navy might play on the exposed coast of Georgia and how best to defend against it.[2]

To protect the Georgia coast and its residents, the authorities conceived of a line of defenses composed of earthworks armed with 32-pounder cannons on the barrier islands at every ship-channel entrance from Tybee Island to Fernandina, Florida, on Amelia Island. It was felt these batteries would offer sufficient defense against coastal raids and serve as visible evidence of defense to apprehensive coastal planters.[3]

While the Southern states banded together through the early spring of 1861, the eyes of the entire nation focused on an unfinished masonry fort on an island in the harbor entrance of Charleston, South Carolina. It was called Fort Sumter, and a contingent of Federal troops there since six days after the state passed an order of secession on December 20, 1860 refused to yield the fort to Confederate demands. The Confederates ringed the harbor with batteries of heavy guns, and the stalemate at Charleston quickly symbolized the national crisis. By April 1861 it was clear that reason would not prevail. Hostilities began in earnest with the bombardment and capture of Fort Sumter on 12 to 14 April 1861.[4]

As war spread across the land, the authorities in the city of Savannah, Georgia, began to look at its situation. With several major water approaches, a strong network of defenses would be needed to deny these routes of approach to an enemy force coming from the sea. During the Revolution the British illustrated the city's vulnerability when they captured it using the seaward approaches. The French later capitalized upon this when their fleet sailed up the Vernon River to land troops, who marched overland to join American forces laying siege to the town. The citizens of Savannah in 1861 had only to look to their past to see what their future might be.[5]

Because Savannah was Georgia's major port, an in-depth defensive system was needed to prevent history from repeating itself. The Savannah River was believed to be sufficiently protected with Fort Pulaski and Fort Jackson garrisoned by Southern forces. However, the Wilmington, Vernon, and Ogeechee rivers remained undefended. The sand batteries on Wassaw and Ossabaw islands covered the entrances to these rivers, but it was decided that additional defensive works would be required to protect important communication routes and lines of travel south of the city. The southernmost anchor of this secondary defensive line would be established at the first high ground above the mouth of the Ogeechee River at a place called Genesis Point.

The Great Ogeechee River begins its journey to the sea as a shallow stream in Greene County in the heart of northeast Georgia about sixty miles west of Augusta. It moves sluggishly through narrow channels and near Millen almost becomes lost in the low, swampy land that marks its course. After passing Millen the river begins its descent toward the Atlantic, striking the coast barely twelve miles below Savannah. In its last miles, the river deepens and widens, its channel sweeping in long, lazy curves through the widening expanse of marshes. In its last reach, before flowing into Ossabaw Sound, the river channel makes one final, dramatic, double hairpin bend, a gigantic reversed S across the marsh, one loop of which covers seven miles. Just before the river reaches its last bend, it passes a small bluff of high ground bordering the south bank. This high ground was Genesis Point, reputed to have derived its name from a Charlestonian named Jennys or Jennist who owned the property at one time. Through the years the property changed hands several times, but the name remained, although slightly altered until its accepted spelling coincided with the first book of the Bible.[6]

Twelve miles due north-northwest from this point was the important Atlantic and Gulf Railroad bridge that spanned the river. Over this bridge passed all the produce, beef cattle, and forage from the southwestern parts of Georgia and Florida; thus the railroad served as a vital communication link along the southeast coast. It started in Thomasville, Georgia, wound its way through Savannah, Charleston, South Carolina, and eventually into Virginia. Its military significance was readily apparent because it could provide transportation for shifting troops and supplies to threatened points along the coast and to the growing theater of war in Virginia as well as providing access to other railroad links connecting Savannah to the interior of the state and beyond.[7]

About a mile farther upstream from the railroad bridge was King's Bridge, an important highway crossing on the coastal road connecting Savannah with Darien and points farther south. Below the highway and railroad bridges were several large plantations, whose owners cultivated cotton on the fertile land along the river and grew rice in the extensive marshes. One of the largest plantations on the river was that of Strathy Hall, owned and operated by the McAllister family, who also owned Genesis Point.

Prior to the war, portions of the point had been cultivated and the marshes opposite turned into rice fields. Midway along the river bluff was a complex of buildings where an overseer lived. When it was recognized that Genesis Point was a strategic location, the McAllisters readily agreed to allow

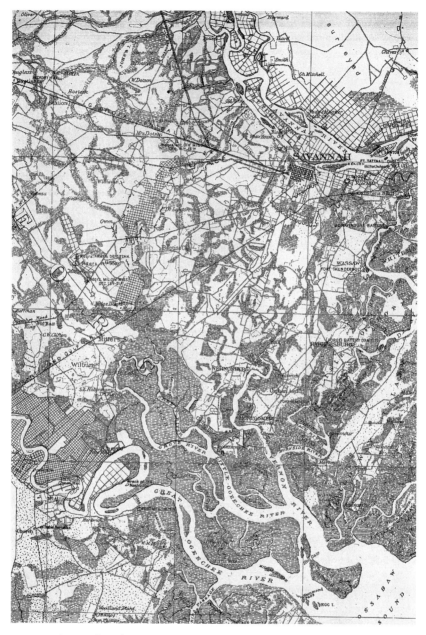

MAP 2. Savannah and Fort McAllister. Courtesy, National Archives

1.1. Joseph L. McAllister owned the property at Genesis Point where Fort McAllister is located. Initially the four-gun battery was known as the Genesis Point Battery but was later called Fort McAllister, because McAllister owned the property and because he was also a close friend of Alfred S. Hartridge, whose unit was in charge of building the battery in June of 1861. Courtesy, Carolyn Clay Swiggart

military defenses to be built there. Construction of fortifications around Savannah and along the Georgia coast continued throughout the summer of 1861. Confederate authorities in Savannah recognized the importance of the Ogeechee River and made preparations to defend the river's entrance. Genesis Point, just above the mouth of the river, was seen as the logical place to position this defense.[8]

On 7 June 1861, Company A of the 1st Regiment, Georgia Volunteer Infantry, the DeKalb Riflemen, arrived at the point to provide a defense force and to assist in the construction of the defenses. This company was commanded by Capt. August P. Wetter[9] with twenty-four-year-old Lt. Alfred L. Hartridge of Savannah as his deputy. Hartridge had attended the Georgia Military Institute for three years but left in October of 1854 before completing his studies and returned to Savannah after his marriage to Julia Smyth Wayne. In early 1861 he joined the Chatham Artillery as a private but was elected first lieutenant of the DeKalb Riflemen and accompanied them when they went to Genesis Point. Hartridge, a close friend of Joseph L. McAllister, initially took up residence at Strathy Hall until a camp could be established at Genesis Point.[10]

Soon after the DeKalb Riflemen arrived, construction began on an earthen battery that would defend the river's entrance. Capt. John McCrady, chief engineer of the 3rd Military District, designed the battery, and his assistant, Capt. James W. McAlpin, executed the plan.[11] Slaves from the local plantations provided the bulk of the labor used to build the battery[12] on a bluff where the river channel flowed past before turning toward the opposite side of the river. Here the guns could command any vessel attempting to pass upstream. The construction of the battery was essentially a matter of rearranging the existing earthen features of the low bluff. Where excavation was necessary, the removed earth was utilized to create walls and covering for bombproofs and magazines. A wooden framework was erected to outline where walls were to be built, gangs of laborers brought the excavated dirt in with wheelbarrows and large wicker baskets, and the dirt was spread out within the wooden framework. Another team of laborers, armed with large wooden pestles, pounded the earth to compact it. This process was repeated until a hard earthen wall was built within the frame, which was then taken down.[13] Bombproofs and magazines whose skeletons were heavy wooden beams and timbers were covered over with layers of earth compacted to a thickness of ten or fifteen feet, leaving only the entrances exposed.[14]

On 2 July 1861, Lt. Hartridge wrote his mother in Savannah and detailed conditions at Genesis Point: "We live very well out here (that is the officers) the planters are very kind in sending us things; particularly Mr. McAllister and Mr. Thos. Arnold; but our men have a pretty hard life of it. Only government rations to eat and nothing to keep [off] the mosquitoes, red bugs, etc. The miserable insects bite very badly and in every occasion, they have caused many of them to get boils and sores from the irritation caused by scratching. . . . I have a good deal to do, but this you know. We rise here at 5 o'clock which makes a day seventeen hours long. We are getting along very well with our battery and fortifications. On Monday the Negroes commenced and every day we have thirty doing good work as they are in charge of our overseer."[15]

By midsummer the Genesis Point Battery, as it had been designated, was complete and four 32-pounder smoothbore cannons mounted in the emplacements, each firing en barbette or over the wall, rather than through embrasures cut in the wall. In August Capt. Wetter was promoted and reassigned to the Confederate Engineers, and Hartridge was elected to command the DeKalb Riflemen. In October, with the threat of an impending U.S. invasion, an additional 32-pounder smoothbore was sent to the battery, and the monthly returns for October noted an effective garrison of two officers and thirty-nine men.[16]

For the people of Georgia the war had been a remote and distant thing through the early months of 1861. They read of fighting and military operations in Virginia and Tennessee and watched as Southern hopes rose. Some of Georgia's troops had been sent to Virginia where they participated in the first great battle at Manassas that July. In August there was news of a successful Federal attack on Cape Hatteras, North Carolina, but this defeat of Confederate forces could not be appreciated by the Southerners who did not grasp the importance of the U.S. naval strategy. Most believed that land battles, not naval victories, would decide the contest.

As soon as the war began, President Lincoln proclaimed his intention to blockade the Southern coast in order to cut off outside commercial, military, and economic aid.[17] However, Lincoln's idea to establish a blockade was ridiculed by many people, both North and South. The Southern coastline was an intricate network of rivers, bays, and inlets and to blockade it seemed nothing less than an impossibility. But Lincoln remained firm in his belief that closing off the Southern ports was vital. For the residents of coastal Georgia, the only physical evidence of the war was the occasional sight of a U.S. Navy blockading ship steaming through the offshore waters, and the Southern people laughed at these first feeble efforts to close their ports. The general feeling was that the war would be over and won before any blockade could seriously affect them.

The first exchange of hostile gunfire on the Georgia coast occurred on 30 October 1861 when the men of the Republican Blues, manning a post on the north end of Wassaw Island, engaged a blockading vessel that had come in close to shore to investigate a grounded blockade runner. The brief exchange of cannon fire served no real purpose, but it was the first test of combat for the Republican Blues.[18] The Blues, organized in May of 1808, were one of Savannah's many legendary militia organizations. When the war came, they had helped garrison Fort Pulaski and had served on Tybee Island and St. Catherine's Island before being sent to Wassaw Island. Their destiny would eventually be found at the little earthen battery at Genesis Point.

By autumn of 1861 the South had intelligence that a large U.S. naval fleet was being gathered to strike at the southeast Atlantic coast. Indications pointed to South Carolina's Port Royal Sound and Hilton Head Island as likely objectives. To counter this possibility, two large earthen forts had been built to protect Port Royal Sound. Fort Walker, on the north point of Hilton Head Island, mounted twenty-three big guns. Across the sound, on the southern end of St. Phillip's Island, another earthen fort, Fort Beauregard, mounted nineteen guns. The Southerners felt these forts should easily be able to repel any attack.[19]

The rumored Federal invasion fleet did exist, and on 4 November it began arriving off Port Royal Sound. On 7 November the attack came, and by day's end the Confederate forces had suffered a resounding defeat. The earthen forts had been battered into submission by concentrated firepower, and only by a stroke of good fortune had the Confederate defenders been able to get off the islands and avoid capture. Federal troops were put ashore, and soon all of Hilton Head and the surrounding area of Beaufort, South Carolina, was in their control. Within a short time a supply depot and repair facility were built to provide support for the naval fleet that enforced the blockade of the southeast coast and for offensive operations against Charleston and Savannah.[20]

Almost overnight the blockade became a more tangible reality to the citizens of Georgia, and the threat of invasion loomed over them as never before. The meager blockade they had experienced in the past months was suddenly stronger and more threatening. The residents of Savannah were especially anxious at this turn of events, because Hilton Head was barely thirty miles from their doorsteps. The presence of so many enemy troops and warships so close to their homes was not a comforting circumstance.

For General Robert E. Lee, commander of the Department of South Carolina, Georgia, and East Florida, the lessons of the Hilton Head Island disaster were plain to see. It was readily apparent that the debacle there could easily be repeated at any of the earthen fortifications that had been so laboriously constructed, armed, and manned on all the major offshore islands on Georgia's coast. Lee realized he did not have the means to support the batteries and troops isolated on these islands. Thus the Federal forces, at their convenience, could easily cut off and capture any of these batteries and their garrisons, and the Georgians might soon find themselves blockaded by their own batteries. This could not be allowed to happen, and the coastal defense plan was reevaluated.

It was determined that a defense of the entire Georgia coast was impractical. Other than Savannah, the Brunswick and Darien areas represented the only other ports on the coast, and these two places were exposed to possible attack. Savannah, the major port city, was not situated directly on the coast but was twelve miles inland with a number of water access routes. It was agreed to give up the lower coast and only defend Savannah in depth. Cavalry forces would then be used to guard the coast south of Savannah and protect against the landing of enemy forces. The Atlantic and Gulf Railroad became an important part of this plan because it would allow for the rapid mobilization and movement of forces to any threatened point. This made the protection of that railroad line even more important. Orders were issued to abandon all the offshore islands, dismantle the sand batteries, and transport all the artillery and stores to Savannah where they would be emplaced to strengthen the city's defenses.[21] This realignment of the coastal defenses made the Genesis Point Battery an even more critical defensive point. After the fall of Hilton Head that November, General Lee visited the battery on several occasions while inspecting the defenses of Savannah and suggested additions and modifications.[22]

While the Federals consolidated their hold on the Hilton Head–Beaufort area, the Confederate forces proceeded with their evacuation of the offshore islands. This shift in the defensive strategy required the construction of new fortifications around Savannah, and the Confederates sought to find an adequate defense that could stand up to the Federal navy. The earthen forts at Port Royal Sound had been deemed almost impregnable, but events there had proved that wrong. The question was raised as to whether any type of earthen fortification would be an adequate defense. Lt. Charles C. Jones Jr., serving with the Chatham Artillery stationed on the Isle of Hope in the Savannah defenses, wrote to his father expressing doubts as to the suitability of earthwork defenses: "It has often seemed to me little less than ridiculous, this idea of endeavoring to fortify every avenue by light sand batteries, which must be silenced so soon as the heavy metal of the Lincoln gunboats is brought to bear. The day belongs to the past when open earthworks and palmetto forts can successfully contend with the heavy batteries of modern fleets. . . . We must expect that these open batteries must yield whenever confronted by the heavy guns of the Lincoln gunboats."[23] It was felt that only thick, masonry-walled forts, such as Fort Pulaski, would be able to withstand a naval attack, and the Savannahians were pleased that Pulaski, considered a modern fort, was still in control of Southern forces.

Through the end of 1861, Federal military operations on the southeast coast lapsed into a period of relative inactivity while the blockade continued to increase in strength and effectiveness. In December 1861, Federal troops landed on Tybee Island, just below the mouth of the Savannah River and within sight of Fort Pulaski. This caused little concern for the Southerners because Tybee was considered to be completely beyond the effective range of artillery, and the fort's thick, brick walls were believed to be more than adequate defense against artillery of any size.

The coming of a new year also brought a new name for the Genesis Point Battery. At some point, probably in late December 1861 or early January 1862, the battery was designated as Fort McAllister. Some sources indicate that the fort was named in honor of George Washington McAllister, the father of Joseph L. McAllister, who now owned the property. Other sources indicate that the fort was named after Joseph McAllister himself because he and Capt. Hartridge were good friends. Whomever the honor was for, the McAllisters owned the property, and their ties to it were quite clear.[24]

On 25 January 1862, Capt. Hartridge wrote his mother a letter headed "Fort McAllister, Bryan Co.," the earliest record of the fort by that designation: "I have been very busy lately arranging my winter quarters. The Departments of our government are very much like a circumlocution office—we have been trying to get lumber and bricks here ever since the first of November but have not yet got enough to finish the officer's quarters. Last week I had the men's tents struck and they moved into their barracks. It is a question of time when we [officers] will be so fortunate. I sincerely trust before long, for the next storm will demolish Head Quarters. . . . Head Quarters is an old tent with sundry patches, which the blow of Thursday has left in a very shattered condition, the rear of it now being propped up with a large board."[25]

Through January and February of 1862, a large U.S. fleet gathered at Port Royal and off Tybee Island. This growing show of enemy strength made the Confederates apprehensive, and an attack on Savannah was anticipated. However, the next Federal moves were sent far to the south, against Brunswick, Georgia, and Fernandina, Florida. Fernandina was captured in February and became a Federal facility to support the blockade. Gradually the blockade tightened its grip on the coast as more and more navy ships prowled the offshore waters, but they shied away from penetrating too far into the inland rivers.[26]

In March 1862, General Lee was ordered to Richmond. Before departing Savannah he issued final instructions concerning Savannah's defenses in which he stated "an obstruction on the Ogeechee has been proposed, and the planters of the river have offered to furnish the necessary labors."[27] This proposal was approved, and two rows of wooden pilings were driven into the river channel and chained together just off Fort McAllister, leaving only a narrow opening under the guns of the fort so that friendly vessels could still navigate the stream.[28] The battery had yet to fire a shot in defense of the river, but it seemed probable that prowling gunboats would eventually find their way into it. The Federal navy would investigate the inland water routes, and it was only a matter of time before they ascended the Ogeechee River.

After Federal forces occupied Tybee Island in December 1861, they began preparations to reduce and capture Fort Pulaski and spent several months building earthen batteries on the extreme northwestern end of the island. The Confederates in Fort Pulaski were not intimidated because the Federal artillery was almost two miles away, considered an extreme distance for artillery of the time. However, unknown to the Confederates, the Federals were about to begin a new chapter of military technology.[29]

1.2. The damaged wall at Fort Pulaski, as seen after the fort's capture, 11 April 1862, shows the effect of Federal bombardment from rifled guns. The fort, which guarded the entrance to the Savannah River, had represented the ultimate in coastal defense. Courtesy, U.S. Army Military History Institute

The Federals emplaced several batteries of rifled cannon of the new Parrott and James patterns on Tybee. These guns had been tested but never tried in combat. Rifled small arms had been used for almost a century before the development of the minie ball for shoulder weapons opened the door for the practical application of this concept to artillery. The concept of rifling was not a new idea, having been used in sporting weapons for many years. Spiral grooves engraved within the bore of the weapon give the projectile a rapid twist upon firing, sending the projectile farther and more accurately than smoothbore weapons. Prior to the war the U.S. government had been experimenting with rifled artillery but now the war presented an opportunity to test under real conditions. It was decided that Fort Pulaski, representing the ultimate in coastal defense at that time, would be the first to feel the power of these new weapons.[30]

On the morning of 10 April 1862, Fort Pulaski was subjected to concentrated bombardment. The Confederate defenders were surprised when the 20- and 30-pound rifled shells slammed into the brick walls with terrific impact. Their surprise turned to dismay when the angle of the fort closest to the Federal batteries began to crumble under the incessant pounding. Attempts to return fire were relatively useless for Confederate artillery could barely reach the Federal positions. The battering soon opened a breach in the wall that was widened until a gaping hole stood where the southeast angle had been. Within thirty-six hours of the beginning of the assault and faced with possible destruction or surrender, Col. Charles Olmstead surrendered his garrison, and Fort Pulaski, defending the Savannah River and ultimately Savannah, fell into Federal hands on 11 April.[31]

This was a devastating development for the people of Savannah and the state of Georgia. Fort Pulaski, which had required over eighteen years of labor to build, had fallen after a bombardment of thirty-six hours. For the Southerners, the question then became, "What can stand up against these rifled guns?" If modern brick forts could not resist the fire of the rifled cannon, how could they expect the earth and sand defenses to be of any value? The day of the masonry fort had come to an end.[32] In a letter to his father, Lt. Charles C. Jones Jr. expressed the thoughts on everyone's mind that April when the news of Fort Pulaski's fall reached Savannah: "If the heavy masonry walls of Pulaski were of no avail against the concentrated fire of those Parrott guns posted at a distance of more than a mile, what shall we expect from our sand batteries along the river?[33] . . . What we greatly need now is artillery of heavy caliber and long range. We are in great want of guns which will enable us to compete successfully with those of our adversary."[34]

While Fort Pulaski was undergoing its ordeal by fire, at Port Royal, Admiral Samuel F. Du Pont, U.S. Navy commander of the Southeastern Blockading Squadron, was initiating a step to strengthen the coastal blockade. With the numbers of available blockading vessels increasing and the offshore islands having been given up by Confederate forces, Adm. Du Pont augmented the blockade by stationing at least one blockader in each of the major coastal sounds. This would give the blockade runners an additional problem to overcome in penetrating the blockade and impede Confederate shipping movements on the intercoastal waterway behind the barrier islands.[35]

Other developments besides the fall of Fort Pulaski and the blockade gave the Confederates cause to worry. Barely a month before, at Hampton Roads, Virginia, two ironclad warships had battled each other for the first time in history. The Confederate ironclad *Virginia,* built from the hull and machinery of the USS *Merrimac,* had run wild amid the wooden U.S. warships there until the U.S. ironclad *Monitor,* a turreted vessel of controversial design, arrived and battled the *Virginia* to a standstill. Although both sides claimed victory, the implications were clear—the day of the wooden warship was also passing.[36] As if the rifled cannon was not enough to worry about, the Federals boasted that fleets of these ironclad monitors would soon be on the Southern coast. The Southerners realized their industrial capabilities could not compete with those of the North, and although the South could build ironclad vessels, Northern technology still placed the South at a disadvantage.

Preparations for a determined defense of Savannah went forward, and a period of feverish construction of defenses ensued. Working parties obstructed river approaches, existing earthwork forts and batteries were strengthened,

1.3. Adm. Samuel F. Du Pont (center) commanded the U.S. Navy's Southeast Blockading Squadron. He was responsible for the capture of Hilton Head Island and Port Royal Sound in November of 1861 and supported operations against Charleston and Savannah as well as supervising the blockade of the southeast coast. When the new ironclad monitors were sent to him for an attack against Charleston, Du Pont decided to test them against Fort McAllister first. Courtesy, U.S. Army Military History Institute

and new ones built. Above all, the importance of Fort McAllister was not forgotten. It constituted the extreme right anchor upon which the entire line of defense rested, and in light of recent events, the battery there was seen to be insufficient.

The Confederate abandonment of the offshore islands and the lower coast meant that additional artillery was available to be incorporated into the defenses of Savannah. A 42-pounder cannon was sent to strengthen Fort McAllister, and work continued on the installation of the river obstructions recommended by General Lee the month before,[37] with Captain Hartridge writing his mother on 16 April, "In two weeks I will have the river so obstructed that the enemy will not be able to pass unless they first silence my batteries."[38] To help defend against enemy landings at points south of the fort, reinforcements consisting of about 200 infantry and 150 cavalry arrived in the area.[39] These forces provided scouting parties and guarded the places where enemy forces might be landed to threaten the fort from the rear. Capt. Joseph L. McAllister's company, the Hardwick Mounted Rifles, provided the bulk of the cavalry in this security force.[40]

The arrival of summer weather brought heat, humidity, and summer rain. The rains and humidity bred mosquitoes in the marshes and low areas with an accompanying increase in the diseases they carried. On 18 June, Captain Hartridge commented to his mother, "The continual rains & general bad weather is making it very sickly here, my hospital is filled all the time with cases of chills & fever, diarrhea etc. One fellow died last night."[41]

In July, Fort McAllister's garrison was strengthened by the arrival of Martin's Light Battery from 3rd Company E, 12th Battalion, Georgia Light Artillery, commanded by Capt. Robert Martin of Barnwell, South Carolina. The unit had been formed at Sandersville, Georgia, in May and sent to Savannah for a period of instruction. In Savannah they received two 24-pounder howitzers and four 12-pounder Napoleons (bronze smooth-bore field pieces named after Napoleon III) and were ordered to take up duties in Bryan County in support of Fort McAllister. One of the members of Martin's Light Battery was Private Isaac Hermann, a native of France who had settled in Washington County, Georgia. Hermann was no stranger to the war, having served a year with the 1st Georgia Regular Infantry in Virginia's Shenandoah Valley. When the unit reorganized at the end of their enlistment, he was asked to join Captain Martin's battery as their bugler.[42]

Hermann returned to Georgia where he found the war on the Georgia coast much different from what he had experienced in Virginia: "We went into camp by the side of the Ogeechee River, about three miles this side of the Fort, which camp we named 'Camp McAllister.' . . . The country surrounding was low, flat, marshy and replete with malarial fever, so that we had to remove our camp several miles further up the river, but still within close call of the fort. This new camp was called 'Camp Arnold,' in honor of Doctor [Richard] Arnold, on whose land we stationed. One morning I was ordered to blow the call, only one man, Sergeant Cox, reported. All the rest of the command were down with chills and fever. There was no quinine to be had, owing to the blockade, such medicines being considered by our adversaries as contraband of war."[43]

Warm weather brought more than mosquitoes, for it was also good sailing weather. Good weather encouraged blockade runners, but it also brought patrolling gunboats poking about the inland waterways.

2

BAPTISM BY FIRE

Fort McAllister had guarded the mouth of the Ogeechee River for almost a year but had only fired its guns in practice, not in anger. With the increasing activity of the U.S. Navy forces on the coast, it was only a matter of time before the fort's defenses were tested. After April 1862, Federal gunboats began exploring the inland waterways and looking for Confederate defenses. Since December 1861, Ossabaw Sound had been kept under surveillance by several gunboats that patrolled the coast between Wassaw and St. Catherine's sounds, but as summer 1862 approached, no vessel had yet been assigned to guard Ossabaw Sound.

The catalyst for the fort's baptism of fire arrived in late June 1862 when a small schooner penetrated the blockade and entered the Ogeechee, anchoring several miles upstream behind the protection of Fort McAllister. The first official notice of the fort by the U.S. Navy came on 1 July 1862 when the gunboat USS *Potomska*, blockading St. Catherine's Sound to the south, entered Ossabaw Sound through the inland water route behind Ossabaw Island. It was on a reconnaissance of the area and searching for the schooner.[1]

The *Potomska*, a three-masted, propeller-driven steamer had been a merchant vessel before the war. It mounted four 32-pounders and a 20-pounder Parrott rifle.[2] Its commander was Lt. Cmdr. Pendleton G. Watmough, who reported, "On opening the Ogeechee River a schooner was discovered at anchor about 7 miles up the river. As soon as the tide served I ascended the river, keeping a lookout for a battery and a row of piles reported to me by a contraband. When within a mile and a quarter of the schooner the battery appeared from a point of woods, its guns (six heavy ones) covering the schooner. It was about the same distance from us as the vessel, only across a marsh, the river making a bend around to it."[3]

Alerted to the *Potomska's* approach, the DeKalb Riflemen scrambled to their battle stations where they readied the big guns and waited as the gunboat gradually steamed into range. The *Potomska* opened fire sending a shell toward the distant schooner and another at the battery. The Confederates replied.[4] Watmough commented, "The battery opened on us, firing with considerable accuracy, one shot going immediately over us. I returned the fire with ten or a dozen shell, but as the channel was narrow and unknown to me, and I away from any support, I deemed it imprudent to prolong the exposure of the vessel to damage, and suffered the ebb tide to drift us out of range. It was my intention to have cut out or destroyed the schooner that night, supposing the piles prevented her ascending the river. In this we were disappointed, as they had either left a channel or the tide had swept away the obstructions, as it is strong, and the bottom sandy. The contraband was positive as to their having been planted across the river. The schooner was moved up the river under sail the same evening."[5]

Watmough decided that Fort McAllister would take more attention than his gunboat could give it and returned the vessel to its station in St. Catherine's Sound. His report of the action was subsequently relayed to Adm. Du Pont, who noted that the presence of a blockade runner in the Ogeechee and of a fort there demonstrated the attraction Ossabaw Sound offered to the runners. As long as the sound remained unguarded, runners could seek shelter behind the fort. On 5 July he ordered Lt. Cmdr. Watmough to take the *Potomska* and assume blockade duties in Ossabaw Sound leaving St. Catherine's and Sapelo sounds unguarded.[6]

On 9 July, Adm. Du Pont issued instructions to Lt. Cmdr. Charles Steedman of the USS *Paul Jones* to make a reconnaissance of the Ogeechee River and with its long-range rifled guns feel out the armament of the fort. Steedman prepared for the undertaking but found no pilots at Hilton Head who could guide him through the intricate coastal waters of the Ossabaw Sound area. The only pilot familiar with the area was Charles Tatnall, but he was at St. Simons Island. Steedman set out in the *Paul Jones* to retrieve him but was delayed with mechanical malfunctions in the boiler flues. It was over two weeks before he was finally ready to undertake the reconnaissance.[7]

Shortly after Steedman set out for St. Simons, the blockade runner *Thomas L. Wragg* arrived in the Ogeechee River with a cargo of arms and ammunition. The vessel, a large side-wheel steamer, had previously been known as the *Nashville,* built in New York in 1854 as a passenger steamer. The vessel came into Southern hands at Charleston in 1861 and was armed and sent forth as a Confederate government-sponsored privateer because its great speed was almost as powerful a weapon as the gun it carried.[8]

The *Nashville* created a small international stir on its first run to England when it overtook and burned the U.S. clipper ship *Harvey Birch* in November 1861 off the coast of Ireland and flew the first Confederate flag seen in European waters.[9] Later the vessel was decommissioned by the Confederate government and sold to the Fraser, Trenholm Company of England, which changed its name to the *Thomas L. Wragg,* although it would continue to be known as the *Nashville* due to its earlier reputation. As a blockade runner, the *Thomas L. Wragg* proved illusive to its pursuers, and it made a number of successful runs through the blockade at several points along the southeast coast. On 23 July 1862 it was thwarted in an attempt to run into Charleston and after a long chase managed to elude its pursuers by slipping into Ossabaw Sound and up the Ogeechee River where it found shelter behind Fort McAllister. The vessel was then taken upriver and its cargo unloaded at the railroad bridge for shipment to Savannah. A return cargo of cotton, pitch, and tobacco was acquired and loaded for the run out. However, getting out would not be as easy as getting in had been.[10]

The navy blockaders in the Ossabaw Sound area became aware from runaway slaves on 26 July of the *Nashville*'s location, and this news was relayed by Cmdr. J. R. Goldsborough to Adm. Du Pont at Hilton Head. A close watch was then established on the entrance to the Ogeechee River lest the *Nashville* escape again. They had the ship bottled up but preferred its capture or destruction, and in order to accomplish this, Fort McAllister would have to be silenced.[11]

By the time Adm. Du Pont was made aware of the *Nashville*'s presence in the Ogeechee, the reconnaissance he had ordered Lt. Cmdr. Steedman to undertake two weeks earlier was ready to proceed. It was hoped that a concentrated bombardment by a squadron of gunboats could silence the fort long enough for the vessels to get upstream within reach of the *Nashville* and the railroad bridge. The four vessels gathered to undertake the reconnaissance included the *Paul Jones,* a side-wheel steamer mounting a 100-pounder Parrott rifle, one 11-inch Dahlgren gun, and two 9-inch howitzers; the USS *Huron,* a screw steamer mounting an 11-inch Dahlgren, one 20-pounder Parrott rifle, and two 24-pound howitzers; the USS *Unadilla,* also a screw steamer, with one 20-pounder Parrott rifle, one 11-inch Dahlgren, four 24-pounder howitzers, and one 12-pounder howitzer; and the USS *Madgie,* a screw steamer mounting an 8-inch Dahlgren and a 30-pounder Parrott rifle. Lt. Cmdr. Napoleon Collins of the *Unadilla* was given command of the squadron.[12]

About 9:00 A.M. on 29 July they ascended the Ogeechee River. Once past Big Buzzard Island, just above the mouth of the river, the vessels began throwing shells in the direction of Genesis Point. They continued shelling the woods as they approached and in half an hour came within range of the fort and began directing their fire upon it.[13]

The garrison of the fort withheld their fire until the vessels crept to a point well within range.[14] Capt. Hartridge outlined his strategy: "Not being able to return their fire I very quietly waited until they came within range & then concentrated my fire upon their leading boat—they returned the fire with great rapidity."[15]

As the gunboats crept closer, the firing of the fort became more accurate, with several shells raking over the *Paul Jones* in the lead. Capt. Hartridge describes the action.

> After playing this game for half an hour & finding that my gunners understood their work, they fell back beyond my range & continued their "long [range]" shooting, but after a little while they seemed to be ashamed of this & started up the river again much to our joy—for it was not pleasant to stand idle & have their shell singing songs over & around us, sometimes filling our faces with dirt & crashing through our quarters—Again I gave the command "commence firing" & again did my brave gunners make a target of their leader—often & often have I beg[g]ed the General who commands this district to let me have a Columbiad & oh, how earnestly did I wish for it.
>
> [The enemy projectiles] would strike the earth & make cavities that were large enough to bury a horse, fall into the water & throw up a column [of water] 100 feet high, bursting in the air they would scatter fragments of iron & flint in every direction. It was a grand sight to look at one of their vessels, see a puff of smoke, a few moments after hear the report & then hear the whizzing shell as it approached you, see it strike the earth or burst in mid-air with a report like a cannon. Sometimes they would pass far above our heads & could be seen whirling far above. Sometimes they would pass so near as to force us to bow with respect until we became more intimate with them & found that we could treat them with contempt.[16]

Lt. Cmdr. Steedman reports his analysis from the *Paul Jones*.

> A spirited fire was kept up on both sides for an hour and a half (firing slowly and deliberately), when, becoming satisfied from the range of the enemy's fire and weight of metal that if I attempted to ascend the river I would have to do so at a great sacrifice of life and perhaps the sinking of one or more of the gunboats, I concluded to withdraw from the contest, for had we continued we would have had to steam up, head on, a distance of more than a mile and a half, with only one gun from each vessel to

return fire; besides this, the river is "piled" across below and in point-
blank range of the fort, effectually obstructing the passage, and to remove
a sufficient number (if possible) to permit passing would require sacrifices
not warranted.

I have been unable to obtain any information of the steamer reported
by Lieutenant-Commander Collins as being up the Ogeechee. I am satisfied, however, that she is still there, and if another vessel could be sent as
a consort to the *Unadilla* to cover the neighborhood, there will not be the
slightest possibility of her ever being able to get to sea.[17]

Capt. Hartridge wraps up the confrontation.

After keeping up the fight for over two hours they abandoned the contest
having thrown four or five hundred of the "most improved projectiles" at
us. That I had no one injured is indeed strange for they shot with accuracy . . . but [their fire] did no damage of any consequence, only "ventilating" our buildings, cutting the tops off trees & digging ditches in our
works. . . . After the fight shell & fragments of every size were picked up
in every direction, some weighing 120 pounds, some 94 [pounds] & a
great many less.[18]

Hartridge had often requested heavy-caliber Columbiads be sent to the
fort to strengthen its armament but his requests seemed to fall on deaf ears.
In a letter to his mother, he said that if he'd only had one Columbiad during
the attack, he "would have made them skulk off sooner than they did, or else
they should have aided in 'obstructing the channel.'"[19] The attack of 29 July
seemed to underscore his requests for the Columbiad. On 30 July he
informed his mother, "The enemy will no doubt, come in larger force next
time, but we will also be better prepared, as the General [Hugh Mercer] has
ordered a Columbiad (large gun throwing a shell of 50 lbs & solid shot of 64
lbs) & I am now expecting it & intend to put it in position in the morning.
The planters, also, are sending their negroes to strengthen the works, so when
the time comes I shall make it a 'tug of war.' The General has sent me word
to call upon him for any force I wish 'infantry or artillery' but I wish to show
my countrymen that 'Yankee Gun Boats' are not such 'fearful monsters' as
some of them have been taught to believe."[20] The additional gun was an 8-
inch Columbiad that had been manufactured at the Tredegar Iron Works in
Richmond, Virginia, in 1861 and designated with serial number 7941. The
longed-for Columbiad was probably placed in a position constructed for it on
the far right of the fort.[21]

The attack of 29 July also focused attention on the strategic position that
Fort McAllister occupied and the necessity of holding it. When the DeKalb
Riflemen were relieved of duty to be assigned to the newly formed 1st

Battalion, Georgia Sharpshooters, they were replaced by elements of the garrison from Fort Jackson near Savannah—the Emmett Rifles and the Republican Blues.[22]

The Emmett Rifles, commanded by Capt. Augustus Bonaud, had been organized by him in August of 1861 and had been at Fort Jackson until their assignment to Fort McAllister. Bonaud, a forty-one year-old native of France, had settled in Savannah, where he operated a dance school, was a liquor merchant, and proprietor of the Marshall House Hotel until the war intervened.[23]

The Republican Blues, organized in 1808, were one of Savannah's oldest and most prestigious militia units. They had been involved in the first hostilities on the Georgia coast in October of 1861 while serving at the Wassaw Island battery. The Blues were commanded by Capt. John Wayne Anderson, a resident of Savannah who was fifty-six years old in 1861 and had led the unit for many years. A native of New York, he had worked as a cotton factor buying and selling cotton and commission merchant, served as director of the Georgia Central Railroad, and been elected a city alderman and member of the Georgia House of Representatives.[24]

At five o'clock on the afternoon of 19 August 1862, the Republican Blues and the Emmett Rifles at Fort Jackson received orders to march to Genesis Point. They departed for Savannah by boat the following morning, where they boarded a train for Way's Station, arriving at midafternoon. Having been at Fort Jackson since November of 1861, the men were all looking forward to the change of duty stations.[25] Twenty-three-year-old 2nd Lt. William Daniel Dixon of the Republican Blues narrated these events in journal entries made several days later.

> At 3 1/2 Oclock we arrived at the station. The Captain sent down to the post to try and get a boat to take the things down. The ride being ten miles from the station we did not hear from it until 6 Oclock. We found that it was 25 miles by water, so we concluded to take up the line of march leaving a guard to take charge of the things. We started on the march in great glee. Not a 6 men in the two companies ever marched such a distance before. We had not marched 2 miles before they began to give out on account of their haveing such loads in their knapsacks. The most of them have been in forts ever since they have been in Service and did not know what weight they were able to carry on their backs, so the most of them filled their knapsacks up and when they began to march they broke down under the weight. It had rained most all day and the road was in very bad condition[26] and the night was very dark. I cannot begin to discribe the scene on the road that night, but I kept up with the head of the column and about 11-Oclock we arrived with 20 men near the Battery at the place of Mr. McAllister. He very kindly furnished quarters for all of us.

After all the men were quartered we were invited into to his house w[h]ere we had a very fine supper which we done justice to. He also furnished us with beds. I was very badly used up so I took a bath and went to bed. Next morning we were so stiff and sore that we were not fit for anything. We came down to the battery and it was turned over to us by Capt. Martin who was stationed here with his light battery. He left here that day but up to today all our men is not in the Battery as there is only quarters for one company so our men are quartered in one of Mr. McAllister[']s houses.[27] Some of our men did not arrive here until one Oclock the next day.

The Battery is very nicely situated. It mounts 7 guns. 5 32 pds, 1 42 and 1 8-in gun. We had no wagons so we have had to throw ourselves on Capt. Martin and Capt. McAl[l]ister for getting up our things, each sending a wagon down for us to bring our things up with, but they cannot make but one trip a day so that it take[s] some time to get our things up. Capt. McAl[l]ister has very kindly thrown open his house to us ever since we have been here. The Captain went up to the city on Thursday for wagons and tents. We expect him today. I am laid [up] with my feet haveing blistered them on our march. The Steamer Nashville is still lying just above the Battery. She run in here some time ago and has not been able to get out since. There is three gun boats lying in sight. . . . The Captain arrived back today with 2 wagons and horses. We will now get our things and get fixed up.[28]

In the 24 August journal entry, 2nd Lt. Dixon describes the *Nashville* captain's determination and a piece of intelligence.

I have not got over my 10 miles march yet. My feet are blistered and cannot wear my boots. The Captain of the Nashville was here yesterday and told us that he would not stay here much longer as he was getting tired of it. He would either get her out or lose the vessel, but not by Yankees, as he would never let them take [it]. He is going down in a small boat tonight to see how things look. He thinks he will try and go out if there is only 2 gunboats off the Bar. And if he gets cornered he will run one down and if his vessel is hurt he will burn her. He is a very determined man.

Capt. McAllister of a Mounted Corps stationed near here while visiting his Pickett yesterday came across a negro that was on board of one of the gun boats that was engaged in shelling the Battery a few weeks since. He states that he was on his way up here to get some medicine for one of the other negroes that was left on the place of McDonalds as they were so old it was thought that they would not be troubled so they were left to mind the place. On his way up the gun boats came across him and took him on board and took him along with them. . . . While there he says he heard the Officers say that they only came up this time to try the Battery and the depth of water to see if they could bring their iron boat up. The next time they came they would take this battery and they [would] burn the bridge and distroy all the crops. . . . I slept down here last night for the first time. My cot and things came up yesterday.[29]

On 29 August 2nd Lt. Dixon, noted, "The Nashville has gone up the river as all her crew are sick."[30] Sickness was only a symptom of one of the problems inherent in Fort McAllister's geographical location. The large expanse of rice fields and surrounding marshes bred mosquitoes bringing malarial fevers. Sickness was already at Genesis Point when the Blues arrived, and it was feared the change in location from Fort Jackson would result in a growing sick list until the men became more acclimated.[31]

The 26 August entry in the Blues' daybook reads, "Our sick list is increasing. It is feared the change down here will make all sick. 17 sick today. . . . We have no Doctor yet at this post." Four miles from the post at the cavalry camp, a doctor was later located who promised to make daily visits to the fort to administer to the sick.[32]

On 9 September, 2nd Lt. Dixon recorded that Capt. Bonaud and 1st Lt. George Dickerson[33] of the Emmett Rifles and 1st Lt. George A. Nicoll[34] of the Republican Blues had been sent to Savannah sick.[35] Sickness continued to hit the garrison very hard, and the Blues daybook clearly documents the alarming decline in unit efficiency and the impact the illness had on the garrison of the post.

19 Sept.—57 men for duty. 20 men sick

20 Sept.—54 men for duty. 26 sick. The camp has become a hospital.

21 Sept.—51 men for duty. 27 sick.

23 Sept.—45 men for duty. 28 sick.

25 Sept.—44 men for duty. 30 sick.

26 Sept.—43 men for duty. 33 sick.

27 Sept.—42 men for duty. 34 sick. Lt. W. D. Dixon sent to the city sick. . . .

28 Sept.—37 men for duty. 38 sick. Captain Anderson taken down with fever.

29 Sept.—36 men for duty. 39 sick. Captain Anderson sent to the city sick.

2 Oct.—30 men for duty. 42 sick.

4 Oct.—29 men for duty. 45 sick.

The day after his 6 October return to duty, 2nd Lt. Dixon commented in his journal, "Our sick list is alarming. We have 63 men down out of the two companies." Just when it looked as though the malarial fever would put the garrison totally out of action, the crisis point was passed, and gradually the sick list began to decline, and the number of personnel able to work increased. On 8 October Dixon noted the change: "Our sick list has decreased today, there being 50 men reported."[36]

Malarial fevers came and went, and the men frequently recovered only to fall ill again, as Dixon found: "I had a slight chill and a very hot fever last night. I am quite weak today,"[37] and on the following day, October 11, "I had a hot fever last night. Today the chill came on me about 10 Oclock and then a fever came on which lasted on me until night. I am Officer of the Day. The officers have offered to relieve me but I will not be relieved. I will try and stick it out. I am taking quinine."[38] Dixon did not suffer a recurrence on the next day: "I think my chill and fever is broken, as I have not had either since Saturday."[39]

The blockade of Ossabaw Sound was firmly established after the 29 July attack on Fort McAllister. The gunboats *Potomska* and *Unadilla* alternated blockading duty paying special attention to the Ogeechee River lest the *Nashville* escape. In September the gunboat USS *Dawn,* commanded by Lt. Cmdr. John Barnes, arrived to assume the responsibility of controlling the entrance to the sound.[40] The activity of the Federal navy in Ossabaw Sound did not escape the notice of Confederate authorities. They deduced that it heralded another attempt against Fort McAllister, and steps were taken to prepare that place to receive it. 2nd Lt. Dixon noted in his journal on 19 October: "Last night at 10 Oclock seven wagons [of ammunition] arrived here from Savannah. Another lot arrived this afternoon. We are now crowded with ammunition besides a lot of infernal machines to sink in the river."[41] The "infernal machines" or river mines, added a new dimension to the defenses of Fort McAllister and one the U.S. Navy would learn to respect.

In late October General P. G. T. Beauregard arrived in Savannah from Charleston to inspect the city's defenses. He had just assumed command of the department and was visiting the posts under his command. His tour of Savannah included a trip to Fort McAllister, which greatly impressed him. Upon his return to Charleston, he issued a summary of additions and changes to be made in Savannah's defenses.[42] For Fort McAllister he recommended, "One of the 32-pounders must be changed in position as ordered, to rake the piling across the river. Its traverses must be raised and lengthened, and a mortar constructed to protect the two 32-pounders now raking the obstruction from being enfiladed. Its magazines must be better protected, and its hotshot furnace reconstructed as ordered. A more efficient commander than the

2.1. Capt. Augustus Bonaud
founded and commanded
the Emmett Rifles, Company
F, 22nd Georgia Artillery.
Bonaud, a native of France who
settled in Savannah, was a liquor
merchant and employed as the
manager of several hotels in the city.
Courtesy, Mary H. Bonaud

present one would, I think, be required for this important position, and who-
ever is sent there should visit first the work at Beaulieu to see its fine condition. . . . A proper sunken battery should be constructed for the protection of
the men and horses of all light batteries intended for the defense of water-
courses. This applies especially to the light batteries now on the Little and
Great Ogeechee."[43]

While the *Dawn* kept watch over the Vernon and Little Ogeechee rivers,
the USS *Wissahickon* maintained a watch on the Ogeechee. The presence of
the *Wissahickon* with the *Dawn* in Ossabaw Sound did not go unnoticed by
the Confederates at Fort McAllister. It was unusual to see two gunboats there
so the Confederates decided to make a reconnaissance. On the morning of
2 November 1862, Capt. Augustus Bonaud and four men of the Emmett
Rifles set out in a small boat to investigate the blockading vessels in the sound.
They cautiously crept downstream until they had approached within about
1,200 yards of the *Wissahickon* and the *Dawn*. About noon their boat was
sighted by lookouts aboard the *Wissahickon*, and Lt. Cmdr. Davis ordered an
armed launch sent out to meet them.[44]

When Bonaud and his party realized they had been sighted, they put
about and began frantically rowing upstream. Once Lt. Cmdr. Davis saw the

small boat fleeing, he ordered the 20-pounder Parrott rifle to send a shot in hopes of bringing them to a halt. This only served to quicken their rowing, and when Davis saw they were pulling away, he ordered the *Wissahickon* to the pursuit. The gunboat went upstream, continuing to shell the little boat with the 20-pounder Parrott.[45] However, by the time the *Wissahickon* began to close the distance, Bonaud's boat was within range of Fort McAllister's guns.

The Republican Blues daybook noted that "Capt B[onaud] with his crew had hard work to get out of reach but arrived at the battery safe though badly used up."[46] 2nd Lt. Dixon's journal fills in details: "The gun boat started after him soon followed [by] the other. The first one run his boat within a mile and three quarters of the battery and cast anchor. The other did not come within range. We assembled the Garrison and took charge of the guns. We both looked at one another for about a half hour, when the vessel let fly one shot at us which struck about fifty yards from the guns on the inside of the battery and bursted but done no damage further than striking the Doctors Tent and knocking over a chair with his pitcher and basin on it. We returned her fire and gave her four more shot with the 8-in gun. The last 2 shots fell just alongside of her, when she put out. We had just sat down to dinner and lost our dinner by the opperation."[47] The fort sustained no real damage, but the men of the new garrison now knew what duty at Genesis Point was all about.

As the year drew to a close, the men of the Emmett Rifles found their enlistments about to expire. On 8 November 1862, they reorganized and elected new officers. It was an extraordinary election in some ways, as 2nd Lt. Dixon relates: "The Emmett Rifles had an election . . . to reorganize. The result was not what they expected. Capt. Bonaud was defeated by the election of Lieut Geo. A. Nicoll of the Blues to the Captaincy. . . . Capt. Bonaud is in the city now having a protest drawn up."[48]

That the Emmett Rifles had elected a man to be their commander who was not even a member of their unit was unusual. Capt. Bonaud had organized the unit, so it was understandable that he was insulted. He would protest the election clear to the Confederate War Department, all to no avail. However, he would go on to contribute valuable service to the Confederate cause.[49]

Election results also made an impact on the Republican Blues, as on 20 October an election determined field officers for the reorganization of the 1st Regiment, Georgia Infantry, their parent organization. Capt. John W. Anderson, who had commanded the Blues for many years, ran against Charles Olmstead for colonel of the regiment. Olmstead, who commanded Fort Pulaski when it was captured, had since been exchanged and was seeking to reestablish his command of the regiment. Anderson and Olmstead apparently did not have a harmonious relationship; Anderson indicated that he would resign if he lost the election rather than submit to command under Olmstead's leadership.[50]

Although Capt. Anderson had support, the last minute removal of the Emmett Rifles from the regiment in exchange for another unit that support-ed Olmstead meant Anderson was defeated in the election. True to his word, he submitted his resignation. On 11 November Anderson bid an emotional farewell to the Blues at Fort McAllister, as 2nd Lt. Dixon noted, "This after-noon after Dress Parade the Captain addressed the Battalion in a few words. He thanked them for the respect and good conduct shown him while in com-mand of them and assured them that if in his punishment he had been too severe he was sorry for it. His remarks were quite touching. When he got through the whole battalion were in tears. He shook each my by the hand and told them good bye. He will leave us tomorrow."[51]

The next day Dixon wrote, "The Captain left here this afternoon. He bid us all good bye. His words to me were God bless you. You have been a good boy to me. There were few dry eyes in the house."[52] With the departure of Capt. Anderson, filling his vacancy would need to be addressed.

On 10 December the garrison received word that the controversy over the election of 1st Lt. George A. Nicoll to the command of the Emmett Rifles had been settled by the Confederate War Department. Orders arrived the fol-lowing day promoting 1st Lt. George W. Anderson Jr.[53] to captain of the Republican Blues. On 30 December, Nicoll was formally assigned to the command of the Emmett Rifles by order of the War Department. This left a vacancy within the ranks of the Republican Blues, and several days later, 2nd Lt. William D. Dixon was promoted to first lieutenant.[54]

In Ossabaw Sound at 5:30 A.M. on 10 November, the deck watch of the *Wissahickon* was alerted to the approach of a small boat coming from up the Ogeechee River. Its occupants, five runaway slaves who had managed to slip away from work details at Fort McAllister, were brought aboard, questioned, and sent to the gunboat USS *Wamsutta* for transportation to Hilton Head.[55]

Although Confederate forces tried to stop the increasing flow of runaway slaves, it was a difficult task, especially when it was necessary to use them as laborers in exposed areas like Fort McAllister. It was not so much the loss of workers and property that concerned the Confederates but the intimate knowledge of the coastal areas the workers possessed. Many of the slaves had been used in constructing military fortifications, and they could provide valu-able intelligence to the Federal forces.

That evening the mortar schooner USS *C. P. Williams* arrived in Ossabaw Sound in tow of the USS *Water Witch*. It relieved the bark USS *Fernandina* that had been doing service between St. Catherine's and Ossabaw sounds. The

C. P. Williams was a sail schooner armed with two 32-pounder cannon and a 13-inch mortar.[56] The 13-inch mortar could lob a two-hundred-pound shell almost three miles from an angle of forty-five degrees.[57]

Aboard the *Dawn,* Paymaster Robert C. Pierce recorded in his diary on 17 November: "One of the officers from the Mortar Sch[ooner] on board and brought their Chronometer, the motion be[ing] so severe when the mortar explodes as to disarrange it. In the evening the Pilot came on board from the Wissahickon, it being intended in the morning to go up and have a look at Genesis Point Battery."[58]

That morning was too foggy and conditions not right for an attack so it was postponed until the next day.[59] But Fort McAllister was more than ready for them. After the 29 July attack, the fort had been strengthened by the addition of an 8-inch Columbiad that was put under the command of 1st Lt. William Dixon of the Blues, who had dubbed it the Pet Gun.[60]

Patchy fog obscured the river when Lt. Cmdr. Davis put the three vessels underway on the morning of 19 November.[61] Aboard the *Dawn,* Paymaster Pierce describes the beginning of the mission: "Got an early breakfast and about seven ocl[ock] up anchor and took the Mortar Boat in tow and steamed up [the] Ogeechee River the Wissahickon joining us when we passed her anchorage. As soon as we opened [the view of] the Battery round the Point, cast off the Mortar boat and she came to anchor and we proceeded a short distance further up and anchored and the Wissahic[k]on above us."[62]

1st Lt. Dixon continues the narrative: "Three gun boats and one mortar boat came up the river but there being such a dense fog at the time they could not be seen and the first notice they had in the battery was the report and whistling of the shells. The men were quickly at their guns and all the tents and sick were removed."[63]

From aboard the *Wissahickon,* Lt. Cmdr. Davis reports: "The enemy disappeared as though they had deserted the battery; all this time they had fired no guns."[64] It was impossible to tell if the battery had been abandoned, so Davis ordered the vessels to advance to a position in the bend of the river about a mile below the fort,[65] as Paymaster Pierce relates: "Fired a few shots from this point when the Wissahic[k]on got up her anchor and steamed slowly up the river we following her, both firing as [we] went and the Mortar also firing. The Wiss[ahickon] proceeded up river till within about 100 yards of the piles driven in the river and then the Battery opened fire and at their first shot put a solid shot into the W[issahickon] 3 ft. below her water line causing of course a bad leak. She then dropped down[stream] a little still firing while we retained our position and though the Battery fired a good many shots and all of them good ones no more took effect though they came near enough."[66]

The leak in the *Wissahickon's* hull caused Lt. Cmdr. Davis some concern because the pumps appeared unable to handle the incoming water. He was afraid they might have to put the vessel ashore lest it sink, and at one point he assembled the crew on the starboard side of the ship in order to list the vessel over enough to raise the damaged hull section out of the water. Davis soon summoned the aid of the carpenter aboard the *Dawn,* and emergency measures were taken to keep the *Wissahickon* afloat.[67]

Paymaster Pierce continues the story: "The Wissahic[k]on got a man overboard and managed to stop the worst of the leak our Carpenter being aboard to help. We anchored and continued firing at intervals. Our expedition was partly to find out where the piles were driven and partly what their guns would do. They have one gun, a good one trained on a certain spot near the piles and can drop a shot on that spot every time; the W happened to get almost exactly on that spot. 30 ft. nearer and the shot would have swept her decks. Our shells must have done a good deal of damage and also the mortar. The W was of no use as far as shooting went, her largest gun, a 11-inch shell not comparing in accuracy or range with our 100–pdr Parrott."[68]

The firing continued until 2:30 P.M. when the three vessels ceased fire and dropped downstream to their anchorage in the sound. The *Wissahickon's* damage had been temporarily repaired, and the vessel resumed its position on station. In the six-hour engagement, the Federal ships fired over two hundred shots at the battery causing some damage to the earthwork and wounding three members of the garrison.[69] Paymaster Pierce said in his diary, "Not many were killed at the Battery for we could see them run for their holes when they saw the flash of our guns."[70]

The defenders of the fort fired only twelve shots in return, but these had been well aimed as the *Wissahickon* learned. The gunners in the fort refused to return fire as long as the vessels remained out of range. 1st Lt. Dixon, who usually commanded the 8-inch Columbiad, was absent in Savannah on business during the action. He wrote upon his return:

There was no one seriously injured with us. One man that was in the battery had his arm cut by a piece of shell. Another [shell] harried [William] Jeffries[71] who had just stepped out of his tent. Was thrown about 5 feet by a shell striking just under his feet. He was hurt by the shock of it and pretty badly scared. Another who was in the tent was knocked down and covered with sand. One of the Emmett Rifles was badly wounded by falling on a bayonet. It penetrated his thigh about 5 in. They are all doing well. The battery was struck in a great many places. One shell struck our shell magazine and tore the whole front off it. One of our men who was in there at the time was shut up for 2 hours before anyone knew he was there. He was taken out safely. One shell went through the roof of the Rifles quarters and bursted inside. It tore the side out of it. Two fragments of shell struck our quarters. One went through the roof, the other took one of our window sashes out.[72]

Once again damage to the fort could be repaired by laboring parties composed of slaves from the local plantations and ammunition replenished with fresh stocks from Savannah. The Republican Blues Daybook states, "Before dark we had the pleasure of seeing we were not forgotten by those in Savannah, as plenty of ammunition has arrived and one morter which will be mounted tonight. A large force of negroes are on the way here. All is quiet but a good look out will be kept up tonight."[73]

The mortar was a 10-inch seacoast mortar, the largest available to the Confederates. Because Gen. Beauregard had recommended a mortar be placed to protect the fort from enfilade fire, it was probably placed in a position to the right of the 8-inch Columbiad. The 32-pounder on the far right was then probably relocated to a new emplacement on the far left of the fort, in a position to rake the river pilings, in compliance with Beauregard's earlier instructions.[74]

The journal of 1st Lt. Dixon describes the scene after the attack: "I found things at the battery in great disorder. . . . A morter was sent down last night and is now ready for them if they return. We have over one hundred negroes at work on the battery and strength[e]ning the magazine and building a bomb proof for the men. The next time they pay us a visit they will find us better prepared. Major [Robert H.] Anderson's[75] Battalion of Sharp Shooters arrived this morning and are encamped about 2 miles from here. They are ordered here in case of a land attack to support the battery."[76]

Ironically, the DeKalb Riflemen were a part of the Battalion of Sharpshooters camped behind the fort. They had departed Genesis Point that summer to join this battalion when it was formed in Savannah, and the Republican Blues and Emmett Rifles had been sent to Fort McAllister to replace them. Now the DeKalb Riflemen were defending the point once again.[77]

On 21 November, repairs and improvements to the fort continued while the garrison made adjustments, as 1st Lt. Dixon describes: "The men have been engaged the most of the day removing their tents outside of the battery as they were in the way of the bomb proof. Some of the boys have emptied a great many of the shells fired in the battery that did not burst. Some of their rifled shells measured 19-in in length. One 11-inch Dalgreen shell was dug up this morning, besides a great many kinds of smaller ones. It seems to me that they tried ev[e]ry kind of shell at us."[78]

On 25 November, Brig. Gen. Hugh Mercer appointed Major John B. Gallie[79] to the command of Fort McAllister. Gallie, a fifty-six-year old native of Scotland, had settled in Savannah to become a successful merchant and cotton factor before the war. He served for many years with the Chatham Artillery, rising from the ranks to the command of that unit. When the war came, he formed the Savannah Artillery and for a time commanded a battalion of state artillery until these units were disbanded due to Confederate government conscription laws. Through the recommendation of Brig. Gen. Mercer, he was appointed a Major in the Confederate service and ordered to assume the command at Genesis Point.[80]

The news of Gallie's appointment to command was not greeted with enthusiasm at Fort McAllister, as the entry from 1st Lt. Dixon's journal relates: "Major Gallie of the Siege Artillery is assigned to duty here and we do not care to serve under him if we can get out of it."[81] The feelings against Gallie were such that on 27 November, Capt. George W. Anderson Jr. went to Savannah to try to have Brig. Gen. Mercer reassign to the Republican Blues to another post.[82] On the morning of 29 November, Maj. Gallie arrived at Fort McAllister, and the following day he took command at morning inspection. It was not an auspicious beginning, as 1st Lt. Dixon noted, "Major Gallie took charge at inspection this morning but as he knows nothing of our drill he made a mess of things."[83] With Gallie's assumption of command also came the news that, like it or not, the Republican Blues were stuck with him. Capt. Anderson arrived back at the post with word that there was absolutely no chance of the Republican Blues being reassigned from Fort McAllister.[84]

The Federal blockaders remained alert for any sign of movement from the *Nashville*. Runaway slaves and deserters continued to keep the naval forces informed about conditions and locations of troops and fortifications, but some of the information they brought out was unsettling. Word was that the *Nashville* was being outfitted as an armed privateer, and the blockade runner *Fingal* was being converted into an ironclad warship intended to break the blockade of Savannah and free the *Nashville* from the Ogeechee.[85]

Following its arrival in the Ogeechee that July, the *Nashville* had been unable to make the run out. After numerous attempts, it returned upstream to the railroad bridge in early September 1862 and discharged its cargo. The Fraser, Trenholm Company then sold the ship to a Capt. Thomas Harrison Baker who refitted and armed it to serve as a privateer.[86] Baker had been the captain of the Confederate raider *Savannah,* a small pilot schooner at Charleston, South Carolina, that was one of the early Confederate privateers. On 1 May 1861 he was issued the first Letter of Marque given by the Confederate government.[87]

It was a brief career, however. On 2 June 1861 the *Savannah* ventured out of Charleston harbor to capture a Northern merchant ship but while returning had itself been surprised and captured by the USS *Perry*. Baker was sent to New York City as a prisoner but after a brief period in jail was exchanged and sent south. Eager to return to action, he acquired the *Nashville* and converted her by lowering the profile and arming her with a 32-pounder cannon and a 24-pounder cannon. On 5 November 1862 he was issued another Letter of Marque, and the vessel was rechristened the *Rattlesnake*.[88] Now all he needed was a chance to get the vessel back to the open ocean again, but the U.S. Navy still held the door closed.

On 27 December, Maj. John Barnwell arrived from Charleston, South Carolina, to inspect Fort McAllister on behalf of Gen. Beauregard. Barnwell was quick to realize the importance of the fort's position.

> Its capture would entail great inconvenience if not actual suffering on all the troops concentrated for the defense of the City and therefore requires that more attention should be paid to the armament of its Battery. It now mounts eight guns.
>
> The right of the work is injudicious, as it is exposed to a perfect enfilade from the Enemy's fire, which has already been practically demonstrated, and to which it must finally succumb, unless it is re-inforced, & that at an early date, by two additional guns of large caliber. At present the uncertain fire of the mortar is the only piece which can reach the Enemy, so long as he avails himself of the advantage of position and heavy metal. The mortar is now within the lines of the work. I would now respectfully suggest that it be moved without the lines and into a sunken work connected to the body of the battery by a flying sap. There is also an oven in the position of the hot shot battery. The gun (32 pdr) for this service is so placed on the left of the work, that it can not be served until the Enemy's fleet is within point-blank [range], where as the gun should be served at the longest range the piece is capable of, as hot shot should lodge to be efficient; besides, if the Enemy is allowed to get within point-blank [range], and use grape, the battery will not be tenable. This has been an axiom in Naval combat with shore batteries, since the time of Nelson: The nearer the ship, the more equal her battery, gun for gun. The new Magazine is well built and arranged. The powder I think has deteriorated, judging from the range of the gun & the fact that at 5-degrees deviation, the shell plunged on smooth water, instead of ricochetting.
>
> The Officers are efficient, in good spirits and determined and therefore, if for no other reason, should receive all the aid the Artillery Bureau can offer.

I am somewhat prolix in the above Report, but outposts are too often overlooked, and I think the importance of the work demands attention.[89]

On 1 January 1863, Maj. Gallie wrote Brig. Gen. Mercer, describing the state of affairs at the fort.

I have the honor to report the two companies comprising this command . . . are well drilled as Infantry, and the guns, viz five 32 pdrs, one 42 pdr, one 8-in. Columbiad and one 10-in. mortar, are handled much to my satisfaction. Their discipline, instruction and Military appearance are highly creditable to the Company officers. Their arms and accoutrements are excellent. The cloth of the [uniforms of the Republican] Blues is tolerable. The uniform of the [Emmett] Rifles is good but the men have no under garments, their shoes are worn out, and there are but few blankets. These are expected to be procured early this month. The Blues had (4000) four thousand [rounds of ammunition] and the Rifles (2396) two thousand three hundred ninety six rounds. There are (898) eight hundred ninety eight rounds for the 32 pdrs, (198) one hundred ninety eight for the 43-pdr, (172) one hundred seventy two for the 8-inch Columbiad in the usual proportion of shot, shell, grape and cannister, and (91) ninety one shells for the 10 inch mortar, inconveniently crowded into two small magazines. . . . When the two new Magazines will be finished (one will be this week) the ordnance stores will be properly distributed. . . . The ambulance with its team of two horses and harness have been condemned. The two wagons are good, but the teams of two horses and two mules, with harness have been condemned. No horses in possession of officers or soldiers. . . . There are two sinks at convenient distances from the Battery, subject to be overflowed on spring tides. The quality of the ration is good, the police [of the grounds] is very good.[90]

The news concerning the construction of Confederate ironclads in Savannah and the conversion of the *Nashville* into a privateer put the Federal forces in Ossabaw Sound on alert. These two events also focused more attention on Fort McAllister. On 28 December the gunboat USS *Seneca*, commanded by Lt. Cmdr. William Gibson, arrived in Ossabaw Sound to relieve the *Wissahickon* for refitting at Port Royal. Two days later, on 30 December, the *Seneca* embarked upon a scouting expedition up the Ogeechee River to view Fort McAllister. Once within sight of the fort, the *Seneca* fired five shells in hopes of tempting a shot from the fort, which did not respond. Not daring to venture any closer while unassisted, the *Seneca* returned downstream.[91]

On the night of 3 January, a 32-pounder rifled gun arrived at the fort. The 10-inch mortar was moved into a position built for it to the far right, outside of the fort, connected by a long earthen wall in accordance with Maj. Barn-well's instructions. The 32-pounder rifle was mounted the following day, pos-sibly in the position vacated by the 10-inch mortar.[92] The 32-pounder rifle was actually a smoothbore piece that had been rifled and an iron reinforcing band placed around the breach. These hybrid weapons were an attempt, by converting the large number of obsolete weapons, on the part of Confederate ordnance experts to offset the advantage the Federal forces had in the manu-facture of new rifled weapons. It was hoped this gun would allow Fort McAllister to gain extra range against the Federal ships in the next attack.[93]

On 9 January 1863, the *Seneca* and the *Dawn* made a reconnaissance to check the status of the *Nashville* and Fort McAllister. Lt. Cmdr. Gibson of the *Seneca* reported to Adm. Du Pont, "I made a reconnaissance . . . up the Little Ogeechee River above Hardee's [Harvey's] Cut, commanding an extensive view of the three rivers. I saw a large side-wheel, two-masted steamer painted lead color, apparently in seagoing order (undoubtedly the Nashville) lying broadside toward us in a reach of the Big Ogeechee, distant not more than 5 miles. . . . She has been much farther up the river, I understand, and has descended since these waters were last reconnoitered. This fact, coupled with the report concerning her and the Fingal, . . . renders it extremely probable that an early attempt at her escape is meditated."[94]

Adm. Du Pont felt that the *Nashville* needed to be dealt with before it got to the open seas, but past attempts had shown Fort McAllister to be a strong work. The threat of Confederate ironclads coming out of Savannah was a concern not only for his vessels in Ossabaw Sound but for his whole blockad-ing squadron in the Savannah area. However, he believed he would soon have the remedy to that problem as new U.S. Navy ironclads were on their way to the southeast coast.

3

SAND AND GRIT

The age of ironclad warships had come, and Federal naval forces on the southeast coast awaited their arrival to reinforce the blockade and combat Southern ironclads known to be under construction. The USS *Monitor,* designed and built by John Ericsson, fought the momentous battle in March 1862 with the Confederate ironclad CSS *Virginia* in Hampton Roads, Virginia. It was then sent for duty on the southeast coast but foundered in a storm off Cape Hatteras on 30 December 1862. Although the *Monitor* was gone, its designs had been tested, and additional ironclads were built that incorporated the *Monitor's* flat deck and heavily armored turret holding two large cannon.

Much was expected of the new monitor-class ironclads (named after the *Monitor*) because the Navy Department thought they would prove invulnerable to Confederate harbor and river defenses. Adm. Du Pont had been preparing for a naval attack on Charleston using the new ironclads, but he had reservations about the assault. In Washington the capture of Charleston was considered more important in political rather than military terms. The latter half of 1862 saw the Northern cause sink to a low ebb. Lincoln was insistent on victories, and the newspapers and magazines continued to draw attention to the promised capture of Charleston. Adm. Du Pont feared the administration was risking everything on one throw of the dice at Charleston, because a naval defeat there might mean a political setback at home as well as breaking the blockade on the southeast coast. Adm. Du Pont was concerned about the actual capabilities of the new monitors, which only added to his growing apprehensions about the operations.[1]

In late January 1863 the monitor USS *Montauk* arrived at Port Royal under the command of Cmdr. John L. Worden, who had commanded the *Monitor.* The *Montauk* was the third of the monitor-class ironclads built by

3.1. Cmdr. John L. Worden, a native of New York, had been sent to deliver secret orders to Northern forces in Florida in 1861 but was captured and imprisoned for several months. Upon his return he was assigned to command the original *Monitor* and took that ironclad into battle against the Confederate ironclad *Virginia* in March 1862. He then took command of the monitor-class *Montauk* and supervised the ironclad attacks against Fort McAllister. Courtesy, U.S. Army Military History Institute

the Navy but it heralded many more to follow. It was two hundred feet long and forty-six feet wide, drawing almost eleven feet of water and almost identical in appearance to the original *Monitor* except that the pilothouse sat atop the turret rather than on the bow. It was armed with two Dahlgren cannons, an 11- and a 15-inch mounted inside its turret. The 15-inch was the largest gun being used at that time and like the *Montauk* had yet to see combat.[2]

Samuel T. Browne, paymaster aboard the *Montauk,* described the ironclad.

> Her flat deck, not more than twenty inches above the water, and pointed at each end. . . . Her deck was protected by a double layer of iron plates, each nine feet by three in surface area, and an inch thick. Her sides were armored with five thicknesses of these iron plates bolted through and through on thick oaken backing, and extending to a point about four feet below the water-line, and there the armor ended, and a sharp right

3.2. The 15-inch smoothbore Dahlgren gun fired a 330-pound shell and required up to fifty pounds of powder to fire the shell. The armament of each monitor was to include one 15-inch gun as one of the two guns in each turret. The men shown here give some idea of how large this gun was. Fort McAllister was the first place the 15-inch gun was ever fired in combat, and the shells easily penetrated the fort's front wall, composed of up to eighteen feet of packed earth. Courtesy, National Archives

angle carried that portion of the vessel known as the "overhang" to the hull of the ship which was constructed of five-eighths inch iron plates.

The distinctive feature of the vessel was amidships, and consisted of a circular iron tower nine feet in height, and made of such plates as above mentioned, placed one over another, until the tower was eleven inches thick. These plates were firmly held together by massive bolts going through and through, on the outside the bolt heads slightly rounded, and with the thread-end and heavy nut on the inside. The roof was made of iron plates perforated and placed upon railway rails, and the rails resting upon massive square beams of iron extending across the top of the tower. This tower, or "turret," as it became known, revolved upon the faces of rings of bronze-metal fitted into a circular channel in the deck, and around an immense iron spindle or shaft that supported the pilot-house standing above the center of the turret. . . . The pilot house did not revolve. It was fitted with funnel-shaped eye-holes nearly five feet above the floor of the pilot-house, which converged from the larger diameter inside, to an aperture an inch in diameter on the outside.

Within the turret were two guns, an eleven-inch and a fifteen-inch—
the latter ludicrously resembling a soda bottle . . . the breech of which is
so thick it prevents looking over it and out of the port, and hence has to
be sighted by the eleven-inch. . . . Its cartridges of walnut-sized powder
[grains] varying from thirty-five to sixty pounds in weight, and its missiles from a three-hundred-and-twenty-five pound unfilled shell, to a
four-hundred pound solid shot! Beneath the turret and guns was the turret-chamber, and here were small engines for working the turret, and also
to operate the ventilating blowers,—for all of the supply of fresh air was
drawn through the perforations in the roof of the turret and forced
through sheet-iron connecting tubes throughout the ship.

All the light admitted below deck, came through thick circular glass
dead-lights set about ten inches below the surface of the iron deck, and at
the bottom of small cavities, perhaps seven inches in diameter, called
"wells." These dead-lights were open when in harbor,—and often even at
seas in smooth weather,—but when engaged in a fight, the "well" was
covered with a thick iron scuttle fitting snugly, secured below and flush
with the deck.[3]

The *Montauk* was fresh from the shipyards, and little was known of its
strengths and weaknesses. The vessel needed to be tested in a close-range
exchange against a land battery to determine how well it would stand up
against direct fire. Fort McAllister seemed to be the most opportune target
because much was to be gained from success there. On 20 January, Adm. Du
Pont wrote to Cmdr. Worden, "The Nashville is up the Great Ogeechee, having been fitted as a privateer, and is lying under a five or seven-gun battery,
waiting to run to sea. We have a report that the Fingal (now called Atlanta)
an iron-clad, will attempt to aid the Nashville in escaping. As the most important operations on this coast must be delayed until other vessels arrive, and
until those now here can be made ready, it strikes me a very important and
handsome thing may be done by capturing this fort on the Ogeechee and in
destroying the Nashville and, should matters go well, in burning the railroad
bridge which the gunboats can lay alongside of."[4]

On 22 January, Worden proceeded to Ossabaw Sound in compliance with
orders.[5] Because the ironclad was not especially seaworthy in open waters, it
was towed by the USS *James Adger,* a sister ship to the *Nashville.* When the
ironclad and its escort approached Ossabaw Sound two days later, Federal
lookouts aboard the blockading ships there were uncertain as to whether the
approaching ironclad was friendly. They had heard rumors of Confederate
ironclads being built in Savannah, and word received only that morning indicated they were headed their way.[6] Paymaster Pierce, aboard the *Dawn,*

recorded the arrival: "About 3 A.M. 4 contrabands from Savannah came on board and brought information that the [Confederate] ram was expected to come down here to day or next day. About seven [A.M.] heard two guns seaward . . . and soon afterwards firing commenced in the direction of Fort Pulaski and continued till noon rapid and heavy. About eight [A.M.] got underway. . . . The Mortar Sch[ooner] signalled ["]Enemy's Gunboats in sight["] and fired a gun. We immediately turned about and with the Wissahickon ran down to the sch[ooner]. She had seen three gunboats in the direction of Warsaw [Island] firing. . . . About noon [we] saw two steamers seaward one of which we supposed to be the Quaker City towing an ironclad. . . . After this fog shut in too thick to make out anything though we suppose the ironclad to be destined for this place."[7]

The firing heard that morning, which they assumed was from naval combat with Confederate ironclads, had actually been salutes fired from Federal gunboats and greetings from the garrison at Fort Pulaski for the *Montauk* as she passed. The *Montauk* entered Ossabaw Sound and anchored at 5:10 P.M. when an intense fog cloaked the vessel.[8] Paymaster Browne details that night.

> Our vessel was now entirely cleared for fighting trim. From stem to stern not a rope or chain, or bolt, in sight, nothing but the round turret and the big smoke-stack. Nothing remained to be done, in case of sudden action, but to close the battle-hatches—the work of a few seconds. An armed watch was stationed on deck, and the alarm rattle laid in one of the turret-ports, ready for immediate use by the officer of the deck. The bright winter moon that flecked the water with flashes of silver, never shone down upon a stranger looking craft. The officers below, in conversation, quietly speculated upon the probabilities of coming contests. The night passed quietly away. In the morning, one of the crew, Isaac Selby, was missing, and it was supposed that during his watch he must have stepped overboard, and the swift stream swept him under.[9]

Cmdr. Worden wrote, "On Monday [25 January] the fog hung with us most of the morning, during which time I called the commanding officers together and arranged our plans of attack."[10] Crews were put to work preparing their vessels for combat. Aboard the *Seneca,* Lt. Cmdr. William Gibson recorded that on the afternoon of 26 January, the crew "commenced preparing the vessel for battle by putting the chains up and down the outside of the vessel amidships; sand bags on the inside of the coal bunkers to protect the engines. . . . Got an iron box on the fore-crosstrees for the lookout. Shifted some sand bags from the port bunker to the starboard side of the deck."[11]

Paymaster Browne noted the arrival of a valuable pilot familiar with the area waterways: "We received on board, from one of the other vessels, a pilot named Murphy,[12] a small, tough-looking Georgian, whose escape from southern authorities was one of singular interest, whose knowledge of those waters proved of immense value to the Union commanders."[13]

While the gunboats prepared, Cmdr. Worden ordered the *Montauk* to proceed: "At 1:30 PM I got underway, with Mr. Murphy as pilot, and stood up the river anchoring just outside of the range of Fort McAllister. During the afternoon the Seneca, Wissahickon, the Dawn towing the C. P. Williams came up and anchored in line astern."[14]

Paymaster Browne described their position.

> The Big Ogeechee is narrow, and very crooked, and low marshy banks border its sides. A mile or more across the marsh, and a little on the left, a spur of woodland conceals a location in the river known as Genesis Point, and here was the Genesis Point battery, better known, perhaps as "Fort McAllister."
>
> The river, which some distance of its course below the fort is hidden by the point of woodland, we could plainly see above the fort as it meandered through the marsh, which, with its tall, sedge grass, extends on the right to, and beyond, the Little Ogeechee, even to the low bluff that forms the bank of the Vernon River, and on which the little hamlet of Beulah is located; near by, a battery of three guns, and not far away, a small camp, possibly of Confederate pickets. Here and there, over this extended marshy basin, we can see columns of smoke rising, either from rice-mills or Confederate camps. Five hundred yards above our anchorage would have uncovered the fort from its concealment behind the point of woods, and bring us near a spot where is flying a white rag from the tip of a rod that sticks just above the grass,—a range mark for the fort, and upon which their guns are bearing. It is more than a mile from the fort, and yet they had obtained such accuracy of practice, that when the gunboat Wissahic[k]on went first to this point, she received the first shot from the fort directly in the centre of her hull.[15]

As darkness settled over the area, Worden initiated further precautions for the coming attack: "At 8 o'clock [P.M.] one boat from the *Seneca* and one from the *Wissahickon,* both in charge of Lt. Cmdr. [Charles] Davis, proceeded upriver to reconnoiter and destroy the range [markers] of the enemy's guns, which were placed near Harvey's Cut."[16]

Paymaster Browne accompanied the nocturnal reconnaissance.

> At nine o'clock in the evening, two boats, fitted for a night reconnaissance, left the ship. Each had a crew of ten men and three officers, and every officer and man was armed with revolver, rifle and cutlass. I accompanied the first lieutenant in the first boat. We shoved away from the ship,

and with oars muffled with sheepskin, quietly pulled along in the broad shadow the grass cast upon the river. The sky was unclouded, and the moon shone clear and bright. Up and up we pulled, with no sound save the pattering of the drops as they fell from the oar-blades upon the river. We supposed the rebels had out scouts along the banks, and we watched for them, but none appeared. Up we continued, half the crew rowing, the other half with arms in their hands, until we reached a line of obstructions that diagonally crossed the river, and effectually closed it, with the channel passage through it skillfully concealed. A third of a mile beyond was the fort, its side toward us dark in the shadow, and the sentry pacing the parapet. Here we remained a while, listening and watching, but nothing broke the stillness of the night, and we returned, removing the range-stakes along the bank as we came across them, and before midnight we reached the ship.[17]

The general conclusion of those aboard the small boats was that the obstructions were protected by torpedoes.[18]

The *Montauk*'s crew rose early on the morning of 27 January to make last-minute preparations. Storekeepers stood by with tools ready for any emergency. Extra men were assigned to the boiler room and engine room and placed in the passageways with lanterns to ensure communication within the vessel. Others were posted in the coal bunkers and bilge pumps to report problems or damage sustained there. Fire hoses were brought out and coiled, ready for instant use.[19] In the vessel's turret, the 11-inch and 15-inch Dahlgren guns were prepared and loaded. The 15-inch gun was about to see its first trial by combat. Much was expected from this new ordnance as it had only been previously tested on gunnery ranges. Firing a 325-pound shell packed with about twenty pounds of powder and propelled by a charge of up to sixty pounds, the piece had a range of several miles.[20]

Among those aboard the *Montauk* on this morning was Bradley S. Osbon, a correspondent for the *New York Herald* newspaper. Adm. Du Pont approved Osbon's presence aboard the ironclad as a civilian observer and allowed him to board the *Montauk* at Hilton Head to observe the new vessel in action but not to report for his paper until after the Charleston operations had concluded. Osbon reported, "At early dawn Commander Worden hoisted the national colors at either end of the Montauk, the Seneca gave another very liberal display of her best bunting, and the rest of the little flotilla were not long in similar demonstrations, of, however, rather more modest proportions. The Montauk soon hove up anchor and stood up the river for about half a mile, then the Seneca, the next in rank, started, followed by the Wissahickon, the Dawn, and the mortar schooner C. P. Williams. . . . The Montauk stood steadily on around the point, presenting to a looker on about as saucy as spectacle as one could well imagine."[21]

From Paymaster Browne's point of view:

We got up anchor, and soon after light started slowly up the river. Three of our boats were trailing astern from a spar lashed across the ship. When well underway, the rattle sounded to "quarters," and officers and men repaired to their stations for action. Captain Worden, the pilot Murphy and myself remained on the turret-top. When we reached the bend in the river where the fort opened to full view, it was [a] clear day and the sun was just shining above the low tree-tops. A little less than a mile ahead was the fort, situated at a sharp angle in the river, the bending of the river above it making of the land on our right a peninsula. Slowly we steamed against the current, and eagerly scanned through our glasses the massive proportions of the fortification, its banks covered with rich green sod, and the muzzles of the guns just visible, pointing at us from the heavily protected embrasures. Between the guns immense mounds of earth or traverses extended back into the rear, effectually covering the guns from an enfilading fire, to which by the approach they were partially exposed. Above the parapet floated the new ensign of this new dominion whose existence we had come to dispute. It being unnecessary and imprudent to remain longer on the outside, we descended into the turret, and from thence climbed up into the pilot-house, and from the funnel-shaped eye holes within, I watched the contest.[22]

Cmdr. Worden noted: "At 7 o'clock this morning I got underway, followed by the vessels enumerated, taking up a position about 150 yards below the obstructions at a point designated by a flag placed there by Lieutenant-Commander Davis last night. The other vessels anchored in line about 1 1/4 miles astern. At 7:35 we opened fire on the fort."[23]

From correspondent Osbon: "The Seneca had the honor of opening the engagement, letting fly a shell from her Parrott rifle. A moment afterwards, the MONTAUK gave the Rebels a sample of the contents of the Yankee cheese-box, followed successively by the Wissahickon and Dawn. The enemy were not long in replying, opening with only two guns, but paying exclusive attention to the ironclad."[24]

Paymaster Browne continues his narrative.

In a few moments we let fly from the eleven-inch gun, a shell that fell a little short and disappeared in the river. Another was tried, that entered the battery and exploded with a loud report, blowing the soil in every direction, and for a moment hiding a portion of the fort in the dust of the explosion. Then a shell was sent from the fifteen-inch gun . . . and this imbedded itself in the parapet, and burst with a heavy deadened report, literally filling the air above the fort with earth and debris. The reports of our guns were like peals of thunder instantly let loose from confinement. Columns of fire fifteen inches in diameter and a rod in length, flashed from the turret; immense bodies of dense smoke shot over the river; and but for its incessant rolling and unfolding looked like masses of granite. For a moment after the discharge of the guns, the turret and turret-chamber were filled with smoke, but the ventilating apparatus soon carried it away. The shock of the discharge, though forty-pounds of powder were used, was not severe or at all injurious within the ship. . . .

Instantly the rebels replied with a ten-inch [*sic*] shot from their pet gun.[25] A flash!—and then a big puff of smoke, out of which a tiny black spot appeared, that rapidly grew in size (or seemed to), describing a low arc, and then for an instant a big black ball was before my eyes, then quick as [a] thought it disappeared, and with a heavy—thud! it struck square in the centre of the turret, making an indentation about as large as a soup-plate. It was evident from their firing the instant our guns were discharged, that they hoped to send a shot into one of our ports, but the immediate turning away of the turret to reload, prevented the working of their plan. We could watch our own shell as they emerged from the smoke, and seemed rapidly to lessen in size and then bury themselves in the earth. Again we gave them an eleven-inch shell that fell within the fort, and again a fifteen-inch that imbedded itself in the solid work an instant, and then exploded, powder, smoke, dust and earth filling the air, and leaving a rent in the work big enough to drive an ox-cart through. Occasionally a shell would scour the top of the fort, and then ricochet into the air, and fall a mile beyond in the dense wood, crushing the trees in its descent. Sometimes a shell would pass through the face of the fort and burst inside. We could only see the rebels as they loaded their guns, and then at the discharge of our own they would drop as though shot, and rush to their bombproofs.[26]

In the fort, 1st Lt. Dixon recounted his experience: "The ball was then open and it continued for five hours and a half. During that time the Iron fell like hail in the Battery. The Iron boat had but two guns one 11-in and one 15-in gun. The shots from her were directed principally at the 8-in gun and the rifle gun. They done their best to dismount both guns but in that they did not succeed. Their fireing was the best, but no harm was done to the battery except the breaking of some of the traverses which would cover us with sand. She was struck twice by my gun. The second time the ball mashed to pieces on her."[27]

Below decks the crewmen of the *Montauk* awaited the results of the gunfire received from the fort. Thomas Stephens, second assistant engineer, reported from the vessel's engine room.

> At 7:35 a rebel shot struck the vessel. At 8:05 A.M. a shot struck the lower section of [the] smokepipe with force, making an indentation, but causing no material injury to it. The firing from the turret seemed slow and deliberate to those in the engine room; the smoke from [the] guns was forced rapidly into the fireroom at each discharge, but was well diluted with air by the fans, and rapidly passed out through [the] furnaces, and smokepipe, causing no unusual discomfort. The temperature during the action did not exceed 104-degrees; average for the whole time of action (four hours), 103-degrees Fahrenheit. The sound or report of our guns was not acute . . . but was heavy and dull. . . . We were aware of this vessel being struck many times by the rebel's shot, but could not distinguish where excepting when striking overhead, and could not then realize any danger from them.[28]

Correspondent Osbon found the firing of the *Montauk*'s guns to be a little more unsettling from a vantage point directly under the big turret: "The sensation below decks was far different than that which I had experienced in the pilot-house. . . . The sound of our own guns was more acute and unpleasant, and well it might be, when it is taken into consideration that the whole volume of sound from the discharge of each gun passed directly over and within a few inches of our heads, and the concussion passing into the system through the brain by the top of the head. I cannot say that it was painful, but it was far from pleasant, and, in addition to this, you were scarcely ever able to hear the word of command when the guns were fired. To hear the officer say, "Are you ready?—Fire!" takes off much of the unpleasantness of the shock; but below you do not have that warning."[29]

Cmdr. Worden's narrative resumes, "After firing our XI and XV-inch guns once the enemy opened a brisk fire upon us. . . . Their practice was very fine, striking us quite a number of times, doing us no damage. Most of their shot struck inside of 15 feet from us.[30] . . . In about an hour from the time of opening the action the enemy's fire had perceptibly slackened, so much so that he was using only two guns at intervals. About 9 o'clock a fresh breeze sprung up, which gradually increased until it blew with such violence as to seriously impede the flight of our shells and effect their range."[31]

Correspondent Osbon, aboard the *Montauk,* analyzed the events recorded by Worden.

> The engagement . . . was, I venture to say, as fine a specimen of an artillery duel as has been witnessed since the war commenced. . . . The

rebels paid exclusive attention to the MONTAUK. For over three hours they did not favor their wooden antagonists with a single shell. They were evidently impressed with the idea that from the "ironclad" they had most to fear, and upon her, accordingly, would they bestow all iron greetings. The Rebel practice was such as to excite admiration from friend as well as foe. Although the precautions had been taken the night before to remove their stakes and other ranges on the river side between us and the fort, they had yet such a perfect range of all points on the river below them that the very first shot fired by the battery struck the turret of the MONTAUK. This was not a chance shot, for each and every one following it was almost equally well directed; if a ball did not hit the vessel itself, it was sure to plow up the water in close proximity to it. But ball and shell were equally thrown away, and, for all real damage done, might as well have been dropped in the neighboring marsh. . . .

During the entire morning the MONTAUK fired but slowly, delivering her shots, on an average, but once in eight minutes. The Rebels . . . did little more than reply to her gun for gun. They soon perceived that their only chance of doing any execution on her iron sides was to get a shot into her [gun] ports, and now universally reserved their fire until the turret came slowly round, fronting them, and then, at the instant the portholes became visible, blazed away. As an example of the accuracy of their marksmanship, I will state that one of these shots, from a ten-inch gun [sic], struck the turret directly between the two [gun] ports, a little over them, yet not more than 18 or 20 inches from the openings. No wooden vessel could possibly have lived in the position occupied by the MONTAUK fifteen minutes. . . .

The working of the machinery of the vessel was all that could be desired. The mechanism of the turret performed admirably. The temperature in the engine room and in the quarters of the officers and men was moderate and no inconvenience whatever was experienced by anyone. In this respect, the MONTAUK proves to be a great improvement on the original Monitor. The rattling of shot and shell above was hardly audible; and were it not for the trembling of the vessel under the discharge of her own guns, one might have been dining on board her without suspecting that a Rebel battery was raining its shot upon her.[32]

But the same could not be said for the garrison manning the fort. The heavy shells from the *Montauk* and the 100-pounder Parrott rifle from the *Dawn* continued to slam into and around the parapets with bone-jarring regularity. The earth beneath their feet shook with each impact and every cannon discharge. When the huge shells smashed into the parapet, tons of sand were displaced in an instant, but in spite of it all, the men maintained a grim sense of humor, as Lt. Col. Charles Jones Jr. relates: "On this occasion a member of the garrison was literally buried upon the explosion of a fifteen-inch shell which penetrated deep into the parapet in front of one of the gun chambers. Liberating first one arm and then his head from the superincumbent mass, and freeing his mouth from the sand with which it was filled, he roared out in stentorian tones: 'All quiet along the Ogeechee today.'"[33]

Cmdr. Worden continues his account: "At 10:35 A.M. we swung to the flood tide, the breeze increasing so that the smoke from the fort drove down upon us so as to affect our vision. The enemy were then enabled to man their guns and hit us frequently. We replied steadily, our shells falling and exploding in the huge traverses and on the parapets, but the admirable construction of the fort precluded our making a rapid impression upon it with our necessarily slow fire."[34]

It was evident to Paymaster Browne that the gunners in the fort knew their business and were not intimidated by the ironclad: "We fired at intervals of six or seven minutes, alternating with our guns, for an hour, when the length of the intervals was increased to ten or twelve minutes. They answered from the fort briskly and with wonderful precision, remembering how small a mark our ship at the distance afforded. Not a shot from the fort struck farther than thirty or forty feet, and the shot and exploding shell threw up from the river columns of water that broke and descended upon the turret like showers of rain. To our astonishment, they would fire some of guns out from the smoke of our exploded shell, when it seemed that the shell had struck precisely where the gun stood."[35]

Correspondent Osbon recorded: "About 10 1/2 o'clock the MONTAUK hove up her anchor and stood a few hundred yards further up the river. This position was within 1600 yards of the fort, and was maintained by her until about 12 o'clock without any apparent effect on her—and I may say as well of the battery either. The gunboats below, in the meantime, having pretty much exhausted their supply of long-range shell, took but an occasional part in the affair; and indeed, for two hours had used their guns very sparingly on this account."[36] From the gunboat *Dawn*, Paymaster Pierce tells of his view: "The Seneca and Wissahickon were of no use whatever with their 11-inch shell guns[,] their shot not reaching or going wide of the battery and the same was the case with the Mortar; our 100 pdr. Parrott made firstrate shots."[37]

Paymaster Browne was also impressed by the garrison's resilience. His observations make clear his growing respect for the fort's defenders. "For three hours we had thrown our big shells into their work. We had carried away their flag, blown into a shapeless mass the parapet and glacis that we had seen in the morning strong and smooth sodded. They still held out, and we began to wonder how long they could stand the explosion of fifteen-inch shell, for the number that remained in our magazine having suitable fuses was small. These were carefully used, and as we watched them, we knew that the havoc they made must be terrible. They continued to fire at us with a spitefulness and snap truly admirable."[38]

Cmdr. Worden realized he would soon have to withdraw from the contest because the supply of ammunition was dangerously low: "At 11:35 A.M., our supply of shells being expended, and finding that our cored shot did not affect the enemy, or at least we could not observe their effect with certainty, I ordered the firing to cease, tripped our anchor, and stood down the river, and . . . ordered the gunboats to discontinue the action."[39]

As the vessels dropped downstream, the fort sent them a parting salute. Paymaster Browne wrote, "As we got underway and were moving down stream, they let fly at us four shot in rapid succession. A few of us had got out on to the deck from one of the smoke-stained ports in the turret. One of the shot fell at our right hand in the river, two fell short, and the fourth came screaming over our heads, and striking in the marsh beyond, threw up grass and mud and water, and ricocheting, flew off high into the air. . . . Officers and men, black and stained with powder-smoke, came from the turret and from below decks, out into the clear noonday air, to see the result of the fight, and to take a parting look at the fort, which not till now had they been able to see."[40]

Correspondent Osbon stated in his account: "About noon a storm, which had been brewing all the morning, came up, with a misty rain and fog, completely enshrouding the fort; and the MONTAUK, too, having exhausted all her shell with the fuse of the required length, the vessels of the flotilla returned to their previous night's anchorage. . . . The affair lasted in all about five hours. During that time there were probably in the vicinity of 350 shot and shell expended by the fleet. The enemy, with the exception of four shells from their mortar with which the Seneca was favored, replied solely and exclusively to the fire of the MONTAUK, and probably expended about half as many."[41]

The *Montauk* came to anchor shortly after 1:00 P.M., then followed the task of inspecting the vessels and tabulating statistics, such as, the number of times they had been struck, extent of damage, and the amount of ammunition expended. Aboard the *Montauk* all seemed secure below decks, as Paymaster Pierce describes: "The Montauk was struck 12 times in her hull & turrett but no further damage was done [other] than a very slight dent where the shots struck. One of the shots struck the turrett and bounced back into their [life] boat and was picked up."[42]

Cmdr. Worden reported to Adm. Du Pont the official count of the *Montauk's* damage. "During the action we were struck by the enemy's shot as follows: Four times in turret, once in smokestack, four times on deck, three times in side plating, once in boat spars, sinking second cutter, also a number of times by fragments of shells."[43]

Paymaster Browne offered a little more detail: "They had carried away one of our flags; riddled another; hammered a score of indentations in our turret and pilot-house; broken off some of the bolts and driven them inside—and two of them, with the nuts attached to them, had passed within three inches of my head, that would have been crushed had they hit it; they had scoured our deck with scars two feet long, indenting and bending the iron plates; they had perforated our smoke-stack in many places, and cut its top into a ragged fringe; they had smashed our boats into splinters; still the efficiency of the vessel was not touched. . . . In the afternoon the ship was cleared and cleaned of powder-smoke, and splinters, and fragments of shell."[44]

Correspondent Osbon accounted the action.

So far as a test of the resisting powers of the ironclad vessel of the Monitor class is concerned, the affair was a most satisfactory one. In all, the MON-TAUK was struck thirteen times, mostly by 10-inch [*sic*] and rifled solid shot. The effect of these shot upon the turret was to leave an indenture of about one-half an inch. One shot which just grazed one side of the turret knocked off the head of one of the numerous bolts, with which the plates are fastened, which was about the only real damage which could be said to have been done. Several shots struck the deck of the vessel and plowed long furrows on the surface of the iron plating, but injured nothing. Two solid 10-inch shot [*sic*] struck in close proximity to one another on the edge of the hull and deck plates, which made the deepest indenture received by the vessel.

So much for the invincibility of the MONTAUK. As to the results of the morning's work, I regret not to be able to speak as flatteringly. How much damage was done to the enemy's works, of course, at present, no one can speak advisedly. But I hardly think it was of so serious a character as to prevent the Rebels from making as good a defense today as yesterday. To many, cognizant of the numerous land batteries reduced by our navy, it may seem very strange that an ironclad, assisted by four gunboats, should, in so long a space of time, have accomplished so little. But it must be remembered that the Ogeechee is no wide stream, permitting of the maneuvering of sea-going vessels."[45]

After checking the magazines of the five vessels, it was found that 378 rounds had been thrown at Fort McAllister. The *Montauk* fired twenty-six of its 15-inch rounds, and the *Dawn* contributed about fifty-five of its 100-pounder Parrott shells. A variety of shot and shell had been fired at the earthen fort but it stood up to the pounding.[46] Lt. Col. Jones recorded, "Despite this . . . enormous expenditure of shot and shell on the part of the enemy, the damage done to the fort was repaired before morning, and not a single casualty occurred among the members of the garrison. Major John B. Gallie commanded the fort during this bombardment, and the guns principally used in replying to the enemy were the eight-inch Columbiad, and the rifle thirty-two pounder gun which had been recently added to the battery . . . On this occasion a fifteen-inch gun was first used in the effort to reduce a shore battery and the ability of properly constructed sand parapets to resist the effect of novel projectiles, far surpassing in weight and power all others heretofore known, was fairly demonstrated."[47]

When Cmdr. Worden received the tally of the ammunition used against the fort, he realized they had severely depleted their supplies of ammunition. It was evident that if Fort McAllister was to be neutralized, it would take a more determined effort.

This attack on Fort McAllister showed that the ironclad's turret provided the gun crews good protection but there were drawbacks. The turret was found to be too small for fast and accurate handling of the two large cannon, which added to the turret's crowded conditions. The same iron-plated housing that provided protection for the gun crews also hindered the range of the guns for targets requiring anything other than low, flat-trajectory rounds. Firing the guns at these low elevations deprived them of longer ranges that could be obtained at higher levels.[48]

The Confederate gunners in the fort noticed the *Montauk's* slow rate of fire and calculated the time it took between shots while reloading its guns. With no fewer than six minutes between rounds, the Confederate gunners could come out of their bombproofs, fire their guns, reload, and return to the bombproofs before the *Montauk* was ready to resume firing. Thus they received the *Montauk's* fire in relative safety.[49]

Almost as soon as the *Montauk* withdrew downstream, the Confederates brought in over 150 slave laborers to repair the damages and further strengthen the fort. With the confusion and the large numbers of slaves at work, it was relatively easy for some to slip away, which situation Cmdr. Worden took advantage of: "[Today] I learned through the medium of a contraband, who has been employed upon these waters as a pilot, the position of the obstructions below the fort and the location of the torpedoes placed upon the pilings of the channel way. This information, with the aid of the contraband, whom I took on board, [will] enable me to take up a position nearer the fort in the next attack upon it."[50]

Paymaster Browne, aboard the *Montauk,* explained, "Contrabands occasionally came to us, some of them directly from the fort, and there was no flaw or contradiction in their story. . . . We learned from a number of refugees that our day's work had almost demolished the fort . . . and that one of our 15-inch unexploded shell was exhibited in Savannah, exciting much wonder, and exerting an excellent moral influence."[51]

On 28 January, Adm. Du Pont wrote to his wife.

> From pretty early in the morning we heard heavy firing in the direction of Ossabaw, and we took for granted Worden was at work. . . . Worden approached to where the Ogeechee was staked and outside of this evidently a row of torpedoes. He was some fifteen hundred yards off, nearly the full range of his 15-inch cannon—fired away his ammunition, and could not see that it had much effect. . . . The other gunboats fired away nearly two-thirds of their ammunition. In short, nothing was effected—but we gained a good deal of information . . . and the invulnerability seemed sustained. There were no casualties at all. Now another of my theories was established. . . . Three regiments or one landing to take the fort in the rear would have so shaken the garrison that a few shells would have sufficed; if met by a larger number of troops, why they had only to fall back under cover of their gunboats. . . . All these things I have clearly stated today in an official letter to the [Navy] Department. . . . I am glad I made the experiment. I suppose the rebels will make the most of having resisted a monitor.[52]

Adm. Du Pont was somewhat upset at the large expenditure of ammunition. With a large fleet to keep supplied, as well as a variety of forts around Charleston and Hilton Head, it was a challenge to maintain sufficient stockpiles of ammunition. He wrote later, "These ironclads soon get out of ammunition for they have not as much pouch as an opossum."[53] The admiral noted his concerns to Cmdr. Worden: "I am sending home for some ammunition. . . . The only fault I find is the tremendous amount of ammunition consumed by the gunboats, particularly by Barnes [of the *Dawn*] with his rifle gun. Unless you can get nearer the fort by the removal of the obstructions and torpedoes, I see no advantage in renewing the attack upon it. You will please order the Dawn up here without delay. I need not add how careful you should be if you make any attempt to deal with the torpedoes."[54]

That Adm. Du Pont was forced to send for more ammunition shows how much impact this little trip up the Ogeechee had on the balance of ordnance supplies at Hilton Head. He was also greatly concerned about what would happen if the Confederate ironclads showed up after the gunboats at Ossabaw Sound had expended their ammunition on Fort McAllister.[55]

He also realized that further operations against Fort McAllister would require more guns, more gunboats, and more ammunition. The ironclad monitor *Passaic* would soon be on hand to reinforce the *Montauk*. In his report to the secretary of the navy, Adm. Du Pont carefully analyzed the information gained.

> SIR: Considering it desireable to test in every way the efficiency of the ironclads that had arrived . . . I sent Commander Worden down to Ossabaw to operate up the Great Ogeechee River and capture, if he could, the fort at Genesis Point, under cover of which the Nashville was lying, now fitted as a privateer and waiting to run the blockade, and in case of success the railroad was also accessible. I enclose a copy . . . of Commander Worden's report. . . . The fort was a very formidable casemated earthwork with bombproofs, and mounting nine guns, the firing from which was excellent.
>
> We have obtained valuable information in the success of the working of the XV-inch gun, and although the Montauk was struck thirteen times she received no injury. My own impressions of these vessels . . . have been confirmed, viz, that whatever degree of impenetrability they might have, there was no corresponding quality of aggression or destructiveness as against forts, the slowness of fire giving full time for the gunners in the fort to take shelter in the bombproofs.
>
> This experiment also convinces me of another impression, firmly held and often expressed, that in all such operations to secure success troops are necessary. . . . The [Navy] Department, however, will observe how difficult if not impossible it will be to remove sunken obstructions and pilings in shallow water under fire.[56]

Although Osbon was only to be an observer, he still filed stories with his paper, much to Adm. Du Pont's chagrin. On 30 January Adm. Du Pont wrote to Cmdr. Worden:

> A long and detailed account of your operations against the battery in the Ogeechee, written by Mr. Osbon, was received this morning too late to go by the *Circassian*. I was of course aware that Mr. Osbon was on board the *Montauk,* but I did not intend that he should be there as a reporter for his paper. . . . This communication is objectionable for the following reasons and cannot, therefore, be forwarded by mail.
>
> 1. Because it is written from the ship and would naturally be supposed to come from one of the officers. . . .
>
> 2. Because it gives information which would be of the greatest value to the rebels. . . . enabling them to perfect their defenses at Charleston.

3. That it magnifies the object of the expedition [and] predicts successes which were not borne out by results. . . .

I have always been liberal to reporters, but I can not permit all our preliminary experiments in view of the attack upon Charleston to be made public.[57]

In spite of Du Pont's objections, Osbon was still aboard the *Montauk,* and he would find ways to get his stories to his paper. He voiced the then–big question: "It seems that upon the iron-clad, or iron-clads, must devolve the principal part of the coming task of reducing Fort McAllister. To do this, however, it will be necessary for [the *Montauk*] to assume a closer proximity to the battery than yet taken by her. In doing this, to be sure, she runs a great risk of grounding and of encountering the torpedoes and other obstructions of the river, near the piles, between us and the fort. I have no doubt Commander Worden will conclude to take these chances and to place his vessel where, in a comparatively short space of time, her heavy guns will render this resort of the grey-coated gentry quite untenable. Upon the coming of ammunition, 'we shall see what we shall see.'"[58]

4

THE NOISE ROLLS LIKE
DISTANT THUNDER

The men of the Republican Blues and the Emmett Rifles felt their faith in the sand defenses had been well placed. But they also felt certain they had not seen the last of the Federal ironclads. Fearful of the consequences that might follow the fort's capture by Federal forces, Confederate authorities took measures to move reinforcements to the area. Col. Robert H. Anderson, commanding the Confederate forces on the Ogeechee River, detailed some of these preparations. "Martin's Light Battery I held in reserve at Hardwick, which is about 1 1/2 miles in rear of the battery. Captain McAllister's troop I also held in readiness about a mile in rear of the battery. The two rifle guns of the Chatham Artillery, under Lieutenant [George A.] Whitehead, I had placed in pits on a commanding bluff on the river about a mile in rear of the battery; the two guns of the Confederate States steamer Rattlesnake, under the command of Capt. [T. Harrison] Baker, I also ordered placed on Richmond Bluff, about 7 miles in rear of the battery. The steamer Rattlesnake . . . was moved to a suitable point in the river and in readiness to be sunk [if] necessity required it."[1]

As January 1863 faded, both sides prepared for the next battle on the Ogeechee. The gunboat *Dawn* and steam tug *Daffodil* carried fresh stocks of ammunition from Hilton Head to the force gathered in Ossabaw Sound, arriving on 31 January. Cmdr. Worden was ready once again to take the *Montauk* under the guns of Fort McAllister.[2]

During the early morning hours of 1 February, the *Montauk, Seneca, Wissahickon, Dawn,* and *C. P. Williams* made their way into the lower reaches of the Ogeechee River and with first light moved into position. Worden reported, "At 6:40 A.M. I weighed anchor and proceeded up the river. The weather was pleasant, but a dense mist hung close over the lowlands, and there was no wind at the time of our starting. We steamed slowly up."[3]

The garrison at Fort McAllister would not be taken by surprise. Col. Anderson described the preparations made to defend the area directly behind the fort: "Before the enemy's boats came within range I ordered Capt. Arthur Shaaff, commanding the 1st Battalion Georgia Sharpshooters, to line the riverbank with his riflemen. His right rested about a quarter of a mile in rear of and west of the battery. As soon as I was satisfied that there was no intention on the part of the enemy to land at Kilkenny [Bluff] on my right flank, and that his intention was restricted to passing the obstructions, I ordered him to deploy his battalion on his right file at ten paces intervals, which enabled him to cover the bank of the river for over a mile with his sharpshooters, who had excellent cover, and would annoy . . . the enemy terribly [should] he succeed . . . in passing the obstructions."[4]

As the gunboats approached within sight of the fort, the sailors were surprised to find it having been greatly built up since their last attack four days earlier. Lt. Cmdr. William Gibson of the *Seneca* commented, "The fort has been enlarged and strengthened with huge traverses within a recent period, and though but an earthwork, is now really colossal of its kind."[5]

Cmdr. Worden gave his account:

> At 7:27 A.M. I anchored about 600 yards below the fort (McAllister), and on the right bank of the river, as near as the shoal water would allow me. The gunboats took a position in line, as on Tuesday last, and about 1 3/4 miles below the fort. At 7:45 A.M. we opened fire upon the enemy, the mist hanging close to the fort, and preventing the smoke of their guns clearing away so that we could see neither their position nor the effect of our own shells. The enemy replied vigorously for some time, when they were obliged to slacken their fire on account of not being able to see us through the smoke. . . .
>
> The C. P. Williams . . . took a position at such a distance from the fort as was believed would enable her mortar to be used with effect, and succeeded in throwing a number of shells in and around it. . . .
>
> At 7:53 A.M. our turret was hit for the first time during this action, at which time the enemy were working their guns with rapidity and precision.[6]

Col. Robert Anderson gave the Confederate perspective of these events: "Our battery opened fire first, but not until the ironclad had approached and taken a position north of and within 800 or 1,000 yards of the battery; their wooden boats lay about 2 miles from and to the east of the fort. The enemy fired steadily and with remarkable precision, at times their fire was terrible.

4.1. Maj. John B. Gallie assumed command at Fort McAllister on 25 November 1862. A native of Scotland, he settled in Savannah and was a successful cotton merchant. He served with the Chatham Artillery for many years and organized a number of artillery units during the war. His death at Fort McAllister during the 1 February 1863 attack by the ironclad *Montauk* was the only fatality suffered by the garrison in seven naval attacks on the fort. Courtesy, Georgia Department of Natural Resources, Fort McAllister State Historic Park

Their mortar firing was unusually fine, a large number of their shells bursting directly over the battery."[7]

The return fire from the fort was limited because the wooden gunboats were at the extreme range of the 32-pounders. The only guns likely to have any effect were the 8-inch Columbiad (the Pet Gun), commanded by 1st Lt. Dixon, and the 32-pounder rifle, commanded by Lt. Francis Willis.[8] The rifled 32-pounder was the only rifled piece in the fort, but it was a hybrid weapon. Capt. Anderson of the Blues found that the gun worked well but the shells were deficient: "We were unable to reach the wooden vessels. Our rifle projectiles are miserable. As soon as they leave the muzzle of the gun they commence to revolve over and over."[9]

Maj. John B. Gallie was observing the fire of 1st Lt. Dixon's 8-inch Columbiad when a shell crashed through the parapet and exploded. He was knocked down, partially buried in the sand, and badly cut in the face by a fragment of the shell. As he was lifted to his feet, someone suggested he seek medical aid but he refused, saying he would "be able to attend to duty in a few minutes."[10] 1st Lt. Dixon described the moment: "A shell from the Iron Clad came through the parapet of my gun. Major Gallie was knocked down.

4.2. The far bank of the Ogeechee River opposite the fort is where the monitors took up position during their attacks on the fort. This gun position is where Maj. Gallie was when a 15-inch shell came over the wall, struck the 32-pounder gun here, and exploded, dislodging a trunnion on the gun. Shrapnel struck Maj. Gallie in the back of the head, killing him instantly. The gun shown is a 10-inch Columbiad, placed here in the summer of 1863. Courtesy, Library of Congress

John Mahon[11] and [Anthony. L.] Robider[12] were knocked down. Jim Barbour[13] was knocked down and buried. They were quickly cared for, Jim Barbour being very near dead. I quickly got two more men and set the gun to work. . . . In a few moments the Major [Gallie] came back to look for his glasses. I saw he had a hole in his nose large enough to put my finger in and the whole nose was badly bruised. But he did not seem to mind it. I told him his glass was buried in the sand and it was impossible to find it. He then left me and that was the last time I saw him."[14]

Maj. Gallie moved on, pausing to encourage each gun crew. Shortly after 8:00 A.M. he was with the crew of the 32 pounder gun located on the left of the battery when a 15-inch shell from the *Montauk* came over the parapet, struck the 32-pounder and exploded. The right trunnion of the gun was broken off, and either the dislodged trunnion or a fragment of the shell struck

Gallie behind the left ear killing him instantly.[15] 1st Lt. Dixon wrote, "He was struck by a shell on the back of the head which tore the whole back off down to the neck leaving only the face. It was indeed a sad affair and it cast a gloom over the entire garrison for he was much beloved by all."[16] This last statement seems curious because, two months before, the Republican Blues sought reassignment rather than serve under Gallie's command. Apparently Gallie had won over their confidence in that two months. Gallie's body was removed, and the command of the fort fell to Capt. George W. Anderson Jr.[17]

Dixon's gun crew serving the 8-inch Columbiad found their position to be the prime aiming point for the *Montauk*'s guns as Col. Robert Anderson noted: "The iron-clad's fire was principally directed at the 8-inch Columbiad, and about 8:15 [A.M.] the parapet in front of this gun was so badly breached as to leave the gun entirely exposed. The detachment did not leave their gun or evince the slightest fear, but in the most gallant and determined manner fought their gun . . . refusing to be relieved. The name of the brave officer who commanded this gun is 1st Lt. W. D. Dixon, of the Republican Blues."[18]

1st Lt. Dixon described his experience.

The fireing still continued. The very next shot from her struck the traverse just on my right. It came very near burying me up. I thought things had begun to look rather serious but we still continued to break our shot upon her. Very soon she began to drop down the river when she again took her stand where she was the last time, where she began to throw shell into us hot and heavy now and then damageing the works a little. She struck one of our guns and broke the wheel the shot comeing through the parapet and knocked a man named [John] Grey[19] down and rol[l]ed over his chest. I think he is seriously wounded. The second time the same gun was struck and the trunnion was knocked off and the carriage all torn to pieces. My gun was worked all the time by six men Corpl [Charles F.] Blancho[20], Priv [John] Mahan, Corpl [Mark] Masters[21], [James] Barbour, [Anthony L.] Robider, [William J.] Baillie.[22] Sergt. [Timothy S.] Flood[23] was the gunner. The whole squad acted well. . . . I never saw men stick to anything so well in my life.[24]

Inside the pilot house of the *Montauk,* correspondent Bradley Osbon found the combat a little too close for comfort. "About half past eight o'clock our pilot-house was hit by a tremendous blow by a shot. Your correspondent was at the instant on one knee writing a paragraph in his notebook. The shock was severe, and afterward he found that the shot struck close to his head. It unbalanced me, and I tumbled over against the side of the narrow pilot-house, when, to my surprise, I was struck by a piece of iron bolt with the nut attached (weighing about one pound), first on the shoulder and then on the knee. . . . In view of such an accident and suffering the shock, I left the pilot-house."[25] Osbon's injury was the only one sustained aboard the *Montauk.*

The gunboats and the ironclad continued the exchange of ordnance until the ebb tide intervened. Aboard the *Montauk,* correspondent Osbon reported, "The Montauk held her position near the piles until nearly low water, and only fell back when it was discovered by sounding that there were but <u>fifteen inches</u> of water under her hull. In another half hour she must evidently have been hard aground."[26]

Cmdr. Worden wrote, "At 8:45 A.M. I sounded in 14 feet, and, knowing that the tide would fall about 5 feet more, leaving about 9 feet under us, I tripped the anchor and dropped down the river to a position about 1,400 yards from the fort and into deeper water. As we were dropping astern, a gentle air sprung up, which gradually dispelled the mist, and we were enabled to resume our fire with accuracy and observed many of our shells to tear up the parapets and crumble down the huge traverses."[27]

The thundering cannonade could be heard far and wide over the Georgia coast. It was Sunday, and the reverberations gave many Savannahians additional cause for prayer. Lt. Col. Charles C. Jones Jr. offered, "The thunder of those hostile guns strangely marred the stillness of the holy day, and with harsh discord invaded even the sanctuaries of the living God. Fervently did the prayers of the assembled worshipers within the respective churches in the city of Savannah ascend to the God of battles in behalf of fathers, husbands, and brothers who were gallantly passing through this fearful ordeal."[28]

John Ash, a nineteen-year-old serving with the Georgia Hussars stationed outside Savannah, entered his account into his diary: "The firing is terrific. The guns sound like broadsides and the noise rolls like distant thunder. The enemy seem determined to take the point. . . . The people in the city who have friends and relatives at the Battery are quite uneasy about them. The cannons roar can be distinctly heard and the windows in the houses of the city shake at every discharge of the guns."[29]

At Way's Station, William Tappan Thompson,[30] editor of the *Savannah Morning News,* and J. R. Read relayed telegraphic dispatches to Savannah as couriers brought status reports from the fort. While the battle raged at Genesis Point, people anxiously gathered in Savannah and other points along the telegraph line to hear the latest dispatches.[31] The thundering of the cannons also brought alarm far beyond Savannah. At the Whitesville hospital near Guyton, about thirty miles west of Savannah on the Central of Georgia Railroad, Pvt. Isaac Hermann was awaiting his release so he could rejoin his unit, Martin's Light Battery, serving near Fort McAllister. Hermann was only one of many men from his unit who had been sent to the hospital suffering from malarial fever. Now after medication and rest, he was ready to rejoin his unit. The sound of cannon fire from the direction of Fort McAllister only proved to be an added incentive: "It was announced that General Mercer of Savannah, and the Board of Inspectors were to come on a round of inspections, when we heard heavy firing, the sounds coming from the east. Presently we heard that the enemy with a large fleet was attacking Fort McAllister. General Mercer and his Board had come up from Savannah on a special train. He called for all convalescent, able to fight to volunteer to go to the front. I presented myself; I was the only one. We cut loose the locomotive and one car and went flying to Savannah at the rate of a mile a minute, crossed the City in a buss at full speed to the Gulf Depot . . . just in time to board the train to Way Station, twelve miles from Savannah. An ambulance carried us to the Fort; the whole distance from the hospital to the Fort was about fifty-two miles. We changed conveyances three times and arrived at our destination in less than two hours."[32]

When Brig. Gen. Mercer arrived in the vicinity of Fort McAllister, he found the mortar battery not being used and ordered Capt. Robert Martin of Martin's Light Battery to take a gun crew into that position. When Pvt. Hermann reported for duty, he found his place on the gun crew was already taken but Capt. Martin still had a job for him.[33] Hermann described the assignment:

> Captain Martin sent me up the River to a bend about half a mile to the rear, which position placed me at a triangle point to the Fort and the gun boats. I was instructed to note the effect of our shots on the enemy's boats. I kept tally sheets as to the hits between the belligerent points. From my observation I counted seventy-five hits by the guns of the Fort, and one hundred and seventy-five hits by those of the boats, which raised a cloud of dust equal to an explosion of a mine . . . while our shots merely made a bright spot where they struck the heavy armored vessels and ricochet beyond. While thus observing I noted a strange move of one of the boats, suddenly I saw an immense flash, and a splash in the river a couple of yards in front of me. The water being very clear, we noted a large projectile at the bottom of the stream, evidently aimed at me, as it was in direct line, as I sat on my horse; undoubtedly they must have taken me for a commanding officer and thus paid me their res—I mean disrespect.[34]

While Pvt. Hermann was at his position beyond the fort, Capt. Martin took his detachment to the mortar emplacement. "I promptly repaired to my post, having first given orders . . . to move my light battery in supporting distance of the fort. I arrived at my mortar battery a few minutes after 9 A.M. and immediately opened fire on the Abolition fleet. At 10:40 A.M. my platform gave way and I was compelled to remove the planking and fire from the second tier of boards, which stood the firing very well."[35]

The *Montauk* received its fair share of attention from Capt. Martin's mortar, much to the dismay of correspondent Bradley Osbon.

> It was just six minutes past eleven o'clock. I was standing in the wardroom, and in conversation with Dr. Brayton, when a most terrific blow was struck upon our deck plating directly over my head. I was driven with much force into a chair, and my whole muscular system seemed for about two minutes perfectly paralyzed. I was faint and could scarcely obtain my breath. I never experienced such an unpleasant sensation in the whole course of my life. It was a heavy shock to my whole system. In fact it exceeded my experience in the pilot-house. . . . And while absorbed in such thoughts Slam! came another such a shot, but, fortunately for me at least, about six feet away from where the first one struck. Weak as I was this again gave me a shock. . . . I soon recovered from the intensive pain I suffered, and resumed my notes, but was continually in apprehension of having the dose repeated. Fortunately, however, it was not.[36]

On the gunboat *Dawn,* the sailors noticed the additional incoming fire received from the Confederate mortar. Paymaster Pierce's diary entry reads, "We got in the Dawn the entire attention of the Mortar and one gun but finally silenced them though they passed the pieces of shell all round us and plenty near."[37]

Capt. Martin and his gun crew serving the mortar were well aware of the incoming fire they received from the *Dawn* and its 100-pounder Parrott rifle. The captain related, "The firing from the fleet was good. My men were frequently covered with sand, and shell and fragments of shell frequently fell around us. My practice was at first bad, owing to the mist, but toward mid-day it improved, the shells bursting over or falling near the vessels. My men stood to their work well." Only one man in the detachment was injured, and his wound was a slight fragment wound in the head.[38]

At one point, incoming shells hit the barracks and started a fire. Fortunately, it was discovered before it had a chance to spread, and a detachment of soldiers extinguished it in spite of the incoming projectiles.[39] All morning the two adversaries exchanged shot and shell, but when the sun reached high into the sky overhead, Cmdr. Worden decided further action was useless: "We continued our fire, with no signs of doing the enemy's guns any damage, until 11:53 A.M., when I ordered the firing to cease and dropped out of their range. . . . We were struck by projectiles forty-eight times, to wit, sixteen times on turret, three times on pilot house, seven times on smokestack, seven times on side armor, eight times on deck armor, once in gig, once in cutter, twice on boat's spars, once on spare anchor, and had two flagstaffs shot away. . . . [40] Two X-inch [*sic*] shot struck in rapid succession within 6 or 8 inches of each other near the base of the turret, immediately after which it was found difficult to revolve the turret until it was raised by driving in the key three-fourths of an inch, when it again revolved quite freely."[41]

The fort's garrison was overjoyed to see the enemy retiring downriver. According to Capt. George Anderson, "At 12:30 o'clock the enemy slowly backed out of range of our guns. The tower of the ironclad was struck several times. We could hear them hammering distinctly evidently mending something which had been broken by our shot. The turret ceased to revolve; whether designedly or not is left to conjecture."[42]

The *Montauk* and the gunboats anchored about three miles below the fort, and the crew came out on deck to check how well the monitor had withstood the pounding. They were also wondering if the problem with the turret was due to the enemy shot. Worden wrote, "The coincidence would suggest this difficulty to have been the effect of these shots, but it is hard to see how such could have been the case, and as after the engagement it was found that only one of the turret engines was working properly, it seems to prove fairly to be attributable to the latter cause."[43]

The thundering of the big guns ceased as abruptly as it began, and quiet settled over the area once again. Both sides assessed the damage and tallied the statistics. Correspondent Osbon gave an optimistic assessment: "The Montauk received . . . no less than <u>sixty-one shots</u>. Her smokestack was completely riddled with balls, her flag-staff at the bow carried away, and upon all sides were signs of the terrible storm of iron to which she had been subjected. But yet no material damage was done, and for all practical purposes was just as good as new. . . . We at least have the cheering assurances that the Monitors are in fact invincible, although it is not allowed us to boast of a victory gained. The mere fact that a vessel having . . . maintained a position for five hours in the face of a strong battery, receiving shots which would have sunk a score of wooden vessels, and then quietly retiring without a man injured and with no damage sustained, is of itself worth no small victory."[44]

But the Confederates laid a firm claim to the day's victory. Col. Robert Anderson reported, "This attack was one of no ordinary character, as will be readily admitted when the class of the enemy's vessels and their superior armament are taken into consideration, as well as the close proximity of the ironclad to the battery. I think that the brave and heroic garrison of Fort McAllister have, after a most severe and trying fight, demonstrated to the world that victory does not, as a matter of course, always perch itself on the flag of an ironclad when opposed even to an ordinary earthwork manned by stout and gallant hearts."[45]

When the *Montauk* and the gunboats withdrew downstream, Pvt. Hermann left his post from where he'd been observing the contest and hurried to the fort. "The Fort was badly dilapidated, our breast works had been blown to atoms, the guns exposed to plain view, all port holes demolished, the barracks injured by fire, which the boys extinguished while the battle was raging; in fact, had a cyclone struck the Fort in its full majestic force, it could not have been worse."[46] The front parapet had been badly torn up in five places and completely demolished in front of the 8-inch Columbiad.[47]

Shortly after the gunboats withdrew downstream, Maj. Henry Bryan arrived on the scene. He reported to Brig. Gen. Thomas Jordan.

The ironclad seems to have fired principally XV-inch shell, one of which went directly through the parapet (17 feet thick) in front of a 32-pounder on the left. At this point the parapet was mostly built of marsh mud, which I infer can not offer sufficient resistance to these missiles. Two shells seem to have struck near the same point on the parapet (made of sand) in front of the Columbiad, and tore away about a third of it, covering several men with sand; one or two were dug out. The resisting power of sand is very great, and, after thick iron, it makes probably the protection most desireable. So far as demolishing earthworks goes, I am inclined to think the XV-inch shell a partial failure. I think a concentrated fire of smaller guns would have been more destructive to us. Had they burst better, however, the result might have been different. Captain George W. Anderson, the officer next in rank to Major Gallie, has proved himself a brave and good young soldier, but I think Captain Alfred L. Hartridge, Company B, 1st Georgia Sharpshooters, who commanded Genesis Point last summer, is the man best qualified to succeed Major Gallie. I will send you by express a brass fuze plug from the XV-inch shell.[48]

The final tally of garrison casualties was surprisingly light. Maj. Gallie was the only fatality; seven men were wounded. From the Republican Blues, John Grey was wounded by shell fragments; John Mahon and James Barbour were knocked down and partially buried in the sand by shells that exploded on the parapet but they were not wounded badly enough to require hospitalization. From the Emmett Rifles, Peter Brady and John Dillon were wounded by shell fragments. John Grey and Peter Brady were wounded badly enough to be immediately evacuated by wagon and taken to Way's Station from where they were taken by train to Savannah.[49]

Repairs to the fort proceeded as daylight slipped away. Pvt. Hermann pro-
vides an image of the activity: "That night we pressed into service all the
negroes on the rice plantations. Spades, shovels and pick axes were handled
with alacrity; baskets, bags and barrels were filled, the enfeebled portions of
the Fort were reinforced by working like Trojans all night long, and the Fort
was again placed in a presentable condition."[50]

The front wall was rebuilt, and the parapet in front of 1st Lt. Dixon's 8-
inch Columbiad was greatly enlarged and strengthened. All that remained
was to replace the damaged 32-pounders, and replacements were soon on
their way. While repairs continued that night, the garrison said farewell to
their commander. Maj. Gallie's body was taken to Way's Station where the
train carried it to Savannah. He was buried in Laurel Grove Cemetery a few
days later.[51]

Quiet settled across the Ogeechee as the *Montauk* and its escort of wood-
en gunboats remained in Ossabaw Sound, and the garrison of Fort McAllister
prepared to meet the next challenge. At dress parade the following day, 2
February, the garrison received a written commendation from Col. Robert H.
Anderson. They also received a 10-inch Columbiad for their armament.[52] On
4 February, 1st Lt. Dixon noted in his journal, "Our whole force with the
sharpshooters have been engaged all day in mounting the 10-inch gun. She is
now ready to bark at all Yankees."[53]

In Charleston, South Carolina, Gen. Beauregard was soon studying the
reports submitted by his subordinate officers. On 6 February, he penned his
own endorsement and forwarded the reports to Richmond. "The results related within of the obstinate attack by an ironclad of the monitor class on our
battery at Genesis Point are important and encouraging. The armament of
the battery in question unfortunately was not heavy nor such as I should have
placed at that point had the proper guns been at my disposition. . . . But,
thanks to the intrepidity of the garrison and supporting force of officers and
men, the battery withstood the formidable attack and the enemy were beat-
en back. I beg to command to the notice of the President the names of all
mentioned in these papers."[54]

Newer and improved weapons soon became part of Fort McAllister's
defenses. Because there was a shortage of heavy guns to fill all of the defensive requirement, Confederate ordnance expert James G. Rains had been experimenting with several different types of river torpedoes that could be
planted in waterways and set to explode upon contact with a vessel passing
over them. Two basic types of torpedoes had resulted. One was the "keg"
torpedo that utilized a small, powder-filled, wooden keg with a sensitive
fuse. The other was the "frame" torpedo, which was a large, 400-pound,

conical-shaped, iron shell, set upon a long wooden timber anchored to the river bottom by a wooden frame filled with rocks or debris. The shell contained twenty-seven pounds of powder and was raised so that the nose was situated below the water surface. In theory, a vessel that ran upon these torpedoes would detonate the powder, and the subsequent explosion would open a hole in the ship's bottom.[55]

Because of the preparations the Federals had been making around Savannah and Charleston, Gen. Beauregard ordered the waterways and harbors in these places protected with the new Rains torpedoes. On 1 February, when the gunners at Fort McAllister were standing up to the guns of the *Montauk,* Gen. Beauregard wrote to Brig. Gen. Mercer in Savannah, "I have ordered nine Rains torpedoes to be sent to you forthwith, to be put in the channel of the Ogeechee within range of Fort McAllister. I hope they will be found to answer for notwithstanding the great importance of that work and of saving the Nashville, which I consider the sole cause of the attacks of the enemy in that quarter, it is utterly out of my power to send a heavy gun to be added to the armament of Fort McAllister."[56] Within two weeks these nine frame-style torpedoes had been mounted and emplaced in the Ogeechee River just downsteam from the obstructions off the fort, near the area where the *Montauk* had taken up its firing position. The next time the ironclad and gunboats ventured upstream, they might have an unpleasant surprise.

The results of the attacks on Fort McAllister focused more than public attention upon the little earthwork. The Confederate military was also quick to grasp the importance of the firm stand made by the fort's garrison and drew attention to the example set by these men. On 6 February, Chief of Staff Thomas Jordan issued General Order No. 23.

> The commanding general announces to the forces with satisfaction and pride the results of the recent encounter of our battery at Genesis Point, Ga., with an iron-clad of the monitor class; results only alloyed by the life-blood of the gallant commander, the late Major John B. Gallie.
>
> For hours the most formidable vessel of her class hurled missiles of the heaviest caliber ever used in modern warfare at the weak parapet of the battery, which was almost demolished; but, standing at their guns, as became men fighting for homes, for honor, and for independence, the garrison replied with such effect as to cripple and beat back their adversary, clad though in impenetrable armor and armed with 15- and 11-inch guns, supported by mortar boats whose practice was of uncommon precision.
>
> The thanks of the country are due to this intrepid garrison, who have thus shown what brave men may withstand and accomplish, despite

apparent odds. "Fort McAllister" will be inscribed on the flags of all the troops engaged in the defense of the battery.

BY THE COMMAND OF GENERAL BEAUREGARD.[57]

Although the fighting was over, the large amount of unexploded shells scattered around the area behind the fort made things rather hazardous. They would eventually be gathered up and salvaged, but until that work was done, the men were cautioned against handling these dud shells. For the garrison of the fort, these large projectiles were nothing new, because they handled them in the course of serving the cannons in the fort. However, the supporting troops encamped to the rear of the fort had a natural curiosity, which made a recipe for disaster. 1st Lt. Dixon noted on 12 February, "There was a bad accident happened here last night in the Sharpshooters. They were fooling with one of the old shells and one of them put a firebrand into it when it exploded killing one Sergt Smith and wounded 2 others very badly. . . . They buried him with military honors."[58]

Lt. Col. Charles C. Jones Jr. visited Fort McAllister while inspecting artillery units stationed in the area. In a 14 February letter to his parents, he said, "The scars caused by the shot and shell fired by the enemy on the 1st inst. are still numerous in and about the fort, and will continue for many days to come. The battery there is now much stronger than it was on the day of the engagement. All damage to the traverses, bombproofs, and parapet has been repaired. In fact, the parapet has been strengthened by the addition of at least three feet of sand, and a ten-inch gun has been added to the armament. An effort is being made to secure torpedoes in the stream below the fort so as to blow up the ironclad when next she takes her position to bombard."[59]

In mid-February, Gen. Beauregard traveled from Charleston to inspect the defenses of Savannah and arrived 21 February at Fort McAllister. 1st Lt. Dixon described the visit: "Genl Beaurigard and Mercer and staff were down here this morning. They were received by the Battalion. Some fireing was done from the battery. . . . Before Gen Beaurigard left, he requested to be introduced to all the officers which was done. He then complimented the whole of us on the gallant defense we made."[60]

The garrison was aware that their defense of the post had attracted media attention on both sides but they were especially interested in what Northern newspaper accounts had to say. On 25 February, 1st Lt. Dixon recorded his reaction: "Yankee acounts say that it is allmost useless to attempt to breech Fort McAllister as the Montauk could not do it. They have concluded that the parepet is 30 feet thick. I hope they will keep on thinking so."[61]

Dixon also noted that James R. Sneed of the *Savannah Republican* newspaper paid a visit to the post on this same day.[62] That meant a chance to tell their side of the story to the public. When the lengthy article was published on 27 February, it was read with great interest at the fort. Besides narrating the events, it handed out laurels left and right.

> Lt. Wm. D. Dixon of the Republican Blues and a resident of this City, is said by his brother officers to have been the true hero of the fight. He had charge of the 8-inch Columbiad, against which the enemy seemed to have a particular spite and served it with a coolness and gallantry that has not been excelled in the war. The entire parapet was shot away by 10 o'clock, yet he and his gallant little band stood firmly by their gun and fought it against an ironclad on an open plain as it were until the last . . . they refused to be relieved until the fight was over. Such men with such a commander would do honor to any service. Lt. Francis Willis also of the Blues and a citizen of Macon, is spoken of by his commander in terms of the highest praise. He had command of the rifle gun, the most exposed in the battery. . . . Sergt. Wm. Moran of the Emmett Rifles, had charge of the 42-pounder and served it with a skill and coolness that commanded the admiration of his commander. Sergt. [Patrick] Cavanaugh of the Emmett Rifles was also at the same gun and distinguished himself by his manly efforts and indifference to danger. Sergt. T. S. Flood was the chief gunner of the 8-inch Columbiad and stood at the rear of his gun from the beginning to the close of the fight. This was the principal gun in the battery at that time and was in the most exposed position. . . . The Mortar battery, which was in a very exposed position was worked by Capt. Robert Martin of Martin's Light Battery with a detachment of his men. . . . They stood their ground manfully through the whole of the fight, with the shells bursting all around and over them, but, fortunately none were seriously hurt. . . . Peter E. Judena,[63] who acted as courier during the fight, passing from gun to gun in transmitting the orders of the Commandant, is said to have discharged his fearful duty with singular coolness and intrepidity.[64]

Although the soldiers of the garrison received acclaim for their bravery under fire, they began to understand that their pile of sand and mud was the real reason they had been able to stand up to the *Montauk*'s pounding. And they knew they could do it all again when the time came. The resiliency of the fort itself gave them confidence in themselves and their ability to resist anything that might come up the river.

The outcome of events at Fort McAllister were not what Admiral Du Pont had hoped for. All the *Montauk*'s attacks had proved was the ship's ability to absorb punishment and the fort's capacity to withstand destruction. The Federals had been unable to destroy it, pass it, reach the *Nashville*, or the railroad bridge upstream. Although the *Montauk* had shown its ability to resist heavy gunfire, it also demonstrated one drawback: the lack of offensive firepower. The wooden gunboats had provided long-range support, but even the added weight of their guns had not proved sufficient to knock out the guns in the fort.

Du Pont felt that if the *Montauk* was reinforced by additional monitor-class vessels, their combined rate of fire might be enough to tip the balance. In a short time he would have three more ironclad monitors ready, the *Patapsco,* the *Passaic,* and the *Nahant.* Because these vessels would also require a combat test, Du Pont decided they would also be brought against Fort McAllister. Until they were prepared for duty, he ordered the *Montauk* and the gunboats in Ossabaw Sound to maintain a respectable distance from the fort.[65]

5

TANGLED MACHINERY AND CHARRED RELICS

The *Nashville* remained a tempting prize for the blockading ships below the Ogeechee River. Adm. Du Pont was determined that the ship remain bottled up or be destroyed, but the vessel remained elusive, often within sight of the blockaders but always out of reach up the river. Through the winter months, the *Nashville* remained anchored near Arnold's Landing, undergoing a change from blockade runner to privateer. By mid-February the conversion was complete. Its deck had been strengthened to take the weight of heavy guns, and 32-pounder and 24-pounder cannons placed aboard. The vessel's silhouette was lowered, its machinery overhauled, and thus the privateer *Rattlesnake* was born.[1]

The *Rattlesnake* (at this point still referred to as the *Nashville* by some) came down the river on the night of 13 February and remained at anchor behind the fort awaiting an opportunity to escape. Apparently all the attention the fort received from the *Montauk* and its escort made Capt. Baker nervous because it was obvious to him that the *Nashville* was their intended target. Baker wanted to make an escape before the ironclad was able to pass the fort but the presence of the *Rattlesnake* behind the fort brought the blockaders even closer to the river's mouth, making escape more difficult. On 17 February, 1st Lt. Dixon wrote down the story: "The <u>Nashville</u> came down nearer the Battery after daylight this morning. In doing so she was in sight of all the Yankee vessels. Soon after we heard them blowing their whistles and two vessels came up to the Iron Clads. There is one vessel in the Little Ogeechee [River] reconnoitreing. She can from her position see the <u>Nashville</u>. I would not be surprised if they made and attempt to get at her."[2]

5.1. Built in 1854 in New York City as a passenger and mail steamer, the *Nashville* worked the east coast and transatlantic routes. When the war began, Southern authorities seized the ship in Charleston and placed it in government service. Armed with cannon, it was sent to England in November 1861 to obtain supplies. Off the coast of Ireland, the *Nashville* overtook and burned the clipper *Harvey Birch,* one of the first Confederate captures by a privateer, and flew the first Confederate flag seen in European waters. Courtesy, Georgia Department of Natural Resources, Fort McAllister State Historic Park

On the morning of 21 February, the *Rattlesnake* moved back upstream to its anchorage near the Atlantic and Gulf Railroad bridge. On the 23rd the privateer took on a cargo of seven hundred bales of compressed upland cotton, seventy-five pounds of resin, and forty boxes of tobacco. When the coal bunkers were topped off with coal, the ship was ready for sea.[3]

The ship's crew was anxious after being marooned up the river for so long. It was difficult to sit and wait for the right opportunity for escape to present itself. On one occasion, a ruse was attempted to fool the Federal blockaders into loosening their watch on the river's entrance. The Savannah newspapers printed stories stating the *Rattlesnake* had already slipped out through the blockade and successfully run into Charleston on a return trip. Similar stories were related with the knowledge that this news, not to mention the newspapers themselves, would find their way to the Federal blockaders in Ossabaw Sound. It was hoped that this effort at deceit would cause the blockading forces at the river's mouth to loosen their hold long enough to allow the *Rattlesnake* to slip out.[4] The Federals were not so easily fooled for they considered their blockade escape-proof and continued to maintain their vigilance. Once Capt. Baker ascertained that none of the schemes had worked, he resumed the routine of steaming the vessel down the river at dusk to await an opportunity to get out and then back up the river every morning when the glow of daylight found them still in the river behind the fort.

In the early-morning darkness of 27 February, the *Rattlesnake* moved downstream once more. The vessel remained anchored behind the fort until about 4:00 A.M. when Capt. Baker ordered the ship back upstream. The ship reversed its engines and maneuvered up the channel backwards rather than turning around.[5] About two miles up the bend, the vessel apparently made its approach to the curve of Seven Mile Bend before it actually got to the curve, thus it crossed the channel and swerved towards a mudbank against the northwest bank of the river. There was a shuddering lurch, and the ship groaned to a halt. Legends persist that the pilot of the vessel was drunk at the time, and this seems plausible as other sources relate that the crew of the ship was mostly foreign sailors and a hard-drinking, hell-raising bunch.[6] Baker ordered the engines forward in hopes of pulling the ship free, but nothing happened. It was held fast in the sand, and only the next rising tide offered any hope of lifting it loose, but the next tide change would not come until much later in the day. Baker realized they did not have that time. The *Rattlesnake* was dangerously exposed, offering the Federals as desirable a target as possible. But he was not ready to give up. As the day progressed, most of the crew was removed, and the steam tug *Columbus* brought downstream to help free the ship.[7]

All efforts failed to free the stranded vessel, and as the sun set on 27 February, it remained aground just north of the fort. The sailors aboard the blockading vessels soon became aware of unusual activity relating to the *Rattlesnake's* predicament. Paymaster Samuel Browne, aboard the *Montauk,* tells the story.

> At three o'clock in the afternoon, the gunboat Wissahickon signaled a movement on the part of the Nashville, lying near the fort. From the gunboat's mast-heads they could see what from our lower position was invisible. We bent our sight eagerly toward the point of woods, and soon discovered thin columns of black smoke ascending from behind the trees, as from a steamer's smoke-stack, and indicating a movement on the part

of the privateer. For a while the smoke increased, and grew thicker, but finally seemed to settle down into a thin broken line, and so remained. The captain and officers went down below to dinner. I remained on the turret, impressed that more was coming out of the matter. In twenty minutes the column of smoke began growing larger, and blacker, and thicker, and to move. . . . Intently I watched the point, and in a moment, from behind the trees came [into view] the famous blockade runner, the rebel privateer Nashville. . . .

I saw immediately that she had waited to go up the river until it was too late, and in endeavoring in the clear light of mid-afternoon,—and we had never seen her so plainly before, her coming and going having been in the duskiness of morning or evening,—had attempted to cut her way through the shoal, and had brought up aground, hard and fast. I immediately sent word below, and the captain and officers came on deck. We went straightaway to quarters, and for a while Captain Worden intended to go directly up the river. The gunboat Seneca was sent up to reconnoitre. She went up the Little Ogeechee to within a mile and a half of the Nashville, and by way of trial threw four or five shell at her, and in half an hour came back again.[8]

At Fort McAllister, 1st Lt. Dixon relates what he saw: "We were surprised this afternoon about dusk by the fireing of a shot towards the battery. We went to the guns but could see nothing. Very soon another shot came and it came from behind the woods, but it was sent at the Nashville. She was lying ashore opposite the battery, where she struck while going up the river today. Three shot was fired at her but they all fell short. The steamer then went down the river. If the Nashville does not get off tonight, I think they will come up in the morning and distroy her as she cannot help herself."[9]

Paymaster Browne continues:

In the meantime the smoke from the Nashville increased, crowding itself up in the air from out her funnel, a dense, expanding, sooty column, and rolling and curling into big black clouds that covered the sky and hurried the coming night, and telling us—how plainly—that they were making a life-struggle to get away. But it was of no use; her engines though a hundred-fold more powerful could not take her off whole. She did not move an inch. The tide, at the ebb when she ran aground, was now falling, and her condition was every moment becoming worse.

Captain Worden would have moved up to attack her if he had thought it judicious, but he saw that she could not get off until morning, with not the slightest probability of her doing so then. Night was fast coming on, and he chose to wait. At dusk a little smoke, mingled with steam, was rising in thin clouds from her funnel. With our glasses we plainly saw men on her deck, at the mast-heads, and in her rigging, and we knew she would be lightened during the night, if possible, and every expedient resorted to get her afloat.[10]

Worden realized that daylight was fast fading, and the risks seemed too great to push on upstream. However, with a full day ahead of them tomorrow, they would have plenty of time to deal with the problem. Paymaster Browne wrote, "The night was mild and hazy, the moon obscured by passing clouds, yet no light was seen in the direction of the grounded steamer, nor indeed in any other direction, not even the usual rebel signal lights seen almost every night on the river above, or at the batteries on Coffee Bluff, or at Beulah; but we were confident they were working on her, and we prepared to make a demonstration in the morning, anxiously hoping that the bird we saw so nicely caught in the afternoon might be still fast at the morrow's dawn."[11]

The crew of the *Montauk* was called to quarters at 4:30 A.M. on 28 February 1863, and Cmdr. Worden ordered the vessel prepared for action. An hour later they proceeded, carefully avoiding locations in the channel thought to contain Confederate torpedoes. The *Montauk* was accompanied by the *Seneca, Wissahickon,* and *Dawn.*[12] Paymaster Browne, in the *Montauk*'s pilot house, recorded the action.

> The morning was just breaking, and it was not light enough to discover whether the <u>Nashville</u> was still on the shoal where last evening's darkness found her. We entered a bend in the river, and slackened our speed somewhat, and soon it became lighter, but we were behind the point of woods, that we were watching with eager eyes, while our passage up the river was opening to our view the point where we hoped to find the rebel steamer still entrapped.
>
> A little farther—and there she is—hard and fast! We can see a number of men on her forecastle, and considerable bustle and confusion. We steam on by Harvee's [*sic*] Cut, by a range-mark that is fifteen hundred yards from the fort, on to a point eight hundred and fifty yards from the fort. . . . From the level of our deck we can see nothing of the <u>Nashville</u> but the paddle-box tops, the smoke-stack, and topmasts; but from the inside of the pilot-house we can see the whole steamer, even below her guards, and nearly to the water. She is newly painted, and is the same light drab color as our own vessels of war. Her masts and spars look well, her rigging is taut, and her figure-head newly gilded. . . .
>
> As we came to anchor, we saw a number of persons get over her starboard side, the one opposite us, after which we saw no living soul on board.[13]

At Fort McAllister the garrison had been preparing to protect the stranded vessel, which 1st Lt. Dixon describes: "As was expected the Rattlesnake Nashville did not get off on the mornings tide. It being the first thing I asked when I got up this morning, and I expected a fight and began to.dress. Before I had time to wash my face the call was made for the Corperal and soon after I heard the ironclad was comeing up. I fixed up my things and sent them off then went to my gun. I saw the iron-clad and three steamers. We had some torpedoes in the channell and thought to see the iron-clad blow up, but she came up very slow and passed over them in safety, but I thought that was on account of the high tide and was certain that she would be blown up when she went out again. She came up to within a mile of the battery and about 3/4 mile of the Rattlesnake and took position. The steamers took their old stand about 2 miles from us."[14]

Aboard the *Montauk,* correspondent Bradley Osbon took notes: "There she lay hard and fast, at about twelve hundred yards distant, a good mark. . . . [The vessel] had a full head of steam in her boilers, and she was blowing off furiously from her escape pipe. At five minutes past seven o'clock we let go our anchor about twelve hundred yards below the fort . . . and in two minutes thereafter we let slip an 11-inch shell at the object of our aims and desires."[15]

The garrison in Fort McAllister took up the challenge once the *Montauk* ventured within range. Realizing that the fate of the stranded privateer was at stake, the gunners did their best to distract the *Montauk.* While the wooden gunboats provided covering fire against the fort, the gunners aboard the *Montauk* calculated the range between them and the privateer. Its masts and upper works could clearly be seen across the narrow neck of marsh separating the channels. Correspondent Osbon wrote:

> The instant we fired our first shot the battery fired three guns at us, and in thirty seconds thereafter another one. But we did not pay any attention to them; and left the battery in the hands of the three gallant gunboats, who threw their shells into it in splendid style.
>
> At eleven minutes past seven fired our 11-inch gun, the shell falling a little over the N[ashville]. In just five minutes afterward the enemy hit our pilot-house, fair and square, with an 8-inch shot, which broke in two pieces, one falling on the turret top and the other on deck, doing no damage and producing no unpleasant sensation whatever.
>
> At twenty-two minutes past seven the 15-inch gun was fired with a 10-second shell, which landed quite close to the N. The fort banged away at us, but they did not exhibit such careful gunnery as on previous firings. We paid no kind of notice to the scamps behind the piles of sand, as we

were bent on blowing up the would-be pirate. At twenty-seven and a half minutes past seven o'clock we fired our 15-inch gun again, with a 10-second shell, which landed plump into the pirate, between her foremast and paddle-box. It exploded beautifully, and there was no doubt in our minds that we should soon see her in flames. This was only our fifth shot. . . . From the turret only the masts and smokestacks were visible, giving, of course, but a very small mark to fire at. . . . After firing our eighth round we were obliged to cease firing, so as to see what the fire was doing on board the <u>Nashville</u>.

To our gratification we were enabled to see a very dense volume of black smoke arising from the forward part of the vessel, and in a couple of minutes thereafter the flames were distinctly visible, forcing their way up, and gradually creeping aft, until they reached nearly to the base of the smokestack. The fog was slowly creeping down upon us, threatening to shut out the glorious sight; but it would light up at intervals, showing us in a few minutes a vast sheet of flames, which shot upward far into the smoky canopy above them. It was not long before the smoke-stack guy wires were burned away, and the huge stack tottered and then fell over on to the port paddle-box, stirring up the glowing embers which rose and mingled with the darkness above the doomed vessel.

Nothing but night, to give a darkened back-ground to the livid flames, could have added anything to the grandeur of the scene before us. . . . Slowly but surely the fire did its work: the rigging caught fire in several places, and torches seemed set, as it were, over a vast funeral pile. We fired occasionally at her until it became evident that we could not add anything more to her speedy dissolution. At intervals the flames would rush up in a body aft and die out forward. . . . All this time the fort was firing at us, stopping only when the fog would entirely hide us from view.

At six minutes past eight o'clock we ceased firing, having only fired fourteen times. We waited, watching for about thirty minutes the burning of the steamer, and then up anchor and stood down the river. At this time the N was entirely enveloped in flames, the paddle boxes were fast crumbling away, and streaks of fire were rapidly making huge crevices in her once graceful hull.

At thirty-five minutes past nine o'clock an explosion took place amidships, throwing up a column of white smoke, which, when its inertia was lost, spread itself out like a huge umbrella. It looked like steam, which escaped from the bursting of her boilers. It probably was the explosion of the 100-pounder rifle gun, from the fact that the outline of the hull was not seriously affected by the explosion.

In ten minutes afterward a terrific explosion took place aft. The fire had reached the magazine, and a spark had, in a flash, set loose the latent power of untold tons. Her hull was not able to withstand a shock like that, and a vast white volume quickly ascended aloft, and spread out . . . when it mingled with the smoke from the burning hull. The mainmast was gone, the quarter torn down to the water's edge, and the hull riven into countless fragments. Some little time afterward the foremast fell, and the destruction was complete. Far away over the lowlands the smoke spread itself. . . . The tide of life was at an ebb and in a short time she would be but a mass of tangled machinery and charred relics.[16]

1st Lt. Dixon was succinct: "About 11 oclock her two guns went off and soon after her powder exploded and the sight was a grand one to look at."[17]

On the *Montauk* Cmdr. Worden wrote, "I . . . had the satisfaction of observing that the Nashville had caught fire from the shells exploding in her

5.2. After the U.S. Navy blockade bottled it up in the Ogeechee River, the *Nashville* was sold, outfitted as a privateer, and renamed the *Rattlesnake*. On 27 February 1863 the vessel ran aground in Seven Mile Bend opposite Fort McAllister, where it was dangerously exposed. On the morning of 28 February, the *Montauk* came up the river, looking for the stranded privateer. While gunners in the fort tried to distract the *Montauk* from its mission, the ironclad focused its attention on the grounded side-wheeler and destroyed it. From *Battles and Leaders of the Civil War*, 4:29

several places, and in less than twenty minutes she was caught in flames forward, aft, and amidships."18

But the *Montauk*'s victory was not without its price. When it was evident the *Rattlesnake* was being consumed by fire, Cmdr. Worden ordered the ironclad downstream. Those in the fort watched anxiously as the *Montauk* approached the area in the channel where torpedoes had been planted. 1st Lt. Dixon observed, "Soon after the iron clad began to drift down. We watched her in hopes she would strike the torpedoes but we were doomed to disap[p]ointment for she passed over them clear. They began to cheer and cheer after cheer went up from the different vessels as they went down the river."19

While it was not evident to those watching in the fort, the *Montauk* did not have an easy ride back over the torpedoes. As it retired downstream, the ironclad ran upon one just above Harvey's Cut but it was not immediately evident to everyone aboard ship. Paymaster Samuel Browne recalled:

> I came out of the pilot-house and was standing on the turret; men and officers had just been relieved from their stations and were gathering on deck The port quarter of the vessel was carried, probably by the action of the current, against the bank of the river, and quite near a small piece of cloth flying from a stick in the grass, which the captain had noticed as we went up the river and called the pilot Murphys attention to it, who said,—"I think I'll give it a wide berth, sir! I am afraid it's a torpedo." As we now touched the bank, I was conscious of a jarring motion, as though she had struck the bank quite heavily, but nothing more. So it was noticed by most upon the deck. There was not much more commotion in the water than might be made by the propeller when close in shore. . . . Before we moved half a dozen rods away from the bank, the chief engineer came up from the fire-room and said to the captain,—"That was a torpedo, sir! It has blown a hole in her hull under the boilers, and the water is within three inches of her fires."20

The sensation produced in the engine room was more pronounced, and the first thought of the crewmen there was that a shot from the fort had penetrated to the engine room. 2nd Assistant Engineer Stephens, who was in the engine room when the torpedo detonated, gives the account.

> A sudden, and seemingly double explosion took place. I instantly called the men from the starboard side to prevent them being scalded, expecting a gush of steam supposing from the locality of the sound that a shot had penetrated or some part of the starboard boiler had given way. While looking at the boiler to see the effect, the dust, debris and smoke came

down from the angle formed by the deck and the smoke pipe on the starboard side, causing the impression for a moment that a shell had penetrated and exploded there. While intently watching for the effect to
develop itself from the starboard boiler, a man stationed in [the] port
passage[way] with a lantern as lookout reported that the port boiler was
burst underneath. Took a view in the port passage[way], saw the water
cascading.[21]

At first Stephens thought one of the boilers had burst, but he could not
ascertain the cause. He set the pumps in motion to remove the water but it
was quickly apparent that the water was gaining on the pumps. There was
obviously more water than would have come from a broken boiler. As they
struggled with the rising water, Stephens was informed of the exact cause of
the problem.[22] "Assistant Engineers R[obert] Potts, [Daniel P.] McCartney,
and [George M.] Greene came from their stations in [the] turret, reporting
that it was a torpedo that had exploded under the vessel. They immediately
went to work to ascertain and repair the damage, if possible, temporarily.
They found the [boiler] pipe broken. . . . They removed the upper piece
amidst the flow of water and got on a temporary stop. We then saw that there
was more water than was due to that leak alone."[23]

It was soon evident that the problem was more serious than first
believed, as Paymaster Browne relates: "We were just passing the gunboats,
whose crews were in their ships' rigging cheering us. Captain Worden
shouted to their commanding officers to send him his men and buckets.
The boats were dropped from their davits to the river; the men jumped into
them; buckets and pumps were tumbled in; and in fifty seconds boats were
alongside, and men, buckets and pumps on board. The tide was about an
hour ebb. Captain Worden turned to the pilot and said to him, 'Murphy,
can't you run me ashore here in some good place?' The pilot answered,
'That I can, sir!' All the remaining steam was crowded on, and after moving about half a dozen lengths, we ran ashore along the river bank, where
the vessel's keel bore evenly."[24]

This action not only saved the vessel from sinking but stopped the water
from entering through the buckled bottom-hull plates. An inspection
revealed the torpedo had detonated directly beneath the vessel, roughly amidships, causing several hull plates to buckle and be driven inward. One of the
hull ribs beneath a boiler had been sprung, striking the bottom of the boiler
and opening a small leak. Assistant Engineer Stephens wrote, "I saw that per-
manent repairs were impossible in our present condition and limited means,
and that the leak was now in a great measure stopped by [our] resting on a
mud bottom; also that any temporary repairs must be done before the tide

raised the vessel. . . . I remained and put wooden and iron shoes and braces between the bottom of the boiler and [the] bottom and ribs of [the] vessel, and made joints of sheet gum, pine wedges, etc."[25]

While Stephens and his men worked to effect repairs to the damaged hull, other crewmembers went over the side to check for other damage. The ebbing tide, which flowed swiftly past the stranded ironclad, clearly showed evidence of the *Rattlesnake's* demise as charred debris and large quantities of loose and scorched cotton drifted past. One member of the *Montauk's* crew noted, "As these silent witnesses of the havoc drifted past us, they seemed to show a determination that, if we would not allow the Nashville to run the blockade as a whole, she was going to run the blockade in pieces."[26]

When the *Montauk's* repairs were completed, the ship was bailed out and the rising tide lifted them off the mudbank. The ship appeared as good as new. Engineer Stephens recorded: "At flood tide the engines were put in

5.3. The Montauk, on its way downstream following the destruction of the *Rattlesnake* (formerly the *Nashville*). A river torpedo detonated beneath the hull of the *Montauk,* rupturing a number of hull plates. Threatened with the possibility of its sinking, the pilot put the injured ironclad on a mud bank where the falling tide left it aground. This action also stopped the water from entering the hull until temporary repairs could be made. By the time the rising tide floated the vessel, it was seaworthy enough to be taken to a repair yard. From *Battles and Leaders of the Civil War,* 4:32

motion . . . at 3 P.M. and run at speed . . . downriver to Ossabaw Sound. Came to anchor at 5 P.M. . . . . I remained under the boiler to see the effect of the engines while in motion, on the temporary plugs and patching. Found that they would do well in smooth water."[27]

At Fort McAllister, the garrison was unaware of the *Montauk's* difficulty and had no idea the ironclad had detonated a torpedo. Capt. Anderson reported to Brig. Gen. Mercer in Savannah that: "The ironclad apparently passed and repassed with impunity over the spot where the torpedoes were sunk."[28] The fort itself sustained little damage in the engagement because it had not been the object of the attack. Capt. Anderson stated that the covering fire from the wooden gunboats "did no damage, but slightly injuring the quarters of the Emmett Rifles and plowing up the dirt in our parade [ground]."[29]

1st Lt. Dixon summed it up: "No damage was done to the battery and no one hurt. They succeeded in doing what they have longed to do, but it was not our fault, for we protected her as long as she kept out of the way. But it seems as if those on board of the R did not care what became of her. Nothing of any value was saved off of her though there was plenty of time to save most ev[e]rything."[30]

That afternoon, 1st Lt. Dixon was placed in charge of a detachment sent up river to see about salvaging material from the wreck.

> This afternoon I went up the river with a detatchment of men to get some things that was saved off the R and while absent getting the things some of the men got hold of some liquor and I suppose they must have had some in them before but they were good and drunk. I had a hard time getting them in the boat, but finally succeeded, but had not got a hundred yards from shore when a fight ensued and for 15 minutes it raged and myself with 3 or 4 others could do nothing with them. I had a boat astern, so I transfered the things into it taking all but two of the sober men in with me. Those I left to take care of the drunken ones. I then cut loose and left them. I had not got more than 200 yards from them when I saw one of the drunken men by the name of [William Patrick] Hunt[31] of the Emmett Rifles jump overboard and strike out to swim and soon after a man named [Daniel] Clancy[32] jumped over after him. I was at this time turning a bend in the river when I saw them take Clancy in the boat and start after the other man. I knew nothing more of them as I came on to the Fort and about dark the other boat came in and they reported this man was drowned. I never want to have such another time with men. I have prefered charges against the most of them and a Court Martial will be ordered.[33]

The following day parties from the fort worked at dragging the river in search of the body of Pvt. Hunt.[34]

At Port Royal, Adm. Du Pont was pleased to learn of the *Nashville's* destruction. On 1 March, he wrote his wife.

> The <u>Nashville</u> is destroyed! A thorn in my flesh—an idea or myth in the public mind—thoroughly fitted as a privateer; her escape and the adding of her capabilities to the destructive powers of the <u>Alabama</u> and <u>Oreto</u>, probably <u>faster</u>, would absolutely have shaken stocks on Wall Street. . . .
>
> Before breakfast this morning [Christopher R. P.] Rodgers knocked at my door and said, "I have some good news for you, Sir—the <u>Nashville</u> is destroyed. Davis is up in the <u>Wissahickon</u>; here is Worden's report!" I had heard the night before she was <u>down</u>[stream], could not account for it; either she had come to be ready for the <u>Fingal</u>, that didn't come, or some mischief was brewing. At one time the gunboat officers were aghast lest she had escaped; Davis had gone up the Little Ogeechee—from which at the masthead you can overlook the Great Ogeechee—and could see her nowhere. There had been fogs and thick weather, and like a deer she could have bounded through an uncovered avenue. The officers felt badly, but a thorough and smart little pilot which we think much of, and came to us from Savannah several months ago, thought there was a bend in the river behind the fort where she was stowed away, to be nearer her leap. . . .
>
> The fire of the fort compared with its previous defense was weak. No one was hurt and the <u>Montauk</u> only hit <u>five</u> times; the firing at the boats was still more wild, as we term it. There was however one contretemps, but I hope of little consequence. While the <u>Montauk</u> was going <u>up</u> towards the obstructions, the pilot pointed out some suspicious-looking bushes, which they kept away from (Worden ought to have fired into them). On their return and in the fog he got near them without being aware of it, and a torpedo went off under the bottom of his vessel. It hurt no one, but set him to leaking. . . .
>
> I think tomorrow Drayton will take the battery itself; we shall see that no steamer is left up the river and the blockade can be made effectual and safe to the vessels left. So much for the <u>Nashville</u>. You can appreciate how much more important her destruction was than the mere running out of a few hundred bales of cotton, by imagining what would be the effect if the news reached the North that either the <u>Alabama</u> or <u>Oreto</u> had been captured.[35]

The residents of coastal Georgia could not appreciate what the loss of the *Rattlesnake* meant and were glad to see it disposed of, believing the ship to be the main cause of all the attacks on Fort McAllister. Lt. Col. Charles C. Jones Jr. wrote from Savannah to his parents in Liberty County, that the destruction of the vessel was "perhaps in many points of view, not an unfortunate affair for us. That vessel, with a drinking captain and a rough crew, has been keeping that neighborhood in hot water for many days."[36] But there was plenty of "hot water" still brewing for Fort McAllister as its most extreme trial lay ahead. The most intense attack yet attempted was being organized and lay in Ossabaw Sound at that moment.

6

A TERRIBLE STORM OF IRON

While the *Rattlesnake* was being dealt with on 27 February, Adm. Du Pont had been issuing the orders to bring Fort McAllister under its most severe attack yet. He wrote to Secretary of the Navy Gideon Welles: "I have determined to test the three ironclads, *Patapsco, Passaic,* and *Nahant,* on the Genesis Point battery, on the Ogeechee. . . . This operation will not retard the great work, but yield us advantages in many ways."[1] Because the *Montauk* had already been tested and its guns approaching what was considered to be the limit for safe usage, Cmdr. Worden was told to hold the *Montauk* in reserve by Du Pont, who ordered, "You will please act as a reserve, and you will have to forego what I know your gallantry and earnest desire would impel you to do, join in. But the Chief of the Ordnance Bureau has just cautioned me by letter against any overuse of the XV-inch gun, none having been fired over 300 times."[2]

The following days were ones of anxious preparation for the garrison at Fort McAllister because it was obvious from the sight of additional enemy gunboats and new ironclads in Ossabaw Sound that the fort was due to receive more attention. 1st Lt. Dixon wrote on 2 March: "We were all certain that the battery would be attacked this morning and was up and had our breakfast by daylight but the attack was not made. I am pretty certain that it will come in force tomorrow as the Pickett report[ed] this afternoon 2 ironclads, 3 mortar boats and 7 steamers, some of them in the river. . . . Later, two ironclads came up in sight of the battery this afternoon about 6 oclock. The alarm was given and all the guns manned, but they cast anchor and were still there at dark. We will be up all night as there is no telling what time the attack will be made."[3]

In Ossabaw Sound the Federal naval forces gathered a powerful array of warships for their next assault on the fort. In addition to the ironclad *Montauk,*

6.1. Capt. Percival Drayton commanded the ironclad *Passaic* during the 3 March 1863 attack on Fort McAllister. At the attack on Hilton Head Island in November 1861, Drayton commanded one of the Federal warships, and his brother commanded Southern forces on Hilton Head. Courtesy, U.S. Army Military History Institute

the new ironclads *Patapsco, Passaic,* and *Nahant* had arrived on the scene. The *Patapsco* was commanded by Cmdr. Daniel Ammen, the *Passaic* by Capt. Percival Drayton, and the *Nahant* by Cmdr. John Downes. The squadron was commanded by Capt. Drayton of the *Passaic*. Drayton was a native of South Carolina whose brother, Thomas F. Drayton, was serving as an officer with the Confederate forces, and[4] his loyalty to the Union was above suspicion. Adm. Du Pont gave the overall command of this expedition to Drayton because "he is much more familiar with ordnance and has a calm, observant and candid mind."[5]

The *Passaic* and the *Nahant,* like the *Montauk,* each mounted a 15-inch and an 11-inch Dahlgren gun. Because an 11-inch was not available for the *Patapsco,* a 200-pound Parrott rifle was mounted next to the 15-inch Dahlgren in its turret.[6] The *Passaic* was a brown-hulled vessel topped by a black turret and smokestack. The *Patapsco* had a lighter-colored brown hull and turret, and its smokestack was ringed by a wide red band. The *Nahant* showed a dark-green hull, turret, and black smokestack, with a wide band of dark green at the top of the smokestack. The different color schemes were intended as a means of allowing the Federals to identify each other, because outwardly, the monitors all looked alike.[7] To support the ironclads, the wooden gunboats *Wissahickon, Seneca, Dawn, Flambeau,* and *Sebago* and the mortar schooners *C. P. Williams, Norfolk Packet,* and *Para* had been assembled. The Federals were so certain of victory that several steamers loaded with troops of the 47th New York Infantry, commanded by Gen. Truman Seymour, had been sent to Ossabaw Sound to take possession of the fort after its capture.[8]

Capt. Drayton was fully informed of what they were going up against because runaway slaves and deserters brought out all manner of information concerning the fort, its armament, and troop locations in the area. Drayton described some of that intelligence: "One of our pilots, an Englishman, deserted from Fort McAllister two months ago. The battery was then an VIII-inch and six 32's. A few days before he left, after a visit from General Beauregard, two rifles and a mortar were sent down, which were about being mounted, and since then a X-inch has been added."[9]

On the night of 2 March, the Confederate forces made preparations to meet the anticipated attack. It had been noticed during the *Montauk's* previous attempts that the ironclad always revolved its turret so that its back was toward the fort while the guns were reloaded. This was easier than closing the gunport shutters, a time-consuming process. The Confederates, realizing the ironclads would probably utilize the same procedure when the attack came, decided to place riflemen in the marsh opposite the points where the ironclads would probably take up position. The call for volunteers passed through the Confederate camps in the area and was answered by Sgt. Stoughton Hayman and Pvts. J .C. Proctor, Wyatt Harper, and Brittain Cobb of Capt. Joseph L. McAllister's company, the Hardwick Mounted Rifles.[10] The detachment was placed under the command of Lt. Elijah A. Ellarbee.[11]

Under cover of darkness the group departed in a small boat and proceeded upriver to a point near where the *Rattlesnake* had been sunk. Here they landed, hiked through the marsh, and arrived at the riverbank opposite Fort McAllister where they dug out a rifle pit in the mud and remained to await the coming of dawn and the enemy ironclads.[12] While the Confederates were busy ashore, Lt. Cmdr. Gibson of the *Seneca* and a party of sailors from that vessel set out in small boats to sweep the river channel for torpedoes. They found none and returned to the *Seneca.*[13]

On 3 March 1863, as daylight spread across the eastern horizon, Capt. Drayton put his squadron in motion. About 7:00 A.M. the steam tug *Dandelion* towed the mortar schooners *C. P. Williams, Norfolk Packet,* and the *Para* upstream to a position about two miles below the fort. Each schooner mounted a 13-inch mortar. The mortar schooners were followed by the *Wissahickon* and the *Seneca.*[14] The three monitors moved to the front.

MAP 3. Area of Fort McAllister at the Ogeechee River entrance. Courtesy, National Archives

The Confederate gunners watched as the ironclads ascended the river and took up their positions: "The 2 iron-clads began to move up the river soon followed by a third from·behind the point of woods. This was one more than was bargained for, but the cry was bring them all at once."[15]

The gunners prepared to greet the ironclads as they approached the fort. On the far left, in a position facing the river, was a 32-pounder smoothbore that served as the hot shot gun. To its right, where the front wall turned away from the river and faced downstream, sat two more 32-pounder smoothbores in a double chamber. On their right was the 10-inch Columbiad, newly emplaced in a separate chamber, followed by the 42-pounder gun, the 8-inch Columbiad, and the 32-pounder rifled gun, all in separate emplacements protected by high lateral traverses. To the far right was the 10-inch mortar in an emplacement connected to the fort by a long earthen wall.

The 32-pounder rifle was commanded by Cpl. Robert J. Smith[16] and manned by a crew from the Republican Blues. The 8-inch Columbiad, the Pet Gun, was commanded, as always, by 1st Lt. William D. Dixon, assisted by Sgt. James Madison Theus[17] and a crew from the Republican Blues. The 42-pounder was in the charge of Lt. Daniel Quinn, assisted by Sgt. J. D. Frazier of the Emmett Rifles. The 10-inch Columbiad was commanded by Lt. William S. Rockwell Jr.[18] of the Emmett Rifles. One of the old 32-pounder smoothbores, crewed by a detachment from the Republican Blues, was commanded by Sgt. Sylvester McGrath and Cpl. John H. O'Bryne.[19]

At 8:30 A.M. the ironclads anchored about twelve hundred yards below the fort, with the *Passaic* in the lead, followed by the *Patapsco* and *Nahant.* The *Montauk* remained downstream in a position to support the attack if necessary but also providing a spectacular vantage point from which to watch the attack, as correspondent Osbon noted: "Our boys were scattered around the decks as passive spectators of an action in which they were very desirous of participating; but as we had done some service before, it was but fair that we should now do some looking on. . . . We had on board Captain John H. Upshur and his clerk and quite a number of the officers of the Sebago, who came on board to witness the scene; and as we lay ahead of all the vessels excepting the ironclads, our turret top offered excellent facilities for observing the firing."[20]

The *Passaic* took a position just above the Confederate range markers in the marsh and no sooner had they anchored when Fort McAllister sent a greeting from the 32-pounder rifle, followed in rapid succession by the 8-inch Columbiad, the 42-pounder, and the 10-inch Columbiad.[21] The squadron of warships replied in return. The Confederate gunners learned from previous encounters with the *Montauk* that it was useless to try to injure the ironclads by directing fire against their thick iron plating. Instead the

Confederates reserved their fire, aiming at the ironclad's gunports when they opened for firing.[22] Aboard the *Passaic,* Capt. Drayton noted this tendency: "I was directly in front of the fort, the guns being, as we looked at them, in the center between high traverses of earth, which were on each side. These, however, as we were placed had no effect in protecting either guns or men. The latter never exposed themselves to our fire, usually discharging their pieces either while we were loading or just as our [gun]ports came in line and before the guns were quite ready."[23]

Atop the *Montauk's* turret was correspondent Osbon.

> The rebels were busy, and at intervals we could see that they hit the Passaic pretty fairly; of course we could not tell what damage was done, but from our experience we felt confident that they could not harm her much. . . . At twenty minutes before eleven o'clock two of [the *Nahant's*] shells landed in the traverses, throwing up the sand to a tremendous height and filling the air with clouds of earth. The crews of the vessels around us gave hearty expressions of their approbation by subdued cheering and loud clapping of their hands.
>
> The rapid fire of the iron-clads caused the rebels to slacken their fire from the three guns and an 11-inch [*sic*] mortar which they had been working with great spirit.
>
> The Patapsco pitched in her shells, doing some execution in the rear of the work, just skipping the parapet in their flight. . . . It was bang, bang, smoke, fire, sand; and I guess but few ever saw such a beautiful sight. Secesh stood up to their guns manfully, and their gunnery was by no means meagre.[24]

Confederate gunners apparently did not have the same respect for the gunnery of their adversary. In great spirit, they served their guns and continually cracked jokes about the quality of the naval gunnery, shouting at them, "Too far to the right" and "Too far to the left" as the incoming shells failed to strike the fort.[25]

Aboard the *Passaic,* the Federal gunners worked their pieces with careful deliberation, although the vessel was practically under the guns of the fort, as Capt. Drayton relates.

> The shot from the fort struck [the ship] in four seconds from the flash, and nearly a second after the report. . . . The guns [of the *Passaic*] were fired immediately after each other, and I [did] not see that the greater rapidity in loading the smaller one [could] be taken advantage of owing to the delay caused from so frequent turning of the turret, and thereby exposing the [gun]ports to be entered by shot, which is an important

consideration, as the enemy . . . almost invariably waits for the [gun]ports to be opened to him before firing. . . .

There was no inconvenience in the turret from either smoke or noise, at least that was not quite bearable, and even less in the pilot house. Below deck the chimneys of two lamps were broken, but no light was extinguished nor any particular jar felt when the deck was struck or our own guns fired over it, nor was the atmosphere below [deck] particularly oppressive, although at times the smoke was quite disagreeable.[26]

Our three mortar schooners kept up a fire . . . from about 4,000 yards distance, but so far as I could observe, without the least effect, the shells generally falling short.[27]

From 1st Lt. Dixon's perspective, "Our shooting up to 11 [o'clock] was as good as could be done striking the <u>Montauk</u> about ev[e]ry third shot. Their shooting was also very good, making the dirt fly thick and fast."[28]

During the course of the action, several problems surfaced on the three new ironclads. Aboard the *Passaic* the pulley broke that worked the chain on

6.2. The *Patapsco* shows how close the Confederate gunners came to hitting their target. The sailor on the left stands by the muzzle of the 15-inch Dahlgren. The other gun is a 200-pounder Parrott rifle. The accuracy of the gunners in Fort McAllister was well known, but their only hope of injuring the monitors was to put a shot into one of the open gun ports of the turrets. The monitors revolved their turrets so the back faced the fort while they reloaded and turned back around to fire. Courtesy, U.S. Army Military History Institute

the sliding shutter for the 15-inch gun, which meant the gun could not be fired for half an hour until the pulley was repaired.[29] Cmdr. John Downes, commanding the *Nahant,* also reported on the others and on the action.

At various times during the action the compressor arrangements of the XV-inch gun became disarranged, the gun twice recoiling so far in that it was with great difficulty, and once only with the assistance of a jackscrew, that we forced it out again; and at the twentieth fire the rivets of the brass guides on the after part of the carriage broke, the guides falling down into the turret chamber below, without, however, disabling the gun. At the thirty-ninth fire of the XI-inch gun the cast-iron yoke snapped at the outer edge of the port trunnion, thereby effectively disabling the gun.

After firing ten charges of 35 pound [each] from the XV-inch [gun], with all the elevation I could give the gun, the shell falling short of the parapet, and not being able to reduce my distance from the fort, I considered it necessary to increase my charge of powder to 38 pounds, after which the practice from this vessel was very satisfactory and the effect upon the earthwork opposed to us apparently very damaging, tearing

6.3. A gun position in Fort McAllister looks downstream to where the ironclads took up positions against the far bank of the river and engaged the fort. Confederate gunners took cover when the ironclads fired, then fired while the ironclads revolved their turrets to face the fort. Courtesy, Library of Congress

away the parapet and traverses and bursting the shells with great certainty inside the work, and very often in close vicinity of the guns.[30]

Cmdr. Ammen on the *Patapsco* observed, "The works of the enemy appeared very much cut up; the parapet was breached in several places and three of the traverses very much injured."[31] Correspondent Osbon, from his vantage point atop the turret of the *Montauk,* gave more detail on the fort's damage: "The outline of the fort, which early in the morning had presented such regularity, now began to assume an entirely different aspect. Huge holes were clearly discernible, and it did not look like the work we saw in the bright glow of the morning's sun."[32]

In spite of the heavy fire from the Federal vessels, the garrison of the fort stood to their posts. The shells screamed over the earthwork and plunged into the parapets and traverses to a depth of eight or ten feet before detonating with an earthshaking explosion.[33]

"At times the enemy would not reply for several minutes, and when he opened afresh the guns would belch out from a different place," Osbon wrote in his articles. "Our shells were doing tremendous execution in the sand, but for some time we thought without damaging any guns. Finally . . . a shell from the Nahant exploded under one of the rebel guns, throwing it up into the air quite a distance."[34]

This 11-inch shell from the *Nahant* entered the gun chamber of 1st Lt. Dixon's 8-inch Columbiad, struck the gun carriage on the right diagonal brace, shattered the carriage, and exploded amidst the gun crew. Miraculously, no one was seriously injured. A fragment of the shell about the size of a hand passed directly between 1st Lt. Dixon and the number-one man of the gun crew, who were standing scarcely twenty-inches apart at the time. The fragment buried itself deep within the traverse behind them.[35] Dixon described the incident: "It all went on very well until about 11 1/2 Oclock when my 8-inch gun was struck just below the trunion and shattered. It was truly Provadential for us that none was not hurt for the splinters flew in all directions and I afterwards found a third of a 15-inch shell just near the corner where we dodged. I raised up quickly and saw at a glance that my gun was useless and that my squad was safe, so I gave them the order to double quick for the bomb[proof] and I went and reported it to Capt. Anderson. It cast a gloom over all as it was a splendid shooting gun and has been in so many fights and allways gave a good account of herself, for which she was termed the pet gun. Up to the time it was dismounted, we had struck the Montauk 13 times."[36] The Republican Blues daybook entry is: "the entire case-mate was filled with [shell] splinters but fortunately no one was hurt."[37]

A short time later the main traverse wheel of the 42-pounder gun was carried away by a shot that entered the gun emplacement. This severely hindered the use of the piece but the problem was solved when a member of the gun crew, Pvt. Carl Hanson of the Emmett Rifles, braved the incoming shells to make his way beyond the rear of the fort to the building where spare parts were located. He retrieved another traverse wheel but it was so heavy he could not carry it. He then proceeded to roll the wheel along the ground and gradually made his way back through the incoming shells to the disabled 42-pounder. The gun was repaired and put back into service.[38]

Another shell entered the gun chamber of the 32-pounder rifle and exploded among Cpl. Robert Smith's gun crew. When the smoke cleared, it was found that no one was wounded, and the gun was undamaged. Only one fragment of the shell was found in the floor of the chamber.[39] 1st Lt. Dixon said, "The rifle gun was of very little use as we had not but 24 projectiles for her when the fight opened and it was then reduced to seven or eight and they fired about once and hour."[40] One of the 32-pound smoothbore guns was also struck, knocking off its traverse wheel.[41]

At this point, according to 1st Lt. Dixon, only the 10-inch Columbiad remained operational. "We only had one gun in the battery that was doing any execution and all the enemys fire was directed on it, the 10-inch being under a perfect hail of fire and we were looking ev[e]ry moment to see her dismounted. Things began to look bad about the battery just then. All the mens quarters were knocked down, the guard house all knocked to peices and 4 guns no use to us. All this time there was a heavy fire kept up on the fort and tearing it up very much, but we soon got on our legs again. The 42 [-pound] gun was again fixed and doing good execution, but we saw it was useless to continue such rapid fireing, besides our ammunition was getting low, so the order was given to fire slow."[42]

The incoming shells did not discriminate, and those serving the guns were not the only ones in danger. A 15-inch shell struck the top of the bombproof, rolled down the bank to the top of the entrance, and exploded above several men gathered at the entry. It knocked them down and burned them from the flash of the explosion, but no one was hit by fragments of the shell, none of which could be found afterwards.[43]

No one living along the coast needed to be told of the fighting. The rumbling of concentrated artillery fire reverberated for miles. From Savannah, people traveled to Coffee Bluff and other points across the marsh opposite Genesis Point to watch the contest. Other people who were too far away could only rely on the ebb and flow of the sounds of the cannons to gauge how the struggle shifted.[44]

While the fort and the fleet slugged it out, Lt. Ellarbee's detachment of sharpshooters, in the marsh behind the ironclads, huddled under cover of their mud rifle pits, directly downrange from the fort's firing. While they awaited the opportunity to take some action, they had ringside seats for the show. The *Passaic* was so close it seemed they could step out on to its flat deck. Capt. John McCrady, chief engineer, reported that Lt. Ellarbee "could distinctly hear the words of command, 'In battery,' etc., and saw the hands of the men and the staff of the rammer protruded through the port in loading. He also reports that in [ironclad] No. 1 [the *Passaic*,] the muzzle of the gun when in battery protrudes about 6 inches from the port. He could see nothing of the same kind in [ironclad] No. 2 and 3 [the *Patapsco* and *Nahant*]. He could observe no injury done by our shot to the turret, the only observable effect being a whitish streak on the iron. The shot either glanced or were broken to pieces. One of our shot is reported to have struck about 6 inches from a [gun] port."[45]

The sharpshooter's patience was soon rewarded, as correspondent Osbon wrote to his readers, "Captain Drayton, of the Passaic, and Lt. Commander [Franklin F.] Miller, were on deck looking at the firing. A piece of something hit the Captain under one of his eyes, and he went inside the turret. A couple of rebel soldiers taking advantage of the exposure of the officers on the iron-clads, fired at Mr. Miller, the ball just grazing him."[46]

According to an account in the *Savannah Republican,* "An officer made his appearance on the deck of the [*Passaic*] with a glass in hand, and presented the long-wished-for target. A Maynard rifle slug soon went whizzing by his ears, which startled and caused him to right about, when a second slug apparently took effect on his person, as with both hands raised he caught hold of the turret for support, and immediately clambered or was dragged in at a port-hole. It is believed that the officer was killed."[47]

Actually, neither officer was injured. "Of course he [Mr. Miller] deemed it prudent to seek shelter inside," Osbon told his readers, "and did so—Mr. Rufus Morrly, our brave and skillful pilot, obtained a rifle and drawing an unerring aim upon the would be guerillas, fired, killing his man. The other scamp skedaddled in short order, probably crawling on his hands and knees through the marsh."[48]

Both sides thought they had injured the other, when actually no harm had been done to either. The *Passaic* replied to the sharpshooter nuisance by raking the marsh with grapeshot in the vicinity from where the shots came. Lt. Ellarbee and his squad had anticipated this response and sought shelter behind their rifle pits as the rounds scattered through the marsh grass around them. No one was injured, and when the ironclad turned its attention to the fort again, they vacated the area.[49]

The wooden gunboats fired wildly, and most of their shots passed over the fort or went wide of their mark. Confederate gunners ignored the wooden vessels beyond their range and continued to direct their fire primarily upon the *Passaic.* The ironclads *Patapsco* and *Nahant* were so completely ignored by the Confederate gunners that many of the crewmen aboard the *Nahant* gathered on deck to view the exchange of gunfire between the fort and the *Passaic:*[50] "The Nahant's people went to dinner as quietly as if not under the fire of the enemy; and after dinner they came out on deck to take a good look at their target. Secesh tried hard to hit her with their mortar but did not succeed. The accurate firing of the Nahant elicited the heartiest commendations from the spectators, who were piled upon our turret and all elevated points of the vessel."[51]

The fort's guns continued to strike the *Passaic,* but Capt. Drayton found the fort's mortar a little more troublesome. The mortar crew, again commanded by Capt. Robert Martin of Martin's Light Battery, was very deliberate in the operation of the piece and took special care to aim each round. Martin realized that common explosive mortar rounds had little or no effect on the ironclads so he adopted a different tactic. Rather than filling each shell with black powder, sand was substituted. It was hoped that the added weight and the velocity gained by the projectile's fall from an extreme height would enable it to penetrate the thinner deck plating of the ironclads. Capt. John McCrady stated, "The firing of the 10-inch mortar was very accurate, all the shells falling near [ironclad] No. 1, [the *Passaic,*] and one filled with sand striking her deck and breaking to pieces."[52]

Capt. Drayton gave his opinion of this attack. "The mortar shell which fell on deck over the bread room, would undoubtedly have gone through had it not struck on a beam; as it was, it . . . completely crushed in the planking at the side of the beam, opening quite a hole through, and had it been loaded with powder instead of sand, might have set the vessel on fire. . . . This certainly does not say much for the strength of the deck." A shot from the 10-inch Columbiad struck the pilot house atop the turret of the *Passaic,* bounced off, hit the rim of the turret top, and rebounded, coming to rest on the roof of the turret.[53]

When the tide began to fall about 3:30 P.M., it was clear that the ships would have to shift their positions or be left high and dry. Capt. Drayton signaled the vessels to cease fire and withdraw downstream.[54] Several factors led him to the decision to break off the fight: "I only withdrew when all my shell with fuses long enough to reach (or over five seconds) had been expended, and when the crew were almost beyond further work, having been occupied for eight hours at the guns without even an intermission to eat, and then I should have remained had I seen the least sign of faltering or slackness of fire on the part of the enemy; but on the contrary, I think that it was, if anything, more rapid toward the last.[55] . . . The fort continued to fire as long as we were in range, which was ten or fifteen minutes after we were underway. I could not observe that their fire was much slackened from the morning."[56]

As the *Passaic* withdrew downstream, Drayton stepped out of the pilot-house on to the roof of the turret just as a 10-inch shot from the fort struck the pilothouse. The shot, which "struck on the opposite side [of the pilot-house] just as we were getting underway, was broken into small pieces without sensibly jarring the pilot house, as I could observe, from being at the time on top of the turret, upside and leaning against it to shelter myself from the enemy's shot." While he was on top of the turret, Drayton recovered the other 10-inch shot that had lodged there previously.[57]

Capt. McCrady, at Fort McAllister, described the incident from his point of view. "The last shot fired at [the *Passaic*] was from the 42-pounder. It was reported to have struck near the water line. Immediately after she was struck a volume of smoke or steam issued from her side. . . . At the same time 3 men rushed out of the turret, but shortly returned. She then blew her whistle three times. . . . Meanwhile both guns of [ironclad] No. 1 were discharged . . . without aim up the river."[58]

Capt. Drayton described the enemy ground as he saw it. "The fort is very solidly built, with high traverses between the guns . . . and contained seven guns and a (X-inch) mortar. One of these guns was, I think, destroyed, the others used until we were out of range. Immense holes were cut into the earth, the traverses and face much cut away, but still no injury done which, I think, a good night's work would not repair."[59]

In Fort McAllister the garrison came out of their bombproofs and took stock of the damage. The *Savannah Republican* later informed its readers, "Considerable havoc was made in the sand banks in the fort, and the quarters of the men were almost entirely demolished. The officers' quarters received two or three shots, but suffered no material damage. Inside the fort, and to the rear and left of it for half a mile, the earth was dug up into immense pits and furrows by the enemy's shell and shot—a large quantity of which has been gathered up and will be returned to the Yankees in a different form should the occasion offer."[60]

Capt. McCrady noted that 11-inch solid shot penetrated the parapet up to nine feet, ten inches, but the 200-pound rifled shells only penetrated three and a half feet. At the roll call it was found that only two men, both from the Emmett Rifles, had been wounded. Thomas W. Rape had been struck in the knee, and William S. Owens slightly in the face.[61]

"It is almost incredible that our troops should have remained under such a fire for so long a time, and not one of them have been killed or seriously wounded," the *Savannah Republican* said.[62] But one member of the garrison had been killed in the battle, Tom Cat, the garrison mascot. It was reported that his loss was greatly felt by the members of the garrison.[63]

There was damage to be repaired all over the walls and traverses, one gun to be remounted and ammunition stocks to be replenished. "The fireing haveing ceased Capt McAllister had a very fine dinner served up which went very good," 1st Lt. Dixon told his journal. "The Sharp Shooters offered their services and went to work repairing the battery and all went on well."[64]

Downstream, Capt. Drayton assessed the damage to his ironclads and tallied the ammunition expended. He noted a variety of damage aboard the ironclads but mostly aboard the *Passaic,* which had been struck thirty-two times. Other damage was caused by the firing of the ironclad's own guns.[65] He sent a report to Adm. Du Pont.

> The injury done to my deck and side armor is so very much more serious than any which the <u>Montauk</u> has suffered that I am at a loss to account for it. . . . Although the attack was an unsuccessful one, it was certainly not owing to any want of zeal and attention to duty on the part of either officers or men. . . . I am satisfied that the natural obstacles are such as to render another [attempt] just as little likely to succeed. . . .
>
> I do not believe that [the fort] can be made untenable by any number of ironclads which the shallow water and narrow channel will permit to be brought into position against it. . . . [Fort McAllister is] nothing as a defense to the river, comparable to the shallow water and piles, as was proved by my being exposed to their fire for eight hours without serious injury, but they answer the purpose, which is simply to prevent the channel being cleared of obstructions. . . .
>
> The conclusion I have come to, both from my attack and that of the <u>Montauk</u> on Fort McAllister is, that if we expect to reduce heavy earthworks, it must be done . . . by a continuous fire by day to destroy, and at night to stop repairs.[66]

Capt. Drayton decided to not allow repairs to be made to the fort unhindered. The mortar schooners *Norfolk Packet* and *Para* anchored at a point downstream from the fort and at about sunset began a slow, steady bombardment, sending a 13-inch mortar shell at the fort every few minutes. This mortar bombardment continued all night,[67] as 1st Lt. Dixon describes.

> All went on well until about half past seven Oclock. We were all sitting in the house talking when we were disturbed by the report of a gun. We jumped up and went out and found that a morter shell was comeing so we got out of the way and it burst just in front of our quarters. We had expected that they would shell us during the night so we were not surprised. They had their morter boats brought back after dark. The most of

us got under cover and all the men were put in the bomb proof. It was a grand sight to see the shells bursting and flying through the air. They had a very good range and kept up a brisk fire. They averaged a shot about ev[e]ry five minutes. Those men that were at work did not mind their shells, but kept at work. . . . We take charge of the Hospital tonight as we will have to sleep to the music of their shells. It begins to look very much like a siege. I suppose they expect to keep us from repairing the battery and resume the attack in the morning but it will take more than two morter boats to keep the men from work. There is 20 vessels reported in sight. Large reinforcements have arrived. . . . The men are in the best of spirits and are ready to go at it in the morning.[68]

The damage done by this mortar attack was unimpressive. While it did prevent the use of slave laborers, it did not prevent working parties from the sharpshooter battalion from accomplishing the work.[69]

"So ended one of the hardest days fighting we have yet had, and all hands went to work to get something to eat as we had not tasted food for 12 hours," the Republican Blues daybook relates. "Col. R. H. Anderson's Battalion of Sharpshooters was brought into the battery and went to work to repair damage, as from the looks of things at dark it is expected they will renew the fight in the morning by which time all repairs will be made. . . . As the garrison is worn out they have been ordered to the bomb proof for rest as the prospect is they have another days work before them."[70]

Later in the night a fresh supply of ammunition arrived from Savannah, and the fort's magazines were restocked and readied for the anticipated renewal of the contest on the following morning.[71] A spare gun carriage was also brought up, and 1st Lt. Dixon's Pet Gun, the damaged 8-inch Columbiad, was remounted in its position. While the new carriage was being emplaced, a heavy timber slipped out of place and fell upon the leg of Pvt. James Mims from the sharpshooters, crushing his ankle. He received medical aid and was sent to the Savannah Medical College Hospital.[72]

The mortar schooners *Norfolk Packet* and *Para* continued their slow, steady bombardment all through the night, but as the light of dawn crept up, they were recalled. When daylight illuminated the area, it was obvious that the nocturnal bombardment had not kept the fort from being repaired as Drayton had hoped.[73] In Fort McAllister, the gun crews waited for their enemy to come up and renew the attack but hour after hour passed with no sign of the Federal vessels. It was evident the Federals had had enough and would not molest the fort anymore on that day. When Drayton surveyed the fort through his binoculars that afternoon, he was astonished to see that little sign of the previous day's bombardment was visible. He noted in the log of the *Passaic* that he "saw large bodies of men at work repairing Fort McAllister."[74]

While repairs had been underway, a variety of Confederate officials and local residents visited the fort to see the damage.[75] Capt. John Mc-Crady, who had designed and supervised the fort's construction, made a detailed report of the attack and subsequent damage: "The whole number of [artillery projectiles] fired at [the fort] was 224, and of these not more than 50 struck any part of our works. Of the 27 which struck the traverses and superior slope only 12 shells exploded, and they did no serious damage. The greatest injury inflicted by a shot was the destruction of the carriage of the 8-inch gun."[76]

Fort McAllister was ready to receive the Federals again by day's end on 4 March, but the Federals did not wish to pursue the issue due to a lack of ammunition and the probability that the results would be the same. A short time later, Maj. D. B. Harris, chief engineer for the Confederate Department of South Carolina, Georgia, and Florida, arrived to inspect the fort. He reported his findings to Brig. Gen. Thomas Jordan: "I have visited the battery since the engagement, and found it in good condition in every respect. It would appear that the iron-clads are not such formidable monsters after all, particularly against vessels, and brick or other walls, the 15-inch shell and solid shot could be used to advantage; but for the reduction of sand batteries the same amount of metal thrown from 8 or 10-inch guns in the same time would, I think, have treble the effect. The firing of the iron-clads was not as accurate as it should have been under the circumstances. The firing of our battery having been directed against one of them alone, the others ought to have fired with all deliberation and care requisite to insure accuracy. I am therefore at a loss to account for their wild firing. The most of their shots passed over the battery. The mortars were fired at a distance of at least 2 1/4 miles without, as usual, any damaging effect upon the battery. . . . The results of this engagement ought to make us feel quite comfortable. . . . I am sure our sand batteries will give a good account of themselves."[77]

On 7 March, the body of Pvt. Patrick Hunt was found. He had drowned in the river during 1st Lt. Dixon's salvage expedition to the wreck of the *Rattlesnake* a week before. The body was recovered and buried with military honors. The other soldiers, against whom Dixon had pressed charges in the same incident, had their cases resolved in an unexpected manner,[78] as related in the 9 March Republican Blues daybook entry: "The prisoners who were to have been tried by Court Martial for riot were released the day of the fight and I don't think anything will be done in the matter."[79]

With the departure of the ironclads and the cancellation of further operations against Fort McAllister, only the *Dawn* and *Seneca* remained to blockade Ossabaw Sound. The two transports filled with troops of the 47th New York Infantry, who were supposed to have occupied Genesis Point after its capture, suddenly found themselves with no place to go and no further orders. Because they could not be kept aboard the transports indefinitely, they were sent ashore on Ossabaw Island and put to work preparing a camp and fortification on Bradley Point. In this way, if it was decided to pursue the attack on Fort McAllister at a later date, the troops intended to occupy that point would already be on hand.[80]

In the days between the attack and March 13, 1st Lt. Dixon noticed the large number of newspaper accounts about the attack. "Ev[e]ry paper that comes to hand now has something in it about Fort McAllister. Today we have something in the way of a Yankee dispatch. It is headed Glorious News, Fort McAllister Taken, and dated New York March 4th 1863. It says Fort McAllister is reported as haveing been captured on the 26th of February togather with a mile and a half of rifle pits. The Forty Seventh New York regiment performed the feat, with the loss of 150 killed and wounded. As the [Savannah] Republican Editor says: It is news in these parts, especially to the garrison of Fort McAllister, whom the Forty Seventh New York, notwithstanding the fall of the Fort on the 26th, have graciously allowed to retain their quarters up to this time."[81]

The soldiers of the 47th New York would probably have been as surprised as the garrison of the fort to have read of their great feat in capturing the place. All they had captured so far was a stretch of beach on Ossabaw Island, and life there was far from the picturesque paradise it seemed at first. By the end of March the Federal troops there had erected a series of large camps and constructed an earthen fortification on the island's north point, which they designated Fort Seymour in early April. These troops remained on Ossabaw Island, and it was as close as they would get to Fort McAllister.[82]

7

LESSONS LOST AND
LESSONS LEARNED

W hen Adm. Du Pont learned the details of the 3 March 1863 attack,
he realized that little would be gained from further operations
against the Ogeechee earthwork. Four monitors had been tested against the
fort and valuable information gained, but with the *Rattlesnake* destroyed, little would be gained from continuing the attacks. The admiral had his attention focused toward Charleston because that was the major operation he was
preparing the monitors for. However, the results of the 3 March attack were
rather disappointing and did not bode well for the anticipated attack on
Charleston.

The attack was not a total loss for the Federals; the operation brought to
light a variety of problems with the new ironclads. One of the main defects
was the poor quality of iron bolts used to hold the plating and in some
instances of the plating itself. In several cases, shot striking the outside of the
turret and pilothouse had caused the large nuts of the bolts to fly loose on the
inside and ricochet at great velocity about the space. Even though the men in
the ironclad's turret and pilothouse appeared to be safe from Confederate shot
and shell, they were often in danger of being injured by the very iron that
protected them. The *Passaic's* experience with Capt. Martin's mortar shells
dropping on its flat deck also illustrated the potential deficiencies of the deck
plating. As a result of this, Adm. Du Pont sent for new iron in order to give
the deck of each vessel an additional layer of plating. Du Pont suspended
active operations with the ironclads until the defects were remedied.[1]

The *Montauk's* experience with the river torpedo also caused Adm. Du
Pont to change his estimation of these devices. He recommended that the
monitors be fitted with a "submarine torpedo exploder," a large wooden raft

fitted over the ship's bow. In theory, these would strike the hidden torpedo before the vessel did, protecting it from the detonation.[2]

Adm. Du Pont justified his withdrawal of the ironclads by stating that unless the fort harbored another Confederate ship similar to that of the *Nashville*, its capture was not really necessary and of "no practical value."[3] However, he could not overlook the fact that he had not been able to capture the fort, even with the biggest guns and the best ships at his disposal. On 4 March, the admiral wrote to his wife, "This experience has added to my conception of the power of <u>endurance</u> in these wonderful [ironclad] vessels, but has also proved that two guns, so large and so slow in loading, particularly the mammoth one, '15-inch' as it is called, that men can avoid them. Drayton fired each gun fifty times in the eight hours, which is about once in nine and one half minutes. I have not yet mentioned the most important item in this experience. Ericsson's high priest, Mr. [Alban C.] Stimers the engineer, was present; it was a great piece of good fortune, he came out to superintend the torpedo destroyers or rafts and the monitors, and I had sent him to see about the injury done to the <u>Montauk</u> by that torpedo the other day. He witnessed all the bombardment and came to the same conclusion that I had long ago: that <u>more</u> [ironclad] vessels would [be] wanted, and is going home to hurry out more. Continuity of fire is the thing; twenty-five minutes of the <u>Wabash</u> broadside, would take that fort about three times a day—wood as she is—if we could get her in. Rodgers and I smiled when we heard this from Stimers—he is very clever, but it was one of those experiences which could only come from actual observation. He will enlighten them more at the [Navy] Department than fifty letters from me would do, because he belonged to the enthusiasts and, like [Gustavus V.] Fox, thought <u>one</u> [ironclad monitor] could take Charleston."[4]

Officials at the Navy Department felt that an assault by massed ironclads might be successful in penetrating the Confederate defenses at Charleston. Accordingly, under pressure from Congress, the Navy Department continued to press Adm. Du Pont to make the attempt. He was less than enthusiastic about the matter, especially in light of the results obtained at Genesis Point.[5]

Adm. Du Pont knew the eight guns at Fort McAllister had proved troublesome to his ironclads but in moving against Charleston harbor, they would face several hundred heavy guns from forts and large batteries concentrated in the area. He held no illusions as to what his ironclad fleet could accomplish against the Charleston forts and attempted to convince his superiors of the foolishness of attacking Charleston with ironclads, noting to William W. McKean:

> The experiments in the Ogeechee with the ironclads, following those of the <u>Monitor</u> on Fort Darling [Virginia], convinced me that these vessels

had no offensive powers against forts—and to add to this, [Admiral] Dahlgren had written me that the 15-inch gun could do but little against earthworks! There is only one brickwork in Charleston; the others are all earth, some seventeen in number.

After Drayton had tried for eight hours with three ironclads to reduce seven guns, what chance was there to overcome between 300 and 400 guns of improved patterns and with every conceivable nature of obstructions with eight ironclads? After our failure on Fort McAllister, I felt as if it was my duty to inform the [Navy] Department what was in store for it at Charleston—though I had never advised in any shape or form this attack. . . . I compromised with my conscience by stating the facts and letting the [Navy] Department judge.[6]

In a 25 March 1863 letter to James Stokes Biddle, Adm. Du Pont discussed what was learned during the failed mission with the monitors.

The testing of the monitors or a sufficient number of them against a live target, as Rodgers called it, in the shape of Fort McAllister, proving here, too, what I had earnestly urged personally in October and by letter since, that the aggressive or destructive powers of these vessels against forts, particularly earthworks, were as much overrated as the defenses of Charleston were underrated. The results were what I expected and what Drayton much more emphatically predicted than I did—with three monitors bombarded eight hours! Worden had tried the fort himself until he had fired away all but three shells. But the experience was invaluable, not alone in reference to measuring the relative strength of forts and ironclads, but in proving how unfit for action these vessels were.

The results in the latter respect were remarkable—for the practice proved that none of the 15-inch guns can be used for more than a day's fight without repairs, and we may be a week before a result is gained at Charleston—a final one, I mean. Four monitors have attacked the fort and three grounded—two concussion boxes were injured, one had a 15-inch gun carriage disabled, the saddle of another was fractured; one was seriously injured by a torpedo (not yet repaired), one by a mortar shell on the deck, very serious, which fortunately did not explode. The injuries to the guns were not by the enemy. Yet you will see that they are not invulnerable even, and Mr. Stimers, Mr. Ericsson's high priest, who witnessed the bombardment, rushed home for more iron plates and they arrived today—sufficient to cover the shell rooms and magazine but will be imperfectly fastened. Now, the above injuries were during an encounter with a seven-gun battery which was not taken.[7]

In a letter to Mrs. Du Pont, the admiral let out more of what he was feeling: "When we weigh the chances, they seem against us. . . . But the operation after all, is an experiment—twenty guns to take two-hundred. . . . The cool certainty with which the thing seems looked upon at home, or rather in the [Navy] Department, always astonishes me."[8]

In spite of everything Adm. Du Pont learned regarding operations on the Ogeechee, the Navy Department insisted he make the attack on Charleston. On the afternoon of 7 April, barely a month after the last attack on Fort McAllister, the U.S. monitors *Weehawken, Passaic, Montauk, Patapsco, Nahant, Nantucket* and *Catskill,* supported by the ironclads *Keokuk* and *New Ironsides,* steamed into the outer approaches of Charleston harbor. In an instant the harbor was transformed into an inferno of cannon fire and smoke. Barely two hours later the Federal fleet withdrew.[9]

The *Keokuk* was struck ninety-nine times and completely riddled. The *Weehawken* was hit fifty-three times, several of which penetrated the hull. Both vessels barely managed to limp out of range of the Confederate guns before the *Keokuk* sank. The *New Ironsides* was hit ninety-five times, the *Passaic* thirty-five times, the *Montauk* fourteen times, and the *Patapsco* forty-seven times.[10]

Adm. Du Pont summed up the whole matter in a note to Charles H. Davis, written the day following the unsuccessful attack on Charleston: "I could never take away from our friend Mr. [Gustavus V.] Fox [assistant secretary of the navy] that extraordinary faith he has in these monitors, they have admirable qualities, but they are dead failures with forts, either brick or earthworks. I presume we shall have Ericsson . . . against us."[11] But inventor John Ericsson was not blind to the drawbacks in his ironclad monitors, mentioning in a letter to Secretary Fox regarding the offensive power of the monitors, "I candidly confess that I cannot share in your confidence relative to the capture of Charleston. . . . A single shot will sink a ship, while a hundred rounds cannot silence a fort, as you have proved on the Ogeechee."[12]

As a result of the defeat at Charleston, Adm. Du Pont assumed responsibility by resigning. He was replaced by Admiral John A. Dahlgren, the inventor of the 15-inch cannon, who realized that Du Pont had not wanted to make the attack on Charleston but had been forced by his superiors, who were unwilling to accept the lessons learned at Fort McAllister until the Charleston fiasco illustrated the same facts Du Pont had learned in the Ogeechee River barely two months before. Dahlgren was determined not to be forced into another such situation.[13]

The results of the attacks on Fort McAllister and at Charleston were reassuring news to the people of Savannah, who had felt threatened since the fall of Fort Pulaski a year earlier. With the large concentration of Federal forces at nearby Hilton Head and the ever-increasing strength of the naval blockade, the Savannah residents were certain that an attack on the city would surely follow. However, the Federal forces were satisfied with holding Fort Pulaski and blockading the water routes because they felt that little would be gained by occupying Savannah. By forcing the Confederates to defend the city, they tied up soldiers and equipment that the Confederates might otherwise have used elsewhere.

Fort McAllister served as a testing ground utilized by both sides to develop the technology of warfare. One of the first attempts by ironclads to reduce and capture a land fort was made upon Fort McAllister but neither heavy guns nor iron ships had been sufficient to destroy the earthwork. The secret of Fort McAllister's success, aside from the determination of its garrison, lay in the fact that it was an earthwork, rather than a masonry fort. Fort Pulaski fell victim to progress, but Fort McAllister ushered in a new era in fortifications. The Confederates made use of readily available materials in building the fort, such as timber, sand, earth, and mud, and discovered the value of these materials as the next step beyond forts built of brick and stone.

Fort McAllister was not a particularly impressive-looking work, especially when compared to the massive brick walls, arched casemates, and symmetry of Fort Pulaski. But when the test of combat was applied to each, and new weapons were brought to bear, it was found that appearances were not what really mattered. As opposed to Fort Pulaski's brick parapets, the resistance of earth, as demonstrated at Fort McAllister, won the admiration of military leaders both North and South. But the value of properly constructed earthwork fortifications was not truly appreciated by either side until demonstrated at Fort McAllister. Very early in the war, the earthen ramparts of Fort Walker and Fort Beauregard, defending Port Royal Sound at Hilton Head, had been blasted away under the guns of a combined U.S. fleet. These forts had not been built in the same manner as had Fort McAllister but the lessons the Southerners learned at Hilton Head had been put to good use as was shown at Fort McAllister.

In later years the Southern people looked back and wondered at what might have happened at Port Royal Sound during those early November days of 1861 if forts of the quality of Fort McAllister had been built there rather than the sorely inadequate works actually constructed. Lt. Col. Charles C. Jones Jr. in his "Historical Sketch of the Chatham Artillery" regarding the Hilton Head attack in late 1861 speculated: "The experience . . . demonstrated the fact that guns in open earthworks, crowded together within narrow limits and unprotected by traverses, could not long withstand a heavy bombardment from well served floating batteries at short ranges. The art of war, as evidenced by the construction of these land batteries, was in its infancy. Had such a battery as Fort McAllister been erected upon the spot occupied by Fort Walker—which could easily have been done—or had the guns in that work been distributed along the shore and thoroughly protected by traverses, the probabilities are that this proud [Federal] fleet would have retired from the contest shattered and discomfited. The military lessons taught by this defeat—dearly bought as it was—the history of subsequent fortifications erected for the defense of the coast, clearly demonstrates was not forgotten."[14]

While the fighting at Fort McAllister had no impact upon the outcome of the war, both sides learned a great many lessons there. Though the Federals ignored these lessons until after the Charleston attack, they eventually implemented changes in tactics and ship design.

The Southern defenders of Savannah put into effect the results of these lessons as soon as possible. Many of the defensive works built around the city had been made of mud from rice fields and marshes for their walls and parapets, and others had been built of sand. At Fort McAllister, both mud and sand had been used to build its walls. It was found that the mud walls were insufficient to withstand the impact of the heavy projectiles the Federals had brought to bear. Sand, on the other hand, tended to absorb the impact of the projectiles better, with less displacement than the mud.[15] The Southern authorities at Savannah went to a great amount of effort to convert the mud defenses to sand by transporting sand to those areas, building a railroad to haul sand from Savannah River sandbars upstream to the city's defenses east of town. The earthwork on the Ogeechee remained ready to take up the next challenge that might come upriver from Ossabaw Sound.

8

A Post of Honor

The ironclads departed Ossabaw Sound leaving the *Dawn* and *Seneca* on station to continue blockade duties but the presence of Federal troops on Ossabaw Island indicated to Confederate authorities in Savannah that Fort McAllister might still be attacked. The fort had shown the value of properly constructed earthworks, but earthworks alone were only as good as the men who stood behind them. The successful resistance of Fort McAllister was hailed far beyond Georgia's borders as a great victory, and the results of the 1 February and 3 March attacks were held up as examples for all Southern soldiers. The garrison received written commendations from generals Mercer, Beauregard, and others. In the Confederate capitol of Richmond, Virginia, the news was received with a great deal of satisfaction.[1] The Confederate government was so impressed that on 1 May 1863, the Confederate Congress approved the following resolution.

> JOINT RESOLUTION of thanks to the officers and soldiers engaged in the defense of Fort McAllister, Ga.
>
> THE CONGRESS OF THE CONFEDERATE STATES OF AMERICA DO RESOLVE, that the thanks of Congress are due and are hereby tendered, to the officers and soldiers engaged in the defense of Fort McAllister, Ga., on the 1st of February and 3rd of March last, for the gallantry and endurance with which they successfully resisted the attacks of the iron-clad vessels of the enemy.
>
> RESOLVED FURTHER, that the foregoing resolutions be communicated by the Secretary of War to the general commanding the Department of South Carolina, Georgia, and Florida and by him be made known in appropriate general orders to the officers and troops to whom they are addressed.[2]

Because the Confederate government had no official program to recognize valor, bravery, or deeds of merit, these commendations were as close as the men of Fort McAllister would come to receiving medals or any award of distinction in recognition of their services.

By mid-April of 1863 a threat of a different nature faced Fort McAllister's garrison. Since George A. Nicoll had been elected captain of the Emmett Rifles and George Anderson had been appointed captain of the Republican Blues, there had been some controversy as to who was the ranking officer and, hence, could lay claim to command of the garrison. The controversy caused ill feelings.[3] Capt. Anderson had petitioned Gen. Beauregard for a ruling, and the general had ruled in his favor. However, Capt. Nicoll had appealed to the Confederate Secretary of War in Richmond, who had ruled in Nicoll's favor. As a result, on 12 April, Anderson went to Savannah to see about being removed from his command because he did not wish to serve under Capt. Nicoll. Nicoll went to Savannah on the following day to see about having the Emmett Rifles removed to a different post and returned to the fort on 15 April with orders to take the Emmett Rifles to Fort Bartow at Causton's Bluff, just east of Savannah.[4] 1st Lt. William D. Dixon wrote, "I am sorry that the companies are to be parted. We have been togather so long that it seems more like one company than two."[5]

1st Lt. Dixon traveled to Savannah on the afternoon of 15 April and returned on the 17th, the day the Emmett Rifles departed. When he arrived at Way's Station on the train from Savannah, he found the Emmett Rifles there awaiting transportation to the city. "I arrived back at the post this morning and things look very lonesome. . . . Those at the post say there was a great deal of feeling exhibited between the companies on parting."[6]

The replacement company for the Emmett Rifles arrived at daylight the following day, 18 April. They were Company E, 12th Georgia Battalion commanded by Capt. J. H. Newsome.[7] 1st Lt. Dixon described his impressions of the newcomers: "They are a hard crowd and want di[s]cipline badly. It will be a long time before we get our garrison as well di[s]ciplined as we have had it. They have never handled big guns and I have to detail men to drill them."[8] The Republican Blues daybook noted, "They are a green lot, don't know anything about di[s]cipline or drill, have never been drilled on battery work, and it will be some time before they will be brought up to the standard."[9]

Throughout the following days, the soldiers of the Blues trained the men from the 12th Georgia in the intricacies of heavy artillery drill.[10] The quality of the men from the 12th Georgia left something to be desired, and the Blues wished for the return of the Emmett Rifles. They were not the only ones with those feelings. On 27 April, 1st Lt. Dixon went to Savannah on business and

8.1. George Wayne Anderson Jr. served with the Republican Blues for many years and took command of the unit when his uncle John Wayne Anderson retired on 11 November 1862. Anderson assumed command of the fort following the death of Maj. John B. Gallie on 1 February 1863. Command of the Blues then fell to 1st Lt. William Daniel Dixon. Anderson remained in command of Fort McAllister until its capture on 13 December 1864. Courtesy, Georgia Department of Natural Resources, Fort McAllister State Historic Park

on his return on 29 April, he reported, "I met some of the officers of the Emmett Rifles in the city. They do not like their new position. They say they would like very much to get back here if they could. I also received a letter from Capt Nicoll and he dislikes his new station."[11]

While Capt. Anderson was absent, Capt. Robert Martin of Martin's Light Battery assumed command of the post. With the removal of the Emmett Rifles, command seniority was no longer an issue. However, Anderson was busy pressing his case, and on 4 May the garrison received word that Anderson had been promoted to major of artillery and assigned duty at Fort McAllister. The Republican Blues daybook commented, "The Company was gratified to hear of his promotion."[12]

On 7 May, the newly promoted Maj. Anderson returned to Fort McAllister to assume command of the post. He relieved Capt. Martin, who departed the post that day with his light battery, bound for service in the

8.2. William Daniel Dixon, photograph in June 1863 in Savannah, joined the Republican Blues in March of 1857, when he was eighteen years old. He rose through the ranks to take command of the unit in June of 1863, when George Wayne Anderson Jr. assumed command of the fort. Courtesy, Georgia Historical Society

Western theater.[13] Anderson's promotion left the Republican Blues without a commander; the vacancy for captain was filled on 23 May when 1st Lt. Dixon was promoted and his commission back-dated to 22 April.[14]

Life at Fort McAllister settled into a routine. Reveille was at 4:30 A.M. followed by a police of the company areas. Sick call was at 5:30 A.M., breakfast at 6:00 A.M., guard mount at 7:00 A.M., battery drill at 8:00 A.M., and lunch at noon. The afternoons were left open for the myriad of duties and drills required to keep the place running.[15] Besides guard duty, drill, and other monotonous details, constant upkeep was required to maintain the earthworks and keep its heavy artillery in top condition. In dry weather the earthworks had to be watered by hand so the grass cover would not die. Erosion was a constant enemy, and no effort was spared in its maintenance. Animal manure was occasionally spread over the grass to fertilize it and cultivate more grass cover. Only designated personnel were allowed to walk on the walls, bombproofs, and traverses of the fort.[16]

The men, the magazines, ammunition, implements, and equipment were frequently inspected. Every day the gun carriages and trucks were cleaned, the axles kept lubricated, and the gun trucks traversed. The heavy guns also were moved frequently so that they would not sit too long upon the same spot, causing settling damage to the carriage, truck, or firing platform. When not in use, the guns were elevated up and down on a regular basis to make certain that elevating devices operated properly. The barrels were depressed, and a tompion placed in the muzzle to keep out dirt and moisture.[17]

In dry weather the men ventilated the magazines by opening the doors in the morning and closing them in the evening. Powder cartridges for the cannons were moved once a week and rolled by hand to prevent the powder from caking. Friction primers had to be protected from moisture and required frequent inspection, especially during damp weather. Only specified personnel were allowed to enter the magazines; lights were only allowed when carried in glass lanterns and then that light had to be carried by the person in charge of the magazine. Swords, pistols, canes, spurs, and the like were forbidden in the magazines, regardless of the rank of the individual. Special moccasins or socks had to be worn when entering a magazine, and if none were on hand, personnel had to enter in their stocking feet. Fire or open flames were forbidden anywhere within the vicinity of the magazines. With the large amounts of gunpowder on hand, no precaution was spared to prevent the chance of an accidental explosion.

Each day, company drill at 6:00 P.M. was followed by a full dress parade at dusk. Just before the retreat sounded, the men designated to man the guns in the event of a night attack paraded at their pieces, and the officer of the day inspected them to see that all their equipment, implements, and ammunition were in order, and the guns in serviceable condition.[18]

When not on duty, the men frequently occupied themselves with pursuits like hunting, fishing, crabbing, and gathering oysters. Bathing in the river was restricted to Mondays, Thursdays, and Saturdays and only after 6:00 P.M. Some tried their hand at gardening, and Capt. Dixon had a "small farm" where he not only gardened but raised some livestock as well. While the garden prospered, the fence around the garden became a bone of contention because some soldiers had been in the habit of taking the fence rails for fire wood. This provoked Maj. Anderson into issuing an order: "The burning and destroying of the rails on the fences around the Post Garden is strictly forbidden and any one found guilty of committing such depredations will be severely punished." While enlisted men could only go a half mile from the post without a pass, the officers could pay social calls and visit friends in the surrounding areas.[19] On 10 May, Capt. Dixon noted, "Major Anderson and myself rode down to Kilkenny this morning and took dinner there. It is 10 miles from here and was the residence of the Rev. Mr. [Charles William] Rogers. It is a very pretty place situated just on the river bank and presents a very pretty view. The Yankee vessels can be seen very plainly from there."[20]

The captain's diary during the summer of 1863 talks of an uneventful, vacation-like time. On 14 June, Maj. Anderson and he took some time to do a little boating: "I went with Major Anderson around to pay our first visit to the wreck of the Nashville. There is nothing left but her ironwork."[21] On 17 June, the captain took a trip: "I went down the river about 8 miles this morning on a fishing excursion and did not get back until 6 this afternoon. We did not get much as we could catch but very little bait. I got pretty well burnt by the sun."[22] On another occasion, "For pass time this afternoon Lieut [Edgar] McDonnel and myself went hunting. The result was a great deal of walking and very few birds."[23] On 31 July, Capt. Dixon started the men of the Republican Blues enlarging the parade ground for drill for several days; the 3 August entry: "I had the company hard at work digging this morning. It is good for their health."[24]

As summer passed, the drudgery and routine of garrison life took its toll. On 10 August five men had "gone off" from camp that Saturday; the following day the absence of an additional man was noted.[25] One of the deserters was brought to the post on 15 August, and Dixon had him confined. Dixon noted on the deserter's court-martial three days later, "Before a Court Martial consisting of Capt. Newsome, Capt Dixon and Lieut [Louis] Wilks, we tried one of my deserters today, and sentenced him to wear a ball and chain for 20 day[s] and 7 days on bread and water diet. Another one of my deserters came in this morning. Maj. Anderson has advertised [for] 2 of them, Priv Barbour and Robider."[26] The two privates had both distinguished themselves during the bombardments, receiving mention in the official reports.

Things remained "all quiet along the Ogeechee" that summer of 1863 as the focus of events shifted to other points such as Gettysburg, Pennsylvania, and Vicksburg, Mississippi. The fighting in Virginia, Tennessee, and Mississippi continued throughout the summer but the fighting around Charleston was much closer to home and kept everyone's attention in the Savannah area. Local units frequently went to Charleston to support operations there. All summer the garrison at Fort McAllister could hear the deep-throated rumbling of guns to the northeast at Morris Island and around Charleston.[27]

The fighting at Charleston finally came home for the garrison at Fort McAllister on 31 October, with Capt. Dixon recording, "Capt Newsome received orders this morning to proceed without delay with his company to Charleston and report to his Major. I am sorry they are going to leave as we have just got settled with them. I think they will leave on Monday."[28] The Blues' daybook commented, "Things are getting warm over there."[29] They departed Fort McAllister the following day.

On 3 November Capt. Dixon ordered his company to begin the task of building log huts because their tents had worn out. The Blues' daybook noted: "We have decided to build winter quarters. Hereafter, when not engaged in Drill, every man will be put to work cutting trees to build 16 log huts."[30] The construction of the huts went on through the balance of the month, and it appeared to be none too soon as on the morning of 11 November, they awoke to the first hard frost. In preparation for winter, the company was issued new clothing on 14 November.[31]

The routine of garrison duty for Capt. Dixon was relieved on 17 November, which would prove to be a turning point in his social life within the local community.

> The monotony of camp life was driven away today by the appearance of two ladies. Miss Anna Patterson[32] of this county and Mrs [Martha] Rowland of Savannah. Miss P inquired for me and I had to go out, though I tried to make the Officer of the day go and it was no go, so I had to go out. When I got to the carriage I bowed to them both and Miss P gave me her name and then introduced me to Mrs. R and Dr. Harris[33] who was with them and then asked to be shown the battery. I went with them and had a very pleasent time of it. Miss P and I was like old friends before she left. While at the battery a boat was reported coming up and I looked and saw a row boat coming under what I took to be a flag of truce, so I had a gun fired which brought it to and I sent a boat out to meet it but before the boat got out they started to come towards the battery. I sent a load of grape[shot] at them which brought them up in a hurry. The boat then spoke [to] them and it proved to be a boat from Rose Dew battery with Maj [Alfred] Hartridge[34] and Capt Anderson[35] on board coming over here. The ladies were much pleased with the firing. I then started up to the quarters and they went into the flower garden and I got a beautiful bunch of roses for them which pleased them very much. They soon after left making me promise to call and see them, which I did though I don[']t much think I will keep the promise. Miss P promised to lend me a lot of books provided I would come for them myself, which I agreed to. Maj Hartridge and Capt. Anderson took dinner with me and started back about 3 Oclock.[36]

The following day he noted receiving some books from Annie Patterson, which would help him pass the time.[37]

On the afternoon of 19 November, Dixon had more visitors[38] at the fort. "I had a visit at the battery from two ladies, Miss [Sally D.] Turner and Miss [Mary A.] White. I was introduced to both and escorted them around the battery. They where accompanied by Lieuts [Brittain] Cobb and [Raymond

H.] Demere."[39] Cobb was one of the riflemen who had positioned themselves in the marsh on the opposite bank of the river prior to the 3 March attack.

On 23 November, Maj. Anderson returned to the post from business in Savannah and brought notification that the garrison would be augmented by Company C, 63rd Regiment, Georgia Infantry, replacing the 12th Georgia, which had been sent to Charleston earlier that month. The 63rd, commanded by Capt. Elijah J. Craven, arrived at the fort the following day. Capt. Dixon's description was "The company is small and they look like hard cases. They know very little about their duties."[40]

By 4 December, the sixteen log-hut winter quarters were completed, and the men moved into them. The new quarters were "very comfortable," no doubt true when compared to living in tents during a cold winter.[41] Soon it was Christmas. Capt. Dixon, who had been absent on furlough the previous Christmas, this year he participated in the festivities at the post: "I have spent a Christmas in camp and taking everything into consideration we done very well. This morning one of the men put up a pig to be shot for, and that consumed the whole morning. A large lot of eatibles came down this morning but they were not cooked so they will have to take their Christmas dinner tomorrow. The things were sent by Mr. E. J. Purse.[42] We had a splendid egg nog last night and a very fine dinner today, and have got plenty of things left for another day. It has been very windy all day." The day after Christmas would see more than one man down with an unrelenting hangover.[43]

New Year's Eve, for the garrison was business as usual, as Dixon related, "We had muster today. Major [Alexander F.] Pope was particular in his inspection. We began at eleven oclock and did not get through until three. While the muster was going on Gen Mercer, Gen [Raleigh] Cols[t]on, Col [Edward C.] Anderson and Capt [William W.] Gordon[44] arrived and inspected the battery. After they got through they called on me to drill my company for them and I was highly complimented on their drilling."[45] On New Year's Day, 1864, the garrison was pleasantly surprised by the arrival of a wagon carrying a fine dinner sent down to them by Thomas Arnold, a county resident who lived several miles away.[46]

The year of 1864 opened with a bleak outlook for the Confederacy, and prospects for victory appeared very faint. Military necessities in other areas took troops from the Savannah defenses and shifted them to threatened points, and the replacements of these troops were often not as strong or capable, little more than old men and young boys. It was a clear symptom of the times.

On the morning of 16 January, the garrison awoke to a mystery. The picket boat sent out the night before had failed to return.[47] Capt. Dixon gave details in his journal, "We were all taken by surprise this morning by eight of my men going off to the enemy last night. The Picket we send down the river, four men, with four others were missing and it is thought the other four secreted themselves in the Picket boat last night when it was going down. The majority of them was some of my best men, though foreigners. I never was more surprised. Their names was Corpl [Simon] Jackson, Privates [Aaron] Mitchell, [Isaac S.] Davidson, [Raiford] Jackson, [William] Jeffries, [Morris] Connell, [James] Dunbar and [Isadore] Cohen.[48] Three jews, two Englishmen and one Irishman. It has reduced my company considerably from 101 to 93. They took the most of their clothing with them and the Picket their guns and accoutriments."[49]

A detail was sent downriver in another boat to investigate but no sign was found of the missing boat or the men. The question remained whether they had deserted or been captured, and the Blues' daybook says that there were many rumors in camp about the incident.[50] A week later the daybook stated, "News received at Savannah from Port Royal reports the arrival there of the 8 men from this Post. They were picked up by a Gun Boat on Ossabaw Sound. As they could not have gotten out there without they pulled to that point, it is supposed they left this post with the intention of deserting."[51]

On the morning of 26 January, the garrison turned out for a visit from Gen. Beauregard and staff. He reviewed the troops, inspected the battery, and indicated he would order improvements made to the rear of the fort.[52] The following day, 27 January, Capt. I. H. Peebles's company, Company E, 63rd Georgia Regiment, was ordered to report to their command and departed 28 January. They were relieved by Company G of the same regiment, commanded by Capt. D. N. Martin.[53] The Republican Blues daybook complained, "This constant changeing of troops here takes the time of all the officers and many of the men in instructing new men."[54]

Cpl. William H. Harden, a member of Capt. Martin's company, had been with the unit since the early months of the war and had served in a number of the fortifications around Savannah. The company arrived at Fort McAllister from Fort Thunderbolt where they had been since early 1863. Harden wrote to his wife, back in Pike County, Georgia, about his change of location. They had taken the train from Savannah, arriving at Way's Station: "Then we left the train and took a steamboat which was waiting for us at the [railroad] bridge. Then we went down the river . . . to Genesis Point, or Fort McAllister. . . . Here we landed, came out and tumbled about here last night. We are in a very good house, but I don't like this place. We can never get to town from here to buy anything that we should need. It is said to be twelve miles to the nearest point of the railroad from here . . . and I don't believe we will get our mail as regular as we have been doing."[55]

Fort McAllister's reputation was well known to the men of Harden's company, and evidence of the bombardments was still visible, so it was to be expected that they would all be intrigued with the location of their new assignment. On 31 January 1864, Harden told his wife, "If you was here to see where they fought last spring, you would be astonished to see where the breastworks were torn up and houses torn to pieces. Just think that you see a ball weighing over 300 pounds—larger than a half bushel. Such balls were thrown here at that time. One of them is here now to show for itself. Then there is another long shell here—it is 21 inches long and about 7 inches thick, weighing 240 lbs. . . . The fortifications here are the best I have ever seen. I don't think the Yanks will ever take this place. . . . We have some of the finest guns here I have ever seen, and some of the largest. You need not be uneasy about me."[56]

The men of the Republican Blues worked with the new members of the garrison, who because they had already been doing service in Savannah's defenses, were familiar with the drill for the big guns. Cpl. Harden was pleased with their new posting, as reflected in an 8 February 1864, letter to his wife: "I think that we will be very well satisfied when we get used to this place. Our duty is lighter in every way. . . . Our provision is scarce, but we make out to live. We are not hungry much, only for something fresh from home. . . . The boys have been hunting all over the battleground for shot and shell and pieces of shell to send to town to have them run over to throw back at the Yanks."[57]

On 18 and 19 February 1864, Maj. James S. Williams,[58] assistant inspector general from Savannah, visited the fort to inspect the garrison and the battery, finding the battery "in excellent condition ready for immediate & active service."[59] Maj. Williams was impressed by the Republican Blues. This unit, armed with the modern, 1855-model Springfield rifled muskets and completely outfitted, presented an appearance that made Williams comment, "Its condition is in every respect admirable reflecting credit upon its officers."[60]

By comparison Maj. Williams found Company G of the 63rd Regiment to be in a deplorable state, their drill "defective," their instruction "imperfect," and much of their equipment "in bad order from neglect. . . . There appears to have been gross carelessness on the part of the men in losing portions of their arms, accoutrement & equipment and great neglect on the part of the officers in failing to check or punish it. Proper steps do not appear to have been taken to replace lost articles or to supply deficiencies. . . . The quantity missing or not accounted for is so great that it appears proper to call attention to it [so] that [a] full investigation of circumstances may be made." The police of their quarters in the McAllister overseer's house was reported as "neglected" and their weapons, the Georgia State rifle from the Milledgeville armory, were totally unsatisfactory.[61]

In closing his report, Maj. Williams offered some defense for the condition of Company G, 63rd Regiment: "In justice to the Commanding Officer of the Post, I must state that this Company has been attached to his command but a short time. Efficient industry applied for a long time can about render it fit to serve as one half of the Garrison of so important a post as Fort McAllister."[62]

On 16 February, 1864, the improvements to the rear of the fort that Gen. Beauregard had ordered during his 26 January inspection got underway with the arrival of Capt. Thomas S. White from the engineer department. He laid out the design of a new rear configuration, and on 21 February a large force of slave laborers began construction of the improved rear defenses. This change created a more compact rear wall, complete with a small dry moat around the land face, that was made by the construction of a glacis, an earthen formation that sloped away from the wall and was designed to protect the wall from incoming artillery fire.[63]

Apparently the deficiencies Maj. Williams noted during the inspection of Company G, 63rd Regiment two weeks prior were thought to be too severe to allow them to remain as members of the garrison, and on 3 March, word arrived that Capt. Nicoll and the Emmett Rifles had been ordered to return to Fort McAllister. The animosities between Capt. Nicoll and Maj. Anderson, evident with their parting almost exactly a year earlier, apparently had been laid to rest. The Emmett Rifles arrived at Fort McAllister by boat on 6 March, which Capt. Dixon described, "The Emmett Rifles arrived here this morning about 9 Oclock. Priv Murphy of that company died on board of the boat last night. He complained yesterday of feeling unwell but nothing was thought of it and this morning he was found dead. He was buried here this afternoon. Capt Martins Co leaves here this morning."[64] With the arrival of the Emmett Rifles and the departure of Company G, 63rd Regiment, the garrison was once again the one that had stood against the U.S. Navy a year earlier.

Cpl. Harden had mixed feelings about leaving Fort McAllister. He had enjoyed the duty there, but with them returning to their former assignment at Fort Thunderbolt, they would be closer to Savannah and would be able to go to the city more often than they had at Fort McAllister. He wrote to his wife, "We got orders to be ready to move. When the steamboat came for us . . . we packed up our mules and put them on board. We stayed on shore until after midnight, when we took up the line of march, went up the river one and a half miles. Went aboard. I and [William] Spencer took it on foot for ten miles in order to get the mail. . . . That night about dark, we took the train."[65]

On 26 March, Lt. Thomas Burdell arrived at the fort to conduct another inspection of the garrison. Regarding the Blues, he wrote, "Too high a

compliment cannot be paid to the commanding officer of the Post, the officers and men for the excellent Military Appearance, di[s]cipline and drill of
Co C 1st Volunteer Regiment of Ga. Also the highest credit is reflected upon
them by the beautiful condition of their arms, which are not equalled by any
in this Military District, nor excelled by any in the Confederate Army"[66]

Fort McAllister continued to be an attraction for local visitors. A group
of four women arrived on 11 April: Ann Caroline Theus, the sister of Lt.
James M. Theus of the Blues, Sarah Miscally, Miss Brown, and Ellen Calvert.
They were escorted around the battery and spent the day there.[67] On 19
April, Capt. Dixon wrote about another group of visitors, "I had a visit from
Misses [Jane E. S.] Ferguson, [Jane H.] Posey and Marshall and the Rev. Mr.
Gilbert today. I rode to the station for them this morning and got back here
at half past ten oclock. We visited the battery and spent a very pleasent time
until half past 12 Oclock when we started for the train which arrives at the
station at half past 2 oclock. I seen them off and there met Miss [Mary A.]
White of this county and she invited me to take a seat in her buggy, so I let
her boy drive mine and I rode home with her and was invited to stay to tea,
but declined. I started back for the battery where I arrived at half past 6
oclock, after spending a very pleasent day."[68]

Spring of 1864 brought more active military operations. The war crept
ever closer to Georgia, and for the first time there was news of Federal operations in North Georgia aimed at the city of Atlanta. Confederate forces were
mustered to meet this threat and sent to this newly developing theater of war.
It was hoped that the Confederates would blunt this thrust aimed at the heart
of Georgia.

By late April of 1864, the Republican Blues had been at Fort McAllister
almost a year and eight months. They were combat veterans, having stood up
to the U.S. Navy and faced the dreary routines of garrison duty. The demands
of war eventually touched them, drawing them to a more active combat theater. Capt. Dixon noted in his journal on 25 April the first indication that
their lives were about to change: "We were all very much surprised this morning on the receipt of an order from Hd Qrs calling on all detatched companies of the 1st Vol Regt Ga to prepare at once to join their regiment to march
to Dalton Ga. Brig Gen Mercer is ordered there and we will go in his brigade.
I am going to Savannah this afternoon to make arrangements for getting my
company equipped."[69] The Blues' daybook commented, "The company is
pleased as they are tired of Battery work."[70]

Capt. Dixon returned to the post the following morning: "I arrived back
from the city this morning and I have had things agoing all day. I am sending ev[e]rything to the station so as I can be ready when the order comes. Gen
Mercer expects to leave on Friday. The 1st, 54th and 57th Regts will form his

brigade. I suppose I will get orders to move tomorrow. . . . I intended to make my last call on my acquaintances in this County this afternoon, but Lt [Thomas] Burdell will be here at 4 Oclock to inspect us and I could not go. I will go in the morning if nothing happens. Later. 4 1/2 Oclock. I have just received orders to join my regiment in the morning. I have just got permission to go tell some friends good bye."[71]

After Capt. Dixon bid farewell to his friends, he returned to the fort only to find that, typical of military life, the situation had changed in his absence. "Later. 12 1/2 Oclock. I have just arrived back and during my absence orders were received countermanding the last and that I would remain at the post for the present. Gen [Jeremy F.] Gilmer[72] I suppose has succeeded in having the regiment detained to take charge of the batteries as there are no other troops here. I do not think we will be removed now. I am greatly disappointed for I would have much sooner gone after getting ready. The large majority of the company are also disappointed for all our things are at the station."[73] The entry for the day in the Blues' daybook reads, "The disap[p]ointment was great as all were anxious to go, and we are now in poor condition everything being sent to [the] station and we don't know whether to bring them back or let them remain there."[74]

Having orders to a more active combat theater was a source of excitement and anticipation for most soldiers, but for others, it was a sobering moment. That next night, 26 April, four of the Emmett Rifles and the guard on the lower point of the battery took the opportunity to make a change in their situation and deserted.[75]

On 30 April, Brig. Gen. Mercer, his staff, and the 54th, 57th, and 63rd Georgia regiments left Savannah bound for Dalton, Georgia.[76] The Republican Blues daybook for 30 April recorded, "Our move very uncertain. Things we are very much in need of at [the] station returned to post"[77] but on May 5 said, "It looks as if we are here to stay."[78] Throughout the month of May, the garrison at Fort McAllister monitored the fighting in North Georgia as Gen. William T. Sherman's Federal armies clashed with Confederate Gen. Joseph Johnston's forces. On 18 May, the Blues' daybook related, "Our Regiment at Dalton seems to be taking part in the fighting. Several killed and wounded. We are looking each day for orders to join them."[79]

On the afternoon of 22 May, several members of the Emmett Rifles devised a scheme to take themselves out of any possibility of being sent to the fighting in North Georgia. The journal of Capt. Dixon gives details: "We have lost a Lieut and four men from the battery. Yesterday four of the Emmett Rifles came and asked Lieut [Daniel] Quinn to go down the river with them for oysters and as they could not go without an officer he went with them and since that time they have not been heard of. Their names [are James] Lanagin,

[Emanuel] Williams,[80] [Stephen] Phillipps[81] and [Carl] Hanson.[82] It is supposed that some of them wanted to desert and they took advantage of Lieut
Quinn for all hand[s] here had the greatest confidence in him. He has a wife
in Savannah, so has Williams and Phillipps. It is not supposed for a moment
that they were captured for it is a very easy matter to get away from anyone
in the creek they were in. The company has lost ten men in a month."[83]

Orders arrived at Fort McAllister on 25 May for the Republican Blues to
report to Savannah for imminent deployment to North Georgia.[84] This time
the orders were not countermanded, and Capt. Dixon predicted: "I am pretty certain we will go this time."[85] Dixon departed that day and traveled to
Savannah to make preparations for the arrival of his company. There was no
time to bid farewell to his friends in Bryan County this time. The company
followed the next morning at 6:00 A.M., and the Emmett Rifles remained to
garrison the fort.[86]

However, they did not remain long as shortly after the departure of the
Blues, the Emmetts received orders for an assignment in Savannah, and the
Terrell Artillery replaced them at Fort McAllister. Maj. Anderson was also
ordered to Fort Bartow on detached duty, and Capt. John W. Brooks assumed
command of Fort McAllister. On 24 June, Company A of the 27th Battalion,
Georgia Reserves, commanded by Lt. Benjamin F. Johnson, was ordered to
duty at Genesis Point to bring the garrison back to its two-company level. On
29 August, Maj. Anderson was ordered back to resume command of Fort
McAllister, and on 12 September the Emmett Rifles and companies D and E
of the 1st Regiment, Georgia Reserves, were ordered to the post to replace
Company A of the 27th Battalion Georgia Reserves.[87]

The 1st Regiment, Georgia Reserves, organized in the spring of 1864, was
commanded by Col. William R. Symons, a fifty-two-year-old tailor from
Savannah who was a native of Devonshire, England.[88] The companies were
made up of seventeen- to eighteen-year-old boys and forty-five-to-fifty-year-
old men. Company D was commanded by Capt. George N. Hendry, and
Company E was commanded by Capt. Angus Morrison.[89] One of the young
boys was fifteen-year-old Samuel Moore, who enlisted that spring in Company D where his older brother, Spencer, was already a member.[90]

While Gen. Sherman was occupied in North Georgia, Gen. Grant's forces
in Virginia began the long, bloody campaign to pin down Lee's army. The
fighting in Virginia was important, but the fighting in North Georgia was a
more immediate concern to the people of Georgia. The residents of Atlanta
and surrounding areas felt confident that Gen. Sherman would be driven
back, but with each day, the Federals were closer to the city. By midsummer
of 1864, the Confederate forces were fighting for Atlanta's very existence.
Gen. Joseph Johnston, commanding the Confederate forces, was replaced by

Gen. John B. Hood in hopes that he could turn the tide. The situation at Atlanta became more critical as Sherman's forces closed around the city. Reinforcements were needed, and Confederate garrisons everywhere were combed for excess manpower to replace the losses already suffered. On 23 September, Maj. Anderson received orders that the "suspicious character of the foreign element" in the Emmett Rifles should be sent to Gen. Hood at Atlanta as replacements for Georgia regiments.[91]

The Confederate forces at Atlanta had been driven completely within the city's defenses, and Gen. Sherman's forces began encircling them. In three desperate battles, Hood attempted and almost succeeded in breaking Gen. Sherman's hold on the city. After realizing his failure, Hood was forced to abandon the city, and by summer's end, Gen. Sherman's army of veterans sat poised in Atlanta, awaiting their next move. All of these events at Atlanta had an impact on the Savannah area, making the threat of the enemy striking Savannah very real. By autumn of 1864 the defenses of Savannah were manned by severely diminished forces, and the quality of personnel steadily deteriorated as old men and youngsters filled the demands for manpower. Though his army was still several hundred miles from the Georgia coast, Gen. Sherman already had his eyes on Savannah and Fort McAllister, as one unknown soldier discovered.

> Weeks before, while the [U.S.] army was yet amongst the hills of Georgia, some soldier, while rummaging among a package of letters which he had found in a house by the roadside came upon a scrap of thin brown paper, marked with curved lines, which to the ordinary eye would have been meaningless; but to any intelligent American Soldier, who had used pick and shovel, it had interest and significance. The writing on the paper ran something in this way:
>
> > "Dear Mother: Here I am in a big fort way off on the Ogeechee River. It is called Fort McAllister, which is the name of a plantation hereabouts. It is a big fort with thirty or forty big guns, which we fire at the Yankee vessels whenever they come up the river. They have tried it on with ironclads and all that, but we always beat them off, and are perfectly safe behind our tall bomb-proofs. You can't imagine how crooked this river is—a snake wriggling is a straight line compared to it. I send you a little drawing which I have made of the bend in the river and the position of the fort. A strong place it is, and the Yanks never can take it so long as they knock at the front door. . . . We don't have much to eat, and its right lonely here."

The soldier gave this bit of paper to his captain, and so it came on through General [Oliver Otis] Howard to General Sherman; and as he carefully examined it I remember hearing someone say: "Fort McAllister! I never heard of such a place before. It must be one of the rebel line of sea defenses."[92]

Gen. Sherman realized the significance of this information because only he knew the direction his army would move from Atlanta and what its ultimate destination would be.

9

A TIME OF RECKONING

Gen. William Tecumseh Sherman's army moved out of Atlanta on 15 November 1864. It was a small city on the move—over 60,000 men, 35,000 horses and mules, 2,690 wagons, and 503 ambulances. Organized into two wings, it moved in two parallel columns that pressed deeper into the heart of the state. They left Atlanta in ashes and cut their line of supply and communication. Without supplies, Sherman's men had to take what they needed from the farms, plantations, and communities they passed through. Confederate Gen. John B. Hood responded by taking the majority of his army into northern Alabama to threaten Federal forces in Tennessee in hopes of drawing Gen. Sherman back out of Georgia. But Gen. Sherman knew there were sufficient forces in Tennessee to deal with Gen. Hood, and he pressed on into Georgia.

Gen. Hood's move left Georgia without an adequate defense force to counter Federal movements, and the Confederate forces left in Georgia had no idea where the Federal leader was going. Indications were that Macon would be threatened or perhaps Augusta. Only Gen. Sherman knew for sure where he was headed. Lt. Col. William E. Strong, Gen. Sherman's inspector general and chief of staff, wrote, "It was understood when General Sherman left Atlanta for the sea, on the 15th of November, that he would strike the coast near the city of Savannah and I think the Ogeechee River was named as the probable point. If no troops from General Lee's army were thrown into Georgia to head off and check him in his march, the gun boat fleet and the fleet of transports laden with supplies and munitions of war, were to be waiting for him off the mouth of the Ogeechee, so as to be in readiness to establish a depot for his army immediately upon his striking the coast; and as I understand it General Sherman hoped and expected that the navy would have reconnoitred the river, captured Fort McAllister, cleared out the obstructions,

9.1. Gen. William Tecumseh Sherman, in the Atlanta defenses in October of 1864, just a month before he departed on his March to the Sea. Whether the hat he wears is the one he traded to Albert G. Browne when they were on the USS *Nemaha* on the evening of 13 December is open to conjecture. Courtesy, U.S. Army Military History Institute

torpedoes etc., and that hard bread, at least, would have been within his reach within a day of his arrival."[1]

The people of Savannah eyed Gen. Sherman's army like the approach of a summer storm. At first it was far away, but each passing day brought it closer. Gen. Sherman's forces captured Milledgeville, the state capitol, and then there was word that Augusta was the target. It looked as if Savannah might be threatened from the west by an army the size of which had never before been anticipated. There was much work to be done to strengthen the city's western defenses to meet this threat. Capt. John McCrady, who had labored for over three years on Savannah's defenses and the construction of Fort McAllister, found more work to be done and time fast running out. Ten years later, he described this: "When Sherman began his march from Atlanta I was on sick leave, but hastened back as soon as I saw Savannah was his objective point. With the aid of previous reconnaissances . . . I chose the line which was actually defended, because, while it was far enough from the city to prevent the city being shelled with field guns, it could be inundated from end to end and this inundation could be made sufficiently deep to enable a small body of men to defend the whole length of it, seven and a half miles. The inundation and fortification of this line were begun as soon as possible after my arrival."[2]

Savannah's geographical location was seen as an advantage against Gen. Sherman's approach. The land mass upon which the city was situated was almost an island, having its only connection to the mainland along a neck of high ground on the south bank of the Savannah River. The Confederates concentrated their defenses along this high ground allowing the marshes and rice fields to the south to provide a natural barrier against assault from the west. In this way, ten thousand Confederate troops mustered together under the command of Lt. Gen. William J. Hardee hoped to hold Sherman off outside the city. If they could prevent him from breaking through to the sea, they might succeed in forcing him to bypass the city and move on.

The Confederate forces were mostly ill-trained militia and arsenal workers supported by a handful of veteran troops, but Lt. Gen. Hardee hoped that with an advantage in heavy artillery and a good defensive position, his small force might prevail against Gen. Sherman. Because the Federals had no supply lines and were living off the land, it would be necessary for them to keep moving into fresh territory. When they arrived outside of Savannah, their army would be held in place by the Savannah defenses west of town, Confederate forces south of the Ogeechee River, and the Savannah River on the north, where Lt. Gen. Hardee had Confederate Navy gunboats and ironclads. If Confederate forces could prevent the Federal army from opening a supply route to the U.S. naval forces, then Gen. Sherman would eventually have to divert his army toward the Federal bases in the Beaufort–Hilton Head, South Carolina, area. It was a faint hope but Lt. Gen. Hardee realized it was the only hope Savannah had. The defending forces had advantages in terrain, prepared defenses, and large numbers of heavy artillery, but Sherman's forces had the advantage in numbers and experience.

However, Southern ingenuity also came to Savannah's defense. Shortly after Sherman's army had left Atlanta, James H. Tomb, chief engineer aboard the Confederate ironclad CSS *Chicora* in Charleston, South Carolina, stepped forward and offered his services, submitting a suggestion to Maj. Gen. Samuel Jones, commander of the District of South Carolina. Tomb was no stranger to danger. At the start of the war, he was in the Confederate Navy at New Orleans.[3] When that city fell, he was reassigned and eventually ended up in Charleston where he was assigned to the *Chicora* and participated in the 30 January 1863 attack on the U.S. blockading fleet by the *Chicora* and the CSS *Palmetto State*.[4] He went on to become involved in the development of semisubmersible torpedo boats.[5] On 5 October 1863 Tomb participated in an attack against the USS *New Ironsides* by the torpedo boat *David*. They successfully exploded a torpedo under the *New Ironsides*'s hull but the torpedo was not large enough to sink the ship.[6] Later, Tomb commanded the *David* when it towed the CSS *Hunley* out to the harbor entrance on its last fateful mission.[7]

On 21 November 1864, Maj. Gen. Jones wrote to Flag Officer J. R. Tucker, in command of the Confederate naval forces at Charleston, regarding the suggestion Tomb had forwarded to him: "J[ames] H. Toombs [*sic*], chief engineer under your command, has suggested that from his knowledge of the use of torpedoes and the roads over which the enemy will probably pass in Georgia that he may be able to delay their advance and inflict serious injury to them. If you can dispense with his services for a short time, and order him to report to me, I will detach him on that service."[8]

The next day Tomb reported at District HQ in Charleston where he was ordered to report to Augusta to "carry into execution the special instructions given him by the major general commanding." At Augusta Tomb assisted in the installaion of torpedoes around that city until it was obvious that Sherman's forces had by-passed them and was moving toward Savannah. Tomb then traveled to Savannah, reported to Lt. Gen. Hardee to explain his mission, and offered assistance.[9] Tomb's plan was to plant torpedoes, or what are termed "land mines" today, along strategic routes of approach to the city of Savannah and in front of designated defenses, such as at Fort McAllister.

No one is quite certain as to what logistical arrangements were made but it appears that Tomb probably obtained a supply of torpedo fuses, possibly from the arsenal at Augusta, which he took with him to Savannah. There he organized working parties from local troops and converted existing stocks of heavy-artillery ammunition into torpedoes by installing the pressure-sensitive fuses in place of the regular artillery fuses. Once buried, these fuses would detonate when walked on or in some cases when walking near them. No one is certain exactly how many or where these torpedoes were buried but it is known that Gen. Sherman's forces encountered these in the roads outside Savannah as they approached, and Chief Engineer Tomb probably buried all he could in the time he had and with the amount of fuses he had to deploy.

For the garrison at Fort McAllister, the last months of 1864 meant a reevaluation of their own defenses. For over three years the fort had occupied a position of strategic importance in Savannah's defenses, but this position was on the south bank of the Ogeechee River while the remainder of Savannah's defenses were located to the north across a wide expanse of marsh and rivers. The approach of an enemy army from the west placed Fort McAllister outside Savannah's immediate network of defensive forts. But McAllister could still be a fort to be reckoned with and with the attentions of Chief Engineer James H. Tomb and his team, the fort would be an even deadlier place to assault. Three years before, only four 32-pounder cannon guarded the entrance to the Ogeechee but in late 1864, the fort was heavily armed. Lt. Col. Charles C. Jones Jr. described the scene: "Its battery consisted of one ten-inch mortar, three ten-inch Columbiads, one eight-inch Columbiad, one forty-two pounder gun, one thirty-two pounder gun, rifled, four thirty-two pounder guns, smoothbore, one twenty-four pounder howitzer, two twelve-pound mountain howitzers, two twelve-pound Napoleon guns, and six six-pounder bronze field guns, with a competent supply of ammunition."[10]

On 20 October, Clinch's Light Battery, commanded by Capt. Nicholas Barnard Clinch, was ordered to Fort McAllister to relieve the Terrell Artillery.[11] The garrison that would see Fort McAllister through its final ordeal consisted of the Emmett Rifles, commanded by Capt. George A. Nicoll, numbering twenty-five men; Clinch's Light Battery, commanded by Capt. Nicholas Barnard Clinch, numbering fifty men; Company D, 1st Regiment, Georgia Reserves, commanded by Capt. George N. Hendry, numbering twenty-eight men; and Company E, 1st Regiment, Georgia Reserves, commanded by Capt. Angus Morrison, numbering forty-seven men.[12] After the "foreign element" of "suspicious character" had been weeded out of the Emmett Rifles in response to orders, only twenty-five men could be mustered; a year earlier, they mustered more than eighty men as part of the garrison at Fort McAllister.[13]

Realizing that his command could be isolated by Gen. Sherman's army, Maj. George Anderson stockpiled supplies. More than 1,000 pounds of bacon, 2,250 pounds of hard bread, and other rations were secured to give the garrison a month's supply. Other supplies, such as forty gallons of whiskey, forty gallons of molasses, fifty pounds of candles, and salt were also obtained; and on 9 December, as Gen. Sherman's army closed upon Savannah, the fort received additional supplies sufficient to sustain the garrison an additional fifteen days.[14]

Before Gen. Sherman had even left Atlanta, the garrison of Fort McAllister worked to prepare for the possibility of an attack. Under the direction of Capt. Thomas S. White, engineer in charge, the camp was dismantled and moved within the fort. An open field for firing at the enemy was cleared behind the fort by tearing down the barracks, workshops, and storage facilities and then cutting all the trees within a quarter-mile of the fort. The fallen trees were to be used to create obstacles to an orderly assault.[15] The garrison apparently had other uses for the tree limbs as on 12 November, Maj. Anderson issued the following order: "In accordance with Special Orders from Maj. Gen. McLaws the garrison will observe great care in not molesting the tops of the trees felled by the Engineers in the rear of the Fort. They are welcome to the trunks but the tops are needed for the defenses of the work."[16]

A palisade obstruction was built in the moat of the fort. Tree limbs stacked around the fort at the foot of the glacis created a closely spaced semicircle of abatis obstructions. Just outside of this line of abatis, at the foot of the glacis, lay a wide strip of land where James Tomb placed torpedoes made from converted 10-inch mortar shells taken from the magazine of the fort's mortar. Because the mortar would be of little use in a land assault across the rear, these shells were an ideal source to be converted into torpedoes. These shells had a flattened section inside opposite the fuse hole that gave the shell a firm base that would direct the force of the explosion upwards into the air rather than dissipating its force in the ground.[17] The torpedoes were attached to the ends of railroad rails buried just below the surface of the ground. One end of the rail lay atop the fuse so that anyone who trod upon any portion of the rail would detonate the mine at the end.[18] Colonel Jones defined the locations of the torpedoes: "A short time before the approach of the enemy a member of the torpedo department had, in obedience to orders, placed in front of the fort and along the direct approach, a considerable number of sub-terra shells."[19]

Construction of Savannah's western defenses progressed at a feverish pace. Because the city's earlier defenses had been focused on the eastern side of the city, all of its heavy artillery was located there. Now, with the threat of Gen. Sherman's forces coming their way, over fifty of these heavy guns were moved from the eastern side of the city to new emplacements being built on the western side. Fort McAllister contributed to this effort. On 21 November, Col. Edward C. Anderson in Savannah ordered Maj. Anderson to remove two 32-pound guns from Fort McAllister and forward them to Savannah for use in the western defenses. Because McAllister had several spare 32-pounders, this request was complied with.[20]

December brought Gen. Sherman's forces closer to Savannah, and there could no longer be any doubt as to his intentions. On 8 December, his advance from the right wing forced a crossing of the Ogeechee River at Jencks Bridge, 20 miles west of Savannah, and proceeded towards the city. With Federal forces converging on the area, Confederate troops in Bryan County realized they were outnumbered and could do little to protect Fort McAllister against the approach of Sherman's army. Since orders had been received instructing Confederate forces south of the Ogeechee to gather on the south bank of the Altamaha River, they evacuated the area and retreated south into Liberty County.[21] With this evacuation of Bryan County, Fort McAllister was isolated. Maj. George Anderson wrote, "Hearing incidentally that the

Confederate forces on the Cannouchee had evacuated that position and retired across the Great Ogeechee, and learning that a large column of the enemy was approaching in the direction of Fort McAllister, I immediately detached a scouting party, under command of Lieutenant T[homas P.] O'Neal, of Clinch's Light Battery, to watch them and acquaint me with their movements. This was absolutely necessary, as the cavalry previously stationed in Bryan County had been withdrawn and I was thus thrown upon my own resources for all information relating to the strength and designs of the enemy."[22]

On 9 December, forces of Sherman's right wing approached from the southwest. After crossing the Ogeechee River, elements of the Headquarters Scouts proceeded toward the Atlantic and Gulf Railroad ahead of the main column.[23] These scouts, an elite unit of hand-picked men from other units, lived life on the edge. George W. Pepper, who wrote one of the first books about Sherman's March, described them: "They are members of an organization of great celebrity in the West, made up of the best men of Western regiments. These daring fellows are known as the scouts of the Army of the Tennessee. . . . The organization is uniformed in Confederate clothing, and the men adopt the dialect of the poor people of the South. Being accepted by the inhabitants as straggling rebels, they are entrusted, without question, with the entire stock of information of military movements which they possess. Many of the scouts have even had the audacity to visit the headquarters of the rebel Generals, and in one instance . . . carried off the officer's monthly return of the strength and equipment of his command."[24]

Capt. William Duncan of Company K, 15th Illinois Cavalry, commanded the Headquarters Scouts. Duncan, a twenty-three-year-old native of Scotland, had been a student at the Elgin Academy at Elgin, Illinois, before the war. He enlisted early in the war but had only been commissioned since April; Company K of the 15th Illinois was his first command.

Duncan and his scouts reached the railroad at two points and began tearing up the track, burning the ties, and bending the rails. While involved in this, they captured an approaching train carrying Richard R. Cuyler, president of the rail line, who was fleeing Savannah. From here the scouts followed the railroad and the coastal highway towards the railroad bridge and King's Bridge on the Ogeechee River. When they arrived, they found both bridges set afire by the retreating Confederates. They managed to extinguish the blaze at King's Bridge, but a large section of the center span had been destroyed.[25]

Gen. Sherman knew his men would need new equipment and heavy artillery before they could reduce the city's defenses, and his concerns about supplies increased daily since there was little to forage in the immediate area.[26] Lt. Col. William Strong, inspector general and chief of staff, reported, "Savannah was deemed almost impregnable, surrounded by a waste of water

9.2. Lt. Col. William Strong served on Gen. Sherman's staff during the March to the Sea and was one of the officers who gathered atop the Cheves Rice Mill to witness the assault on Fort McAllister and accompanied Gen. Sherman and Maj. Gen. Howard to the fort after it was captured. His after-action report of the final assault on Fort McAllister was submitted to the general and remains in Sherman's papers today. Courtesy, U.S. Army Military History Institute

and approachable only by a few narrow causeways which were filled with torpedoes and thoroughly commanded by artillery. It was generally conceded that it would be almost impossible to carry it by direct assault—certainly not without great loss of life. So long as Fort McAllister blocked up our route to the sea, preventing our forming communication with the transport fleet, just so long would Savannah hold out. The fort was the key to the city and both armies were well aware of it."[27]

Gen. Sherman knew that his first priority was to tell the navy his army was on the coast. At his headquarters near the Ogeechee River at its junction with the Savannah and Ogeechee Canal, Gen. Sherman charged Maj. Gen. Oliver Otis Howard with the responsibility of opening communications with the navy and informed him that Brig. Gen. Judson Kilpatrick's cavalry would assist him.[28] The major general made preparations to send a courier downstream to get a message through the Confederate lines to the Federal

9.3. Maj. Gen. Oliver Otis Howard, a native of Maine, had served in the eastern theater of the war, losing an arm in 1862 at the Battle of Fair Oaks. Sent to the western theater in early 1864, he served admirably under Gen. Sherman, commanding the right wing of his army during the March to the Sea. When the army reached the coast, Maj. Gen. Howard was responsible for opening a route to the sea. He sent scouts downriver in a small canoe in an attempt to reach the navy ships offshore and then focused on capturing Fort McAllister, the last obstacle. Courtesy, U.S. Army Military History Institute

navy.[29] This was another job for the Headquarters Scouts, as it would be a dangerous mission with no guarantee of success or survival. It was the type of challenge the scouts thrived on. Capt. Duncan agreed to personally carry these communications through the Confederate lines. Maj. Gen. Howard penciled dispatches to Secretary of War Edwin Stanton and to Adm. John Dahlgren.

Headquarters Army of the Tennessee
Near Savannah Canal, Georgia
December 9, 1864

SIR: We have met with perfect success thus far. Troops in fine spirits and nearby.

Respectfully,
O. O. Howard
Major-General Commanding
Right Wing of Army[30]

He concealed copies of these messages in a plug of tobacco and entrusted them to Capt. Duncan, who was about to embark upon a potential suicide mission with the fate of thousands resting on its outcome. Duncan chose two men from his scouts to accompany him: Sgt. Myron J. Amick of Company K, 15th Illinois Cavalry, and Pvt. George W. Quinn of Company F, 31st Illinois Infantry.[31] Sgt. Amick was a twenty-two-year-old native of Kane County, Illinois, who had been a printer before the war.[32] Pvt. Quinn, also twenty-two years old, was a native of Jefferson County, Illinois, who had been a carpenter before the war.[33]

Maj. Gen. Howard was confident that Duncan could get the messages through despite the risks. On 8 December, Gen. Sherman personally interviewed the men shortly before their departure to impress upon them the importance of their mission. The following evening Capt. Duncan and his two companions departed from the Savannah and Ogeechee Canal junction near King's Bridge. According to George Pepper, "Embarking in a frail dugout [canoe], which they found, they launched out on the rapid waters of the Ogeechee River, and with the assistance of paddles, made their way down stream as rapidly as possible."[34]

"Captain Duncan, the bravest, and most skillful scout in our command," Lt. Col. Strong wrote, ". . . accompanied by two of his most trusty men, undertook the perilous task of reaching the sea in an open boat. It was known to all that the river was well filled with torpedoes, and that picket boats were thickly stationed about the fort; placed there on purpose to pick up any daring adventurer from our army who should be foolhardy enough to attempt to run the gauntlet and reach the sea. It did not seem possible that Duncan could get through safely; but he knew no fear and was eager to attempt it. When I shook his hand that night and bade him good bye, I never expected to see him again."[35]

The dugout canoe with its three passengers glided downstream until darkness settled about them. They made their way ashore and huddled in the underbrush, not daring to light a fire for fear of discovery.[36] George Pepper wrote: "The next morning they continued on their voyage, making good time. On several occasions they were observed on the shore by negroes, who, supposing them to be escaped prisoners, did not detain them. On the same afternoon, they landed and proceeded to a house, near the stream, in quest of food. They had scarcely entered before a party of rebels rode up in search of them. The negroes, ever faithful friends of the Union soldiers, hid the scouts under the floor. The rebels surrounded the house, declaring if the three men were found they would hang them. The scouts kept their cover, and the rebels disappointed in not finding them, soon left. The negroes now released the scouts from their hiding place, gave them food to eat and an ample supply for future use, escorted them to the river and saw them safely in the current, paddling away to their destination."[37]

While Capt. Duncan and his comrades paddled along the Ogeechee River, Gen. Sherman's forces continued taking up positions opposite the Confederate defenses of Savannah. Lt. Col. Strong described the action: "On the 10th of December when we reached Savannah, our supply trains were quite exhausted of hard-bread, sugar, and coffee and the country, for nearly thirty miles west from the Ogeechee had been swept of provisions and forage. During the last three or four days of our march we were moving through the 'Pine Barrens,' a poor country and very thinly settled, and the foragers had poor opportunities for accumulating provisions of forage. . . . Within two hours of the time the Army of the Tennessee developed the enemy's works on Little Ogeechee December 10th the signal corps had reconnoitred the peninsula between the two rivers and had selected for a signal station the great rice mill on the Cheeves [sic] Plantation some ten miles from the main army and the nearest available."[38]

Capt. James McClintock, chief signal officer with Gen. Sherman's forces, established a signal station at Cheves Mill. He wrote, "On the 10th of December . . . I accompanied a party to reconnoiter the country between the Ogeechee Rivers, with a view of opening communication with the fleet, which was supposed to be in the vicinity of Ossabaw Sound, but failed to see anything of our vessels. On the 11th Lieutenant [Jacob] Sampson and myself established a station of observation at a rice mill on the Great Ogeechee two miles and a half north of Fort McAllister. From this point we obtained a good view of the rebel works. . . . [A] strict watch was kept during the day, while rockets were sent up at certain intervals through the night to attract, if possible, the attention of any vessels that might be in the sound near the mouth of the river."[39] Out beyond Fort McAllister were the glistening waters of Ossabaw Sound and beyond that the sea. Couriers brought word that slaves had seen strange lights and shooting stars in the sky while fishing in the sound at night. That could only mean signal rockets indicating the fleet must be close at hand.[40]

With Gen. Sherman's army pressing against Savannah's defenses, Lt. Gen. Hardee made it plain that he was not going to give up the city without a fight, and Confederate artillery commenced shelling the Federal positions while sporadic gunfire resounded all along the line. Eventually, Gen. Sherman established his headquarters at Berwick Plantation, across the road from where Gen. Howard and the 15th Army Corps would establish their headquarters at Lebanon Plantation on the coastal road south of Savannah. Ironically, Lebanon was Maj. George W. Anderson's home, where he had grown up and lived before the war. Brig. Gen. Judson Kilpatrick would also set up his headquarters at Lebanon, and he was no stranger to the place. While a cadet at West Point, one of his classmates had been Robert H. Anderson, Maj. George W. Anderson's brother. During one summer vacation, Brig. Gen. Kilpatrick had visited his classmate at Lebanon and was well acquainted with the family and George W. Anderson. Now the house sheltered Federal officers while George W. Anderson and the men of Fort McAllister awaited their arrival.[41]

Capt. Duncan and his two companions continued their trip down the Ogeechee River as darkness approached on 10 December. George Pepper noted: "During the night of the 10th, the little canoe glided noiselessly by a rebel gunboat [the *Columbus*], so close that its occupants could see the rebel sentinels on watch, and, as they passed, they heard the cry of 'all's well.' Our gallant party being landsmen, were more accustomed to land navigation; and, consequently, experienced, upon their approaching the sea, much difficulty with the tides. However, a little care saved them from catastrophe. They had no trouble in passing Fort McAl[l]ister, and the tide now being in their favor, they were borne down Ossabaw Sound and out to sea."[42]

They reached the open waters of Ossabaw Sound by sunrise on the 11th but rough water threatened to swamp their canoe. According to George Pepper, "Their craft might be considered a staunch one for inland service, but [for] the boisterous waves of the ocean, it was no match. As they were beating about at the mercy of the waves, expecting momentarily to founder, they caught sight of a vessel bearing the ensign of the United States. If they could reach this they were all safe; if not, and night should close in upon them, they were certainly lost, for every moment they were drifted farther and farther from the land. To reach the gunboat . . . was therefore the impulse which nerved their energies to the greatest exertion."[43]

The gunboat USS *Flag* had been patrolling in Ossabaw Sound looking for signs of Gen. Sherman's approach. On the morning of 11 December, the sound of heavy gunfire was heard to the distant northwest, and the second cutter was sent off about 8:30 A.M. to scout the lower Ogeechee. As the *Flag*'s cutter approached the entrance to the Ogeechee River, the crew's attention was attracted by three men struggling to keep a small canoe afloat in the choppy water.[44] Capt. Duncan and his companions were overjoyed to see the cutter approaching. George Pepper stated, "Steadily it came towards them, and so elated them that they waved their hats and shouted for joy. . . . Scarcely had they done so, however, when they were capsized by a huge wave. . . . Presently the scouts could hear the encouraging shouts of their rescuers bidding them . . . to hold out to the last. . . . The next moment the rescuers had swooped down the watery hill side. . . . A rush of water, a quick order or two, a rounding to of the boat and a strong hand was on each scout—all was well."[45]

By 9:30 A.M. the three soldiers stood safely on the deck of the *Flag* where they enjoyed a warm welcome. Once Capt. Duncan's mission was made known, the commander of the *Flag* set about getting them on their way to Hilton Head. Capt. Duncan and his two scouts, accompanied by two Confederate deserters who had been held aboard the *Flag*, went aboard the gunboat *Dandelion* for transportation to Hilton Head, arriving there the following day.[46] Duncan was then taken to Washington, D.C., to personally carry the dispatches to the secretary of war. On the basis of these dispatches, the Northern press would, three days later, announce to the world the safe arrival of Gen. Sherman's lost army.

But conditions were still far from comfortable for Gen. Sherman's army. Food supplies continued to be their biggest problem, and each day made the situation more acute. Lt. Col. Strong told of the hardships: "On the 11th of December . . . many of the horses belonging to the right wing were sadly reduced, and the men were living on short rations of rice gathered from the plantations around us; but even this supply was limited and a week or ten days at furthest would exhaust it, and what then? We expected to draw hardbread and forage from the transport fleet within two days of our arrival and three had already elapsed and there were no signs of relief. Fort McAllister lay between us and our supplies, its parapet bristling with heavy guns."[47]

In his diary, Lt. William H. Pittenger of Company O, 39th Ohio Volunteer Infantry, summed up the situation facing Sherman's army: "Our last issue of bread expired last night which makes it necessary to do our work quickly. Must eat to fight. We must take Savannah or reach a base very soon. Time is precious."[48]

Gen. Sherman was unaware of Capt. Duncan's success in carrying the dispatches to naval authorities at Hilton Head. The route to the sea was still blocked, and he had yet to see any sign of the navy. The need to move against Fort McAllister was apparent, and the general discussed the situation with his commanders. He wanted to send Brig. Gen. Kilpatrick's cavalry against the fort, but Kilpatrick was opposed: "General, I am sorry but I don't think a regiment will take that fort." Sherman was surprised by this estimation: "Why the hell don't you? There are only 250 men in the garrison." Kilpatrick replied, "Yes the garrison is not large, but I know the man commanding, and he is damn fool enough not to surrender." Sherman remained unconvinced and ordered Kilpatrick to move the bulk of his cavalry command into Bryan County to scout the approaches to Fort McAllister and, if feasible, to assault the fort.[49]

Brig. Gen. Kilpatrick accepted the orders but felt that he would require infantry support to ensure the success of an attack. While moving his command toward the Ogeechee River to comply with Gen. Sherman's orders,

Kilpatrick went to Maj. Gen. Howard to request the assistance of his infantry in the proposed movement against McAllister. The major general promised his support if Gen. Sherman would approve of the revised attack. Although Howard was willing to aid Kilpatrick's attack, he felt that nothing short of an infantry assault would succeed. Kilpatrick communicated his evaluation to the general and requested approval.[50] Howard wrote, "It was after this visit of Kilpatrick, made to me, without a doubt, on his way over the Ogeechee to carry out his instructions, that I went in person to Gen. Sherman and represented to him the necessity of sending infantry to take the fort. My impression has always been clear that I asked him, contrary to his instructions to me, which were to destroy King's Bridge utterly, to allow me to rebuild what was already demolished, and send a division of infantry to take the fort. The General asked me which division I would choose, agreeing with me that it would be next to impossible for the cavalry alone to storm the fort. I answered 'Hazen's.' To this proposition the General agreed."[51] Within a short time after this conference, repairs to the damaged portion of King's Bridge began, and Gen. Sherman sent new orders to Brig. Gen. Kilpatrick.[52]

On the morning of 12 December, the 9th Pennsylvania, 2nd, 3rd, and 5th Kentucky, 8th Indiana, 9th Michigan, and 5th Ohio Cavalry crossed the Ogeechee and Canouchee rivers on pontoon bridges and moved toward Fort McAllister. At the same time, Maj. Anderson and a small scouting party left

9.4. Brig. Gen. William B. Hazen commanded the 2nd Division of the 15th Army Corps. This division was Sherman's old unit, which he had commanded early in the war at Shiloh and other battles. Gen. Sherman was confident in their ability to take Fort McAllister and in Hazen's ability to make it happen. Hazen was a proven veteran of many hard-fought campaigns. Courtesy, U.S. Army Military History Institute

the fort to reconnoiter the area.[53] Anderson wrote, "On the morning of the 12th of December, 1864, I accompanied Lieutenant [Thomas P.] O'Neal on a scout, and found the enemy advancing in force from King's Bridge. We were hotly pursued by their cavalry, and had barely time to burn the barns of Messrs. Thomas G. Arnold and William Patterson, which were filled with rice. The steam tug Columbus—lying about three miles above the fort—was also burned."[54]

The Federal cavalry pursued Maj. Anderson's party all the way to the vicinity of Genesis Point but halted short of the causeway. Maj. Anderson made his return in safety while Brig. Gen. Kilpatrick's men weighed the chances of success in an unsupported attack on the fort. A short time later a courier arrived bearing Gen. Sherman's revised orders for Kilpatrick that countermanded previous orders calling for a cavalry assault on the fort. Sherman ordered Kilpatrick to fall back from the fort and to send a portion of his forces south in an attempt to open communications with the navy ships in St. Catherine's Sound. The remainder were to move south into Liberty County to take possession of the next access to deep water at Sunbury and to begin foraging operations.[55]

If Fort McAllister withstood attempts to capture it, Sherman recognized that he would need an alternate route for a supply line to the naval fleet. The harbor at Sunbury was the next logical point that could be used. During the colonial period, Sunbury had been a major port city, but by 1864 the city was gone, nothing but a memory, although the high bluff and deep-water channel remained. It was also obvious that several weeks might elapse before a supply line was established and enough provisions stockpiled to support the army. Until then forage had to be found, and the only source lay to the south of Savannah, in Liberty County, which had been all but abandoned by Confederate forces.

Brig. Gen. Kilpatrick complied with Sherman's orders, establishing his headquarters at Strathy Hall, the home of Lt. Col. Joseph L. McAllister, and sending the 9th Michigan Cavalry south of the fort to take possession of Kilkenny Bluff in anticipation of making contact with the U.S. Navy from there.[56] The remainder of Kilpatrick's troopers fanned out through the area. One of their first acts was to burn the Episcopal Church in an attempt to signal the U.S. Navy forces offshore. The Demere House, several miles west of Kilkenny Bluff, was also burned in a similar attempt. At Kilkenny Bluff the Federal troopers of the 9th Michigan Cavalry swarmed over the area and occupied the Kilkenny House. They made themselves at home with no regard for its lavish interior of marble mantles and massive mahogany folding doors that soon became kindling for the troopers' fires.[57] The soldiers camped in the yard and viewed the panorama of Ossabaw Island, St. Catherine's Sound, and the Atlantic Ocean to the east. In the distant sound, the blockading schooner USS *Fernandina* rode quietly at anchor appearing to be totally unaware of events taking place ashore.

The troopers practiced similar depredations at Strathy Hall, where Kilpatrick set up his headquarters. The McAllister home was ransacked, valuables taken, and Lt. Col. McAllister's library scattered all over the house, yard, and up the road leading to the home. They also focused their attentions on the slave quarters and outbuildings, and the rice mill was burned. Many area plantations suffered the same fate, and some, such as the neighboring Clay plantation home, were burned by the marauding troopers.[58]

While Brig. Gen. Kilpatrick's forces probed the area around Fort McAllister, the fort came under fire from a different direction than usual. A section of Battery H, 1st Illinois Artillery, a light battery of 20-pounder Parrott rifles under the command of Capt. Francis DeGress, had been set up near the signal station atop Dr. Cheves's rice mill on the northwest bank of the river.

These were the same guns that had fired the first shell into Atlanta on 20 July 1864 and around which desperate fighting had swirled two days later when the battery was overrun during the Battle of Atlanta. But the guns had been recaptured, and on this December morning at the Cheves Mill, the section began firing on the fort at long range, while the other section accompanied Brig. Gen. William Hazen, commander of the 2nd Division of the 15th Army Corps. The fort briefly replied to the fire but the two and a half mile range was too great a distance, and the fort's guns soon fell silent. Federal artillery continued an intermittent fire on the fort throughout the day, partially to harass its garrison but also to attract the attention of the navy gunboats offshore.[59]

"So soon as the enemy opened fire upon the fort from the opposite side of the river," Maj. Anderson wrote, "it was evident that two of the magazines were seriously endangered, and it became necessary to protect them from that fire by the erection of suitable traverses. The labor expended in their construction, in the mounting of guns on the rear of the work, and in removing debris . . . occupied the garrison constantly night and day, for nearly forty-eight hours immediately preceding the attack."[60]

"We knew that our time would come the next day," Samuel L. Moore of Company D, 1st Regiment, Georgia Reserves, recalled, "and the necessary preparations were made to give Mr. Sherman as warm a reception as we could."[61]

While Kilpatrick moved his cavalry into Bryan County on this day and Sherman looked for some sign of the U.S. Navy, events were taking place that morning at Hilton Head that would bring the navy to Sherman. Capt. Duncan and his companions arrived early that morning, and Maj. Gen.

John G. Foster, in charge of Federal forces there, was relieved to finally have some word of Sherman's status. Armed with Duncan's knowledge of the area where Sherman's army was closing upon the coast, Foster wanted to travel to Ossabaw Sound and attempt to open communications with him, but the vessel he generally used for water transportation was unavailable, and no replacement was at hand. Customs Agent Albert G. Browne offered the use of his revenue cutter *Nemaha*. Foster accepted, and soon they were preparing to depart.

One of the officers who accompanied Foster was Capt. Jesse Merrill, chief signal officer of the department, who brought a detachment of ten privates and a noncommissioned officer from the signal service under the command of Lt. George A. Fisher.[62] The *Nemaha* left Hilton Head at 10:30 on the morning of 12 December and traveled to Fort Pulaski where they stopped to check for any further news of Sherman and to get some signal rockets. They left for Ossabaw Sound, arriving late that afternoon to meet the *Flag* on blockade duty there.[63] Lt. Fisher was ordered to take two men from the detachment, board the *Flag*, and scout the waterways with the intention of establishing contact with Sherman. Fisher described his obstacles: "I . . . proceeded on board the Flag with Sergeant George Hardy and Private Cornelius Smedes, and was introduced to Captain [James C.] Williamson, commanding, by Maj. John F. Anderson, chief of staff to General Foster. Captain Williamson promised to render me every assistance in his power, but had no picket-boats to send out, but as soon as the tug Dandelion returned would let me have her to proceed up the [Little] Ogeechee and Vernon Rivers. Finding I could no nothing that night in reconnoitering, I induced the captain to fire his heavy guns six times in rapid succession, after which I threw up several rockets in rapid succession, and closely scanned the horizon inland for some answering signal. After waiting some time a faint shoot of light was seen to arise in the direction of the Ogeechee River, but not being satisfied, I threw up two more at once, and again saw the response, but at so great a distance as to be almost indiscernible."[64]

The steam tug *Dandelion* eventually returned, and Fisher wanted to board her and start his reconnaissance, but the captain of the *Flag* had orders to take the remainder of the signal detachment to the north end of Ossabaw Island to erect a signal tower there the next day, also in hopes of establishing contact with Sherman. Fisher would have to wait until the next morning.[65]

As the sun set on 12 December, Gen. Sherman arrived at the home of William King near King's Bridge on the Ogeechee. Here he found Maj. Gen. Howard with Brig. Gen. Hazen, whose division of the 15th Army Corps was camped nearby.[66] Sherman knew that this was the division for the job of taking Fort McAllister. The 2nd Division of the 15th Army Corps was, he said, "the same old division which I had commanded at Shiloh and Vicksburg, in which I felt a special pride and confidence."[67]

Hazen's division, composed of units from Ohio, Illinois, Michigan, Indiana, and Missouri, was typical of the veteran units that made up Sherman's army. Virtually all of Hazen's units had been organized at the outbreak of the war and had seen hard service from Fort Henry, Fort Donelson, Shiloh, Corinth, Stones River, Vicksburg, Chattanooga, Knoxville, and the battles of the Atlanta campaign. These men were as diversified as the battles they had fought.

Some, like Capt. John M. Groce of the 30th Ohio were already considered heroes. Groce had seen it all from the very beginning. A native of Circleville, Ohio, born there 13 April 1840, he became a teacher and was pursuing a law career when the war came. He enlisted for a ninety-day term and served as an orderly sergeant with his company at the first battle of Bull Run in July 1861. The following month, the twenty-one-year-old sergeant reenlisted in the 30th Ohio Infantry, eventually being promoted to lieutenant, then captain when Company H was formed. He participated in the campaigns in West Virginia and was sent west with the unit in the spring of 1863.[68]

At Vicksburg, Groce personally led 150 handpicked men on the first assault of the Confederate defenses. Only twenty-three men survived the attack, and Groce himself, terribly wounded in the left arm, lay in the ditch below the Confederate fort all day. That night he managed to return to his own lines under a hail of Confederate gunfire. After a long and painful recovery, he returned to his command in January of 1864 and led his men throughout the Atlanta campaign. Now, one more battle lay ahead of him.[69]

Groce's heroism was only one such example. Although he received high acclaim for his devotion to duty, many other men were just as devoted and suffered merely as a part of the burden they carried as a soldier. Like Capt. Groce, Pvt. James Horner also enlisted in the 30th Ohio Infantry at the age of twenty-one in August of 1861. A native of Perry County, Ohio, Horner had worked as a farmer and sought no commission as an officer. He followed Company D, 30th Ohio, through its campaigns in the east and was wounded in the left arm at South Mountain, Maryland, on 14 September 1862. He suffered a debilitating illness that winter that required hospitalization; he recovered and followed the 30th Ohio west to the fighting at Vicksburg and Chattanooga. In February of 1864 he reenlisted for three more years and followed the 30th Ohio on the Atlanta campaign.[70]

Another veteran of the 30th Ohio was 1st Sgt. Lyman Hardman of Company I. A native of New Philadelphia, Ohio, he answered the first calls for volunteers, enlisting as a private on 22 August 1861 at the age of nineteen.

He followed the 30th Ohio through its campaigns in the eastern theater, suffered through illness and recuperation, participated in the unit's service in the western theater, and on 1 February 1864 at Larkinsville, Alabama, reenlisted as a veteran volunteer.[71]

Some men, like Capt. Abner B. Smith of Company E, 48th Illinois Infantry, had seen a side of the war that few of his comrades had experienced. A resident of Illinois when the war came, the twenty-two-year-old enlisted September 1861 as a second lieutenant in Company E. Promoted to captain a year later, he followed the 48th Illinois through all of its campaigns. On 21 July 1864 he was captured on a skirmish line outside of Atlanta and sent to Andersonville Prison where he languished for several months. When Atlanta fell, the Confederates began transferring prisoners to other points. Shuttled about on rickety railroads while crammed aboard dismal boxcars, Smith finally ended up in Columbia, South Carolina, where he managed to effect his escape. Over the next few weeks he eluded his pursuers and on 27 November rejoined the 48th Illinois near Millen, Georgia.[72]

Another soldier of the 48th Illinois was twenty-eight-year-old Capt. Stephen F. Grimes of Company I. Before the war he had been a teacher and medical student. He enlisted in September 1861 as a second lieutenant with the 48th Illinois. At the Battle of Shiloh he was badly wounded when a bullet passed through his right shoulder and lung and lodged in his back between his spine and shoulder. He would recover but the bullet could not be removed, and Grimes would carry it for the rest of his life.[73]

Grimes participated in the fighting at Corinth, Vicksburg, Chattanooga, Missionary Ridge, and Atlanta where he was slightly wounded in the right shoulder. Asher Goslin, surgeon of the 48th Illinois, said that Capt. Grimes "was as brave an officer as we had in Sherman's Army—was always detailed on all hazardous service."[74] With the pace of the war changing, Grimes found that his outlook in life changed as well. In September 1863 he obtained leave to return to Illinois to marry. When the 48th Illinois embarked on the Atlanta campaign that spring, Grimes was aware that he was also to become a father. He pressed south from Atlanta with Sherman's army but had no word from his wife, so it was understandable that on this December evening, Grimes wanted the army to break through to the coast and communications opened up with the outside world. He was unaware that two weeks before, while he was marching through Georgia, his wife had given birth to a healthy baby girl.[75]

Other men had left their homes in Europe and fought to preserve their adopted country. Charles Bateman had been born in Ireland and while still a child immigrated to the United States with his parents, settling in Hamilton County, Ohio, where they took up farming. Bateman grew up on the farm, and as his father's health declined, Charles, as the oldest child, found himself taking on more and more of the responsibilities of running the farm and supporting his parents, two brothers, and two sisters.[76]

Charlie watched other young men his age march off to the grand adventure when the war came, but he remained home to tend to his parents and the farm. For two years he followed the course of the war until he could stand by no longer. The twenty-two-year-old man arranged for others to care for the farm and his sickly parents, and he then traveled to Cincinnati, Ohio, where on 23 February 1864 he enlisted in Company D of the 70th Ohio Infantry. Charlie then found himself in the war, seeing combat in earnest through the Atlanta campaign, but he never forgot his parents and regularly sent home a large portion of his monthly pay.[77]

These were only a few of the forty-five hundred men who made up the 2nd Division of the 15th Army Corps. They were a mixture of old veterans and new recruits and represented a cross section of life from the Northern states. On the evening of 12 December, they remained in camp at King's Bridge while Sherman, Howard, and Hazen conferred on the plan of action for the next day.[78] The repairs to the bridge would be complete by sunrise, and troops would be able to cross the river. With Hazen's division on hand and the bridge repairs close to completion, things were in order for the move against Fort McAllister. Sherman describes his strategy: "I gave General Hazen, in person, his orders to march rapidly down the right bank of the Ogeechee, and without hesitation to assault and carry Fort McAllister by storm. I knew it to be strong in heavy artillery, as against an approach from the sea, but believed it open and weak to the rear. I explained to General Hazen fully, that on his action depended the safety of the whole army, and the success of the campaign."[79]

10

A Perfect Chaos

During the early morning hours of 13 December 1864, the repairs to King's Bridge were completed, and Brig. Gen. Hazen's division began crossing the river. At the same time, Brig. Gen. Kilpatrick's cavalry was moving out of the area. The 2nd, 3rd, and 5th Kentucky and 9th Pennsylvania cavalries pressed south on the coastal highway towards Midway in Liberty County. Brig. Gen. Kilpatrick, accompanied by the 5th Ohio Cavalry, prepared to depart for Kilkenny Bluff to join the 9th Michigan Cavalry already there.[1] Gen. Sherman gave details of the day.

> Having seen General Hazen fairly off, accompanied by General Howard, I rode with my staff down the left bank of the Ogeechee, ten miles to the rice-plantation of a Mr. Cheeves [*sic*], where General Howard had established a signal-station to overlook the lower river, and to watch for any vessel of the blockading squadron. . . .
>
> On reaching the rice-mill at Cheeves', I found a guard and a couple of twenty-pound Parrott guns, of DeGress's battery, which fired an occasional shot toward Fort McAllister, plainly seen over the salt-marsh, about three miles distant. Fort McAllister had the rebel flag flying, and occasionally sent a heavy shot back across the marsh to where we were, but otherwise everything about the place looked as peaceable and quiet as on the Sabbath.
>
> The signal-officer had built a platform on the ridge-pole of the rice-mill. Leaving our horses behind the stacks of rice-straw, we all got on the roof of a shed attached to the mill, where from I could communicate with the signal-officer above, and at the same time look out toward Ossabaw Sound, and across the Ogeechee River at Fort McAllister.[2]

Capt. McClintock and Lt. Sampson still manned the signal station atop the rice mill. One of the officers with Sherman on the roof of the shed was Maj. George Ward Nichols, who recorded in his diary: "As General Sherman and his staff stood all day on the top of Cheves rice mill looking through their glasses at the fort they saw the Confederate flag continue to fly over it. They discussed the probability of its being lowered. One of the staff officers knew Maj. Anderson, they having been schoolmates. He said to General Sherman 'George Anderson is in command, General, and the flag will never be lowered. You will have to capture that fort.'"[3]

Lt. Col. William E. Strong, also among the group on the roof of the rice mill shed, gave his perspective

> What an exciting day it was for us! . . . Twenty officers or more with field-glasses, swept the horizon seaward. Signal officers with their powerful telescopes labored with untiring industry to make out a sail, or a mast, or a smoke stack, or a wreath of smoke. The signal flags from the cupola above us waved and fluttered in vain. At intervals of five minutes a twenty pound shell from DeGress's battery went whistling through the air, and more than one of them burst in close proximity to that huge fort bristling with cannon which guarded our only approach to the sea.
>
> There it lay, in plain view, two and one-half miles away, sullen and silent, like a great lion at bay—conscious of its own strength, yet not deigning to speak to us. The key to the city, which we were besieging. Again and again did every officer present adjust his field glasses and gazed long and steadily. The situation was not desperate, perhaps, but it was perilous. The men were living on short rations of rice gathered from the plantations about us and many of the artillery horses . . . were sadly reduced for want of forage. No fleet of gun-boats in sight, no transports, no depot of supplies! No wonder General Sherman was anxious and no wonder he strained his eyes to pierce the space that separated him and his army from the sea.[4]

While Sherman and his staff scanned the eastern horizon for some sign of the navy, Hazen's division was approaching Fort McAllister. Hazen related:

> The day was bright, and the march, after leaving the rice farms, was along a lovely road of shells and white sand, under magnolias and wide branching live-oaks draped in long, hanging moss. About midway we passed the old McAllister mansion, called Strother [Strathy] Hall, whose inmates I had known before the war. There was their home, but they had gone. Kilpatrick's Cavalry had been there before us, and the contents of

the house were strewn upon the floors or scattered about the lawn. I saw a few familiar articles, and was recognized by an old auntie who had been with the family at the North. The negro servants showed no disposition to put things to rights again thinking perhaps, that it would only invite further mischief. After I had taken steps to prevent my command from adding to the disorder, we went on, and soon met Kilpatrick at the head of his men, returning from a reconnaissance of the fort. He gave me such information of it as he had gathered.[5]

The division proceeded toward Fort McAllister with the 47th Ohio Infantry leading the column. In advance of the main body was a small group of mounted scouts from the 47th Ohio commanded by Capt. Henry Breenfoeder of Company B. The twelve men arrived about 6:30 A.M. at the head of the causeway leading over to Genesis Point. There was little sign of life on the other side so they decided to make a hurried dash across the causeway along the tree-lined shoulder of the road so as not to show themselves any more than necessary.[6]

Located on the other side of the causeway was a small defensive work with a few Confederate soldiers on a picket line scattered along the marsh. The Confederates knew that the enemy was in the area but they felt confident since Chief Engineer Tomb had mined the causeway road with torpedoes.[7] It did not seem likely they could be surprised by the Federals but their confidence also resulted in a lack of vigilance. They were unaware that Federal scouts had already arrived in the treeline on the opposite side of the causeway. Lt. Col. Strong tells what next occurred.

> Genl. Hazen reached a point some two miles from the fort, at a quarter to seven A.M., in which position he remained for several hours. Pending this halt, a small squad of men attached to the 47th Ohio, rode further on, crossed a narrow causeway on one side of which flowed the Ogeechee and on the other side a great salt march; dashed through a belt of timber in the skirt of which was an abandoned outwork and captured an outpost of the enemy. On the return of this party, the prisoners, who were compelled to march in advance on the causeway, were seen to file to its extreme edge. They were halted and required to state the cause of their cautious movements, when [Pvt. Thomas J. Mills of Clinch's Light Battery] answered that torpedoes were buried in the bed of the road; and upon further inquiry disclosed the fact that torpedoes were buried all along the road. They were then forced to point out the particular localities and in some instances were compelled to dig up and remove them. Guards were then stationed over these infernal machines and brigade

commanders notified so that the troops passed over the causeway without the loss of a man.[8]

Pvt. Mills realized that the war was over for him and took the oath of allegiance when it was offered.[9] Brig. Gen. Hazen wrote, "I withdrew the command a half a mile to the Middleton House, where dispositions were immediately made for the assault. I made no formal demand for surrender, believing that it would merely advertise our intentions, and be met by a boastful refusal."[10]

When the causeway was cleared of mines, the regiments detailed to assault the fort began crossing and moving into position. They found the terrain extremely difficult with thick woods and low swampy areas so that much time was required. While the designated regiments made their way through the woods, skirmishers went forward.[11] Maj. Gen. Howard reported, "Leaving eight regiments [in reserve], nine were carried forward to about 600 yards from the fort and deployed, with a line of skirmishers thrown sufficiently near the fort to keep the gunners from working their guns with any effect—those firing to the rear being in barbette. The grounds to the right of the fort being marshy, cut through by deep streams, rendered deployment of that part of the line slow and difficult."[12]

"At about 12 P.M. our regiment arrived within about one-half mile of the fort, in a piece of timber," Sgt. Joseph A. Saunier of the 47th Ohio Infantry wrote. "The regiment was immediately formed in line of battle and ordered to remain there on the banks of [the] Ogeechee River, and the division formed on us. Capt. Wm. E. Brachman of Company F. was ordered by Colonel [Augustus C.] Parry to take his company out and deploy as skirmishers."[13] While the Federal line deployed, Lt. William H. Sherfy of the Signal Corps located Brig. Gen. Hazen's headquarters and established a signal station from where he could communicate with Gen. Sherman across the marsh to the northeast.[14]

G. Arthur Gordon of Savannah recalled in later years what Maj. Anderson had told him. "It was known that an assault would be made from the land side by Gen. Hazen's division. Maj. Anderson assembled the garrison and requested the older men and the married men to leave the defense to the younger men. This left a garrison of less than 200 men to withstand an entire division, as Maj. Anderson had resolved to refuse to surrender the Fort and to force the Union troops to take it by assault."[15] Samuel L. Moore of Company D, 1st Regiment, Georgia Reserves, said, "The roll was called . . . and 155 men answered for duty."[16]

It was not until the skirmishers opened fire on the fort that the garrison realized the Federal forces were close at hand. Sgt. Saunier of the 47th Ohio gives the account: "We deployed and Captain Brachman advanced on the fort, but not a shot was fired until the writer got his platoon of said company within gun shot range and under the enemies guns bearing directly on our brigade, he fired his musket (which was the first shot) at a gray mule and killed the mule; that shot opened the skirmish."[17] An unknown recruit of Company F, 47th Ohio Infantry, said in later years, "Sergeant J. A. Saunier . . . said, 'Watch me make the Johnnies get off the works,' and he brought to his shoulder his trusty rifle and opened the fight."[18]

Maj. Anderson describes the fight from the fort.

> About eight o'clock A.M. desultory firing commenced between the skirmishers of the enemy and my sharpshooters. . . . Receiving from headquarters neither orders nor responses to my telegraphic despatches, I determined, under the circumstances, and notwithstanding the great disparity of numbers, between the garrison and the attacking forces, to defend the fort to the last extremity. The guns [of the fort] being en barbette, the detachments serving them were greatly exposed to the fire of the enemy's sharpshooters. To such an extent was this the case that in one instance, out of a detachment of eight men, three were killed and three more wounded. The Federal skirmish line was very heavy, and the fire so close and rapid that it was at times impossible to work our guns. My sharpshooters did all in their power, but were entirely too few to suppress this galling fire upon the artillerists. In view of the large force of the enemy . . . holding the fort was simply a question of time. There was but one alternative—death or captivity. Captain Thomas S. White, the engineer in charge, had previously felled the trees in the vicinity of the fort, and demolished the mortar magazine which commanded the fort to a very considerable extent. For lack of the necessary force and time, however, the felled timber and the ruins of the adjacent houses, which had been pulled down, had not been entirely removed. Protected by this cover, the enemy's sharpshooters were enabled to approach quite near, to the great annoyance and injury of the cannoneers. One line of abatis had been constructed by the engineer, and three lines would have been completed around the fort, but for the want of time and materials. . . . At the time of the assault, the men were greatly fatigued and in bad plight, physically considered, for the contest. . . . At ten o'clock the fight became general, the opposing forces extending from the river entirely around to the marsh on the east.[19]

"About 10 o'clock in the morning the enemy entered the woods and began to form in line of battle," wrote Moore of Company D. "We could see the Yankees behind the big trees near the little dairy (McAllister dairy) and the dairy itself was as full of them as it could be. Our sharpshooters would take a crack at every 'Blue Coat' that exposed himself. One of the boys asked permission to put a cannon ball through the dairy, which was granted, and a thirty-two pound rifle shot was sent through the center. Then business picked up!"[20]

Capt. Stephen F. Grimes of the 48th Illinois Infantry commanded the 3rd Brigade skirmishers holding the center, where they found the fire of two 32-pounder smoothbore cannon covering the rear of the fort extremely annoying. Grimes instructed his sharpshooters to concentrate on the gunners manning the two pieces. Within a short time the guns were silenced.[21]

"The fort was an enclosed work," Sherman wrote, "and its land front was in the nature of a bastion and curtains, with good parapet, ditch, Fraise, and Chevaus-De-Frise, made out of the large branches of live-oaks. Luckily, the rebels had left the larger and unwieldy trunks on the ground, which served as a good cover for the skirmish line, which crept behind these logs, and from them kept the artillerists from loading and firing their guns accurately."[22]

It was not long before some of the units on the skirmish line began to run low on ammunition. Pvt. Louis Shuttinger of Company A, 47th Ohio Infantry, volunteered to go for more. He went to the rear to locate an ammunition resupply point.[23] Sgt. Joseph Saunier described Shuttinger's endeavor: "When he got to where the ammunition was, he pulled off his blouse and filled it with packages of cartridges, and returned under cover of the River bank until [he] reached the end of the [skirmish] line, which deployed at right angles to the river; here he was compelled to get on top of the bank, and in full view of the enemy, so he called out, 'Keep them down, boys, here I come' and deliberately walked along the line dropping the cartridges to the men as he passed. Even the Confederates seemed to think him too brave to shoot at."[24]

While Hazen's men skirmished with the defenders of Fort McAllister and the assaulting forces deployed, Brig. Gen. Kilpatrick and the men of the 5th Ohio and 9th Michigan Cavalry, at Kilkenny Bluff several miles to the south, attempted to establish communications with the navy blockader in St. Catherine's Sound. At 10:00 A.M. the 5th Ohio arrived at Kilkenny, where they joined the 9th Michigan already there in camp. From the bluff they could see a vessel anchored in the sound but all attempts to attract its attention had failed.[25] The vessel anchored in the sound was the bark *Fernandina*, commanded by Lt. Cmdr. Lewis West. Although the cavalrymen at Kilkenny Bluff felt that they had not attracted the attention of those aboard, the crewmen of the *Fernandina* knew something was happening on the coast. The day before they had sent scouts upriver in boats to search of signs of unusual activity ashore, and that evening the crew saw rockets to the northwest of them and heard the sound of cannon to the north.[26]

At Kilkenny Bluff, six of Kilpatrick's officers, from the 5th Ohio, rowed the ten miles out to the *Fernandina* in two small canoes that had been located nearby. Arriving at the anchored vessel shortly before noon, they received a hearty welcome, spent several hours aboard, and for their return trip were provided an escort and a cutter. One of the ship's naval officers accompanied them in order to report personally to Brig. Gen. Kilpatrick.[27] At 1:30 P.M. Kilpatrick penned a dispatch to inform Sherman of these developments and recommend they utilize the landing at Kilkenny to bring in the needed supplies from the fleet. This was the first direct communication between Sherman's forces and the Navy and the first point at which Sherman's army actually reached the sea, clearly visible from Kilkenny Bluff.[28]

While Kilpatrick was communicating with the *Fernandina* in St. Catherine's Sound, Sherman hoped to accomplish the same thing in Ossabaw Sound. Atop the Cheves rice mill, he and his staff anxiously eyed the eastern horizon for any sign of the naval vessels while they awaited developments at Fort McAllister. Sherman wrote, "About 2 P.M. we observed signs of commotion in the fort, and noticed one or two guns fired inland, and some musket-skirmishing in the woods close by. This betokened the approach of Hazen's division, which had been anxiously expected, and soon thereafter the signal-officer discovered about three miles above the fort a signal-flag, with which he conversed, and found it to belong to General Hazen, who was preparing to assault the fort, and wanted to know if I were there. On being assured of this fact, and that I expected the fort to be carried before night, I received by signal the assurance of General Hazen that he was making his preparations, and would soon attempt the assault. The sun was rapidly declining, and I was dreadfully impatient."[29]

It seemed to Sherman that Hazen was taking far too much time in deploying his troops. Skirmishing had been going on all day, but as of yet, there appeared to be no sign of an assault. Only a few hours of daylight remained, and Sherman feared night would fall before the fort did. However, it was no easy task for Hazen to get his troops into position for the assault because there were a number of obstacles to overcome. As Hazen's division converged upon Genesis Point, the causeway presented a bottleneck to their approach so that the column of troops began to back up. Also, the land along the south side of Genesis Point was broken up with creeks and marsh, making the movement of troops through this area slow and uncertain. It also took time to organize the assaulting forces in the order of their approach to the area, and it took the better part of the day to get them across the causeway and deployed into a line of battle.

Hazen's division comprised three brigades and on 13 December 1864 numbered about forty-three hundred soldiers. A portion of each brigade was held in reserve, and nine regiments, numbering a little more than three thousand men, made up the assaulting force. The three brigades had been instructed to form a single line of battle. The 1st Brigade, commanded by Col. Theodore S. Jones and composed of the 6th Missouri, 116th Illinois, and 30th Ohio Infantry, would hold the extreme right of the line, with the right flank of the 30th Ohio positioned along the river marshes below the fort. The 2nd Brigade, commanded by Col. Wells S. Jones and composed of the 47th and 54th Ohio and the 111th Illinois infantry, would hold the extreme left of the line, anchored on the Ogeechee River bluff behind the fort, with the left flank of the 47th Ohio on the river bluff. The 3rd Brigade, commanded by Col. John M. Oliver and composed of the 48th and 90th Illinois and the 70th Ohio infantry, would hold the center of the line.[30]

While events moved forward at Genesis Point, Lt. George Fisher, out in Ossabaw Sound that morning, was scouting the upper reaches of the water routes looking for Sherman. He and his detail boarded the steam tug *Dandelion* at 8:00 A.M. and left the gunboat *Flag* in the mouth of the Ogeechee River about 9:00 A.M.[31] According to the *Dandelion*'s logbook, they proceeded up the Vernon River and entered the Little Ogeechee from where Fort McAllister could be observed across the marsh. However, the Little Ogeechee was guarded by a strong battery on Rose Dhu Island, and the captain of the *Dandelion* was unwilling to stir up that hornet's nest by getting too close. Fisher relates their mission.

[We] proceeded up the [Little] Ogeechee River, looking closely in every direction . . . for some signal or sign of General Sherman's army. We proceeded up the river to a point just out of range of . . . Fort McAllister and the batteries on the opposite side of the Little Ogeechee River. Here the captain was afraid to proceed any farther on account of the cross-fire which the different forts could bring upon him; but desiring to reconnoiter their position, I obtained the use of a small row-boat, and, accompanied by Sergeant Hardy and Private Smedes, and four men to row, I proceeded up along the shore until I arrived nearly opposite Fort McAllister's guns, and had passed the forts on the Little Ogeechee. Here I put the boat into a small creek,[32] where we were concealed from the enemy by the high grass of the marsh. I then made a careful and close reconnaissance of the forts and the surrounding country. . . . I soon heard musketry as of skirmishers advancing in the woods above Fort McAllister, and soon a few heavy guns were fired from the fort inland. I then looked about and saw, about three miles northwest of where I was lying in the marsh, a flag upon the top of an old rice mill, but there being no air stirring I was unable to make out of what nature it was. I could then indistinctly see persons through a broken part of the roof, one of whom, taking hold of the end of the flag, drew its folds out so that I could see our own glorious Stars and Stripes. I then immediately returned to the boat and rowed back as rapidly as possible to the tug-boat. I then gave orders for the tug to be moved up past an opening in the woods through which Fort McAllister had the range of the river. As soon as the anchor was got up the tug was put under full head of steam. . . .[33]

The *Dandelion* dropped down the Vernon River, passed through the Hell Gate, entered the lower reaches of the Ogeechee River and ascended the river. Savage Island shielded the tug from the fort as they approached closer to a bend in the river.[34] Fisher wrote, "I could then distinctly see the rice mill, with the Stars and Stripes waving over it; and raising my white flag I had the general call made."[35]

At Fort McAllister the skirmishing continued all afternoon, providing a backdrop of noise to the deployment of the assaulting forces. About 3:30 P.M. the 2nd Brigade commander, Col. Wells S. Jones, and his adjutant general, Capt. John H. Groce, scouted the ground in front of their skirmish line, across which their men would have to charge. Col. Jones, a thirty-four-year-old physician from Ohio, had never been afraid to go where the fighting was heaviest, and Capt. Groce, the young hero of Vicksburg, had always been in the thick of the fighting. As the two men made their way through the fallen timber, a single bullet passed through both of them, killing Groce instantly and severely wounding Col. Jones, who fell with a wound through his right breast. He was removed from the field and taken to receive medical attention but there was doubt about his recovery.[36] The news cast a pall of gloom over the men of the 2nd Brigade, but there was little time to mourn. The death of Capt. Groce and the wounding of Col. Jones left the 2nd Brigade without its commander at the most crucial moment of the imminent attack. Command of the brigade went to the next ranking officer, Col. James S. Martin of the 111th Illinois Infantry.[37]

While the battle line formed up, Sherman and his staff remained atop the rice mill, waiting for the attack to take place and intently watching for the first sign of any vessels offshore. Among the group gathered atop the rice mill was Lt. Col. Strong.

> Twenty times or more during those eleven hours of anxious watching had different officers of the staff and members of the signal corps discovered something that bore resemblance to a gun boat. Notwithstanding the perilous position we were in, and the intense anxiety pervading the heart of every soldier present from the highest to the lowest, we had many a hearty laugh over the descriptions given every few minutes, of the long

looked for boat. There were more phantom ships seen that 13th of December than Maryatt ever dreamed of; they went floating by on every cloud and seemed to sail as well on land as on sea.

It was about 4:30 P.M. when Captain Bleckly [Samuel Bachtell], Chief Signal Officer of the army, whose eye had scarcely left his telescope since daylight, reported, in a quiet tone, to General Sherman that he felt certain he could make out a blue wreath of smoke curling up above the tree tops, many miles below McAllister, and indicated the exact position just to the left of a cluster of pines that fringed the bank of the stream. After careful scrutiny through his own glasses, General Sherman became satisfied that the young officer was correct. Five minutes later, everyone present by the aid of a strong glass could trace the naked outline of what appeared to be a gun boat and men could be seen walking to and fro upon her deck and a little later the stars and stripes could be distinctly seen.[38]

From Sherman's pen is: "Someone discovered a faint cloud of smoke, and an object gliding, as it were, along the horizon above the tops of the sedge [grass] toward the sea, which little by little grew till it was pronounced to be the smoke stack of a steamer coming up the river. 'It must be one of our squadron!' Soon the flag of the United States was plainly visible, and our attention was divided between this approaching steamer and the expected assault."[39]

Lt. Col. Strong continues.

Fifteen minutes later a group of signal officers collected on her forward deck and the first signal was sent. Flutter, flutter, up and down, right and left and our signal officer read the dispatch out loud so that all could hear it: "Who are you?"

ANSWER: "McClintock, General Howard's signal officer [with] General Sherman, who are you?"

Flutter, flutter, up and down, right and left.

REPLY: "Admiral Dahlgren and General Foster. Is Fort McAllister captured? How can I get to you? What troops are at Fort McAllister?"

ANSWER: "No it is not, but will be in twenty minutes. We are now investing Fort McAllister with Hazen's division."

"What can we do for you? We are ready to render you any assistance."

GENERAL FOSTER: "Can you assist us with your heavy guns?"

GENERAL SHERMAN: "Being only a tug-boat, no heavy guns aboard."[40]

And as the last word was telegraphed, a dozen heavy guns opened fire simultaneously on Hazen's division which was forming for the assault, some three-quarters of a mile from the fort; and then, for the first time, Major Anderson sent us his compliments in the shape of an eight-inch shell. We heard it coming and instantly all eyes were turned from the gun boat to the fort. The shell fell short a quarter of a mile or more and burst as it struck among the reeds and rushes.[41]

"The Right Brigade found itself behind a long stream, or sluice," Brig. Gen. Hazen said in his account, "and was a long time getting across and into position. This was especially annoying, as Gen. Sherman's last injunction was, not to find myself behind any creek, so that we could not get forward. I waited till nearly sundown, and then, with the Right Brigade still being reported not ready, I determined to assault with the other six regiments. Each officer and man was instructed to advance rapidly but in order until the enemy opened, and then to charge with a rush, every man for himself. . . . To make the chance of hits by the enemy as small as possible, the formation was in a single rank, resembling a close line of skirmishers."[42]

"General Sherman walked nervously to and fro," reported Maj. George W. Nichols in his diary, "turning quickly now and then from viewing the scene of conflict to observe the sun sinking slowly behind the tree-tops. No longer willing to bear the suspense, he said: 'Signal General Hazen that he must carry the fort by assault, to-night if possible.' The little flag waved and fluttered in the evening air."[43]

Lt. Fisher aboard the *Dandelion* also read the signal: "This was about 5 P.M. During the time these communications were being sent the musketry about the fort became more distinct. I then saw the signal made from the station I had been communicating with to some station in the woods near Fort McAllister, to General Hazen: 'It is absolutely necessary that the fort be taken immediately. The Stars and Stripes must wave over the battery at sundown. Sherman, General.' The answer came back: 'I am ready, and will assault at once!'"[44]

"I replied to go ahead," Sherman wrote, "as a friendly steamer was approaching from below."[45]

Lt. Col. Strong continues.

And now a deathlike stillness prevails at the rice mill; not a word is spoken—every officer is pale with excitement. The hands of the watch are creeping along towards 4:56—the sun is fast sinking to rest and Hazen is always prompt. He had just sent General Sherman word that the column would move at the sound of the bugle. And now the skirmishers of the grand old Second Division can be marked distinctly by the little round puffs of blue smoke that roll out from the cover . . . full rifle range away from the Rebel Fort, and which float lazily up towards the tree-tops—and now the troops can be plainly seen forming for the attack—the left flank of the division resting on the river below the fort, completely encircling the little garrison and all the time fully exposed to a deadly fire from those heavy guns; shell[,] grape[shot] and canister were hurled at the gallant command; every gun that could be brought to bear was opened on Hazen and was worked with the greatest rapidity. The fort was a perfect sheet of flame and the dense columns of smoke that hung about the parapet and floated over and above the bombproofs and magazines for a time fairly hid the work from our view.[46]

From the diary of Maj. Nichols, the narrative continues. "From out the encircling woods there came a long line of blue coats and bright bayonets, and the dear old flag was there, waving proudly in the breeze. Then the fort seemed alive with flame; quick, thick jets of fire shooting out from all its sides, while the white smoke first covered the place and then rolled away over the glacis."[47]

"At that instant of time," Sherman said, "we saw Hazen's troops come out of the dark fringe of woods that encompassed the fort, the lines dressed as on parade, with colors flying, and moving forward with a quick, steady pace. Fort McAllister was then all alive, its big guns belching forth dense clouds of smoke, which soon enveloped our assaulting lines."[48]

Yerby R. Davies of Company B, 70th Ohio Infantry, stood in the ranks waiting for the imminent assault. He had just recently rejoined his unit after being furloughed due to a wound in his right ear during the fighting at Atlanta that summer.[49] As with many of these soldiers, he was a veteran of much service with the 70th Ohio, but some among them were just then facing their first taste of combat, which he described.

In a southerly direction from the fort lay an open field, 1000 yards more or less in width and almost perfectly level. There was no fence but it was skirted by a pine forest, at the edge of which the 70th Ohio was drawn up in line of battle, with another regiment on its right and one on its left. . . . The guns of the fort were belching forth their thunder of ball and shell into our ranks and into the forest behind us. . . . An incident occurred which left an indelible imprint on my mind. It seemed to be a foreboding—a kind of presentiment—a few minutes prior to the advance, of what was going to happen.

Col. Henry Phillips, standing in front of the regiment, said, "My comrades, knowing that you have been prompt in the discharge of every duty, I deem it a waste of words to urge upon you the importance of continuing to do so." Then, pointing to the fort, he continued: "You see what is before you, and you know your duty."

These words were hardly spoken when John [Compton], color-bearer, who, up to the fall of Atlanta, had been detailed as regimental teamster, therefore had never been directly engaged in any of the numerous battles, approached Col. Phillips and said, "Colonel, you know I am not used to this kind of work; please excuse me." He answered: "John, were it in my power God knows I would gladly excuse every man in this regiment."[50]

Most of the Federal soldiers drawn up in the assaulting line had experienced this moment before as each man, alone with his thoughts, standing on the threshold between life and death, made peace with his Maker. John L. Compton, a thirty-one-year-old farmer from Ohio had served with the 70th Ohio since late 1861, having been through the battle at Shiloh and the advance on Corinth, Mississippi. Shortly after that he was detailed as a regimental teamster, and the remainder of his service had been in the rear areas. He stayed with the army, returning home only when word reached him of his wife's death. When the army left Atlanta, Compton was returned to the ranks, and at Fort McAllister he found himself at the front, bearing his unit's colors and fighting back an uneasy fear that welled up from within him as he looked across the open field toward the blazing furnace of Fort McAllister, beckoning them to come on.[51]

Lt. Col. Strong continued. "Four minutes of five o'clock; the sun is just going down! The western horizon is fairly flooded with the last rays of one of the loveliest sunsets I ever looked upon. . . . It seemed as though the sun was struggling fiercely to witness the assault about to be made."[52] The sun slowly slipped below the horizon, throwing its last rays of light into the eyes of the defenders of the fort, obscuring their view of Hazen's 2nd Brigade approached from the west. Brig. Gen. Hazen reported, "The 'assembly' was then sounded by the bugle three successive times, followed by the 'forward,' and as with a great impulse the line advanced. To my great surprise and joy, the Right Brigade, under Col. Theodore Jones moved out accurately at the same moment. It had crossed the streams and formed in line just in time to receive the order."[53]

"Captain [William] Brachman seeing the division formed for the charge at 5 P.M.," related Sgt. Saunier of the 47th Ohio, "passed the order along his skirmish line to fire on the enemy as fast as possible, and when the regiment came up to our skirmish line every one in Company F was to come together and take their place in the regimental line . . . and at 10 minutes to 5 o'clock P.M., the bugle was sounded, and the division advanced on the double-quick; with cheers the enemy opened rapidly with his inland guns, but so effective was the fire of our skirmish line under Captain Brachman, that altogether . . . very little damage was done."[54]

Across the marsh at the Cheves's rice mill, the assembled group strained to see the unfolding drama at Fort McAllister. Lt. Col. Strong describes the charge, "Four minutes of five o'clock! and across the river comes floating the bugle notes and away they go. Ye Gods! I never saw the like. . . . With a fierce

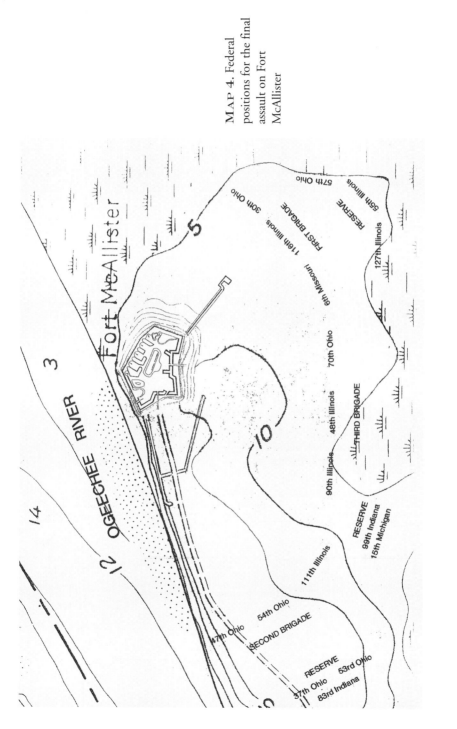

MAP 4. Federal positions for the final assault on Fort McAllister

10.1. The Confederate perspective of Gen. Hazen's forces forming along the tree line is captured in this 16 December 1864 photograph. This view across the rear of the fort shows the open ground over which the 54th Ohio Infantry and the 111th Illinois Infantry crossed to reach the fort. The 47th Ohio Infantry, posted along the river bluff at right, moved to the exposed beach below the bluff to avoid crossing through the scattered obstructions. In this view the obstructions have been piled up to be burned off. The 12-pound mountain howitzer (right of the sentry on the wall) is the same one mentioned in Lt. Col. Strong's account. Courtesy, Library of Congress

and infectious rush to the fort and with a gallantry almost unparalleled and with a wild cheer which I can never forget, away they went."[55]

"The line of blue moved steadily on," Maj. Nichols recorded in his diary, "too slowly, as it seemed to us, for we exclaimed, 'Why don't they dash forward?' but their measured step was unfaltering. Now the flag goes down, but the line does not halt. A moment longer, and the banner gleams again in the front. We, the lookers-on, clutched one another's arms convulsively, and scarcely breathed in the eager intensity of our gaze. Sherman stood watching with anxious air, awaiting the decisive moment. Then the enemy's fire redoubled in rapidity and violence. The darting streams of fire alone told the position of the fort. The line of blue entered the enshrouding folds of smoke. The flag was at last dimly seen, and then it went out of sight altogether."[56]

At this moment the assaulting lines west of the fort moved into a natural depression of the land behind the river bluff. From Sherman's distant vantage point, it appeared as if the fire from the fort had shattered the attackers for they disappeared momentarily from sight. It was a moment of uncertainty for Sherman, who exclaimed, "They are repulsed . . . must try something else."[57] He lowered his binoculars as if unable to watch the failure of the assault. "No, by Heaven!" yelled someone beside Sherman, "there is not a man in retreat— not a straggler in all the glorious line!"[58] Sherman looked back as the assaulting lines moved out of the depression of land and reappeared. The depression had actually served to protect them from the fort's fire as most of it passed over their heads at this point.[59]

"I have seen many gallant assaults made on fortified positions; but none like that," Lt. Col. Strong continued. "Not a straggler in sight. Every officer and enlisted man in that grand division proved himself a soldier and a hero. Of course the formation was broken the moment the column came in contact with the network of slashed timber, and after this no attempt was made to preserve an alignment; but every officer and soldier worked his way surely and certainly to the front and every eye was fixed upon the prize in front. It was a perfect chaos of smoke and flame and bursting shells and shrieks and shouts—Here and there . . . the men tore aside the chevaux-de-frise and worked their way over and through the abatis . . . over the huge 10-inch shells made into torpedoes which were sown among the obstructions, more than one-hundred and fifty in number and lying buried just beneath the surface of the ground so that the pressure of a soldier's feet would explode them. . . . The torpedoes exploded as they were trodden upon and many a gallant soldier was mutilated and fairly torn to pieces."[60]

Pvt. James S. Horner of Company D, 30th Ohio Infantry, was part of the 1st Brigade units approaching on the far right of the assaulting lines. "I remember very distinctly of jumping over a pile of fresh earth while on the charge. The man just behind me jumped over it all right, but the man behind him struck the cap of the torpedo as he ran and it exploded and blew off his foot above the ankle joint. When I heard the report of the shell I looked back and saw the poor fellow as he fell back in the hole the torpedo made when it exploded."[61]

First Sgt. Lyman Hardman was also with the 30th Ohio as they made their way through the obstructions and into the torpedo line. In the rush, he was one of the unfortunate ones who trod upon a torpedo and in the next instant was thrown violently to the ground, his left foot badly lacerated with shattered bones and his leg burned.[62] Hardman related the incident: "I had arrived near the edge of a small ditch around a mortar bed, when I exploded a torpedo that had been placed in the ground by stepping on it. On recovering from the effects of the shock I found that the shoe of my left foot was entirely blown off and my foot badly burned. My knee was slightly cut, the small finger and the one next to it on my left hand also cut and the hand burned. My face and one ear considerably cut and burned. My eyes swelled shut in a short time."[63]

Pvt. Charles C. Degman of Company F, 70th Ohio Infantry was in the 3rd Brigade in the center of the assaulting line. He remembered seeing "at least five brave boys in blue torn into fragments and scores hurled to the ground around the crater. Charles Bateman, an intimate acquaintance, . . . was one of the unfortunate victims of a cruel torpedo there in the battle front. Many were thrown over and into the abatis, which was just in the rear of the line of torpedoes."[64]

"When within about 150 yards of the fort we opened fire and soon silenced their guns," Pvt. Davies recalled. "Some 50 yards from the fort we crossed a line of torpedoes buried in the sand and John [Compton], stepping on one of them, was instantly killed. His body was mangled almost beyond recognition."[65] The young color-bearer who only moments before had asked his colonel to be excused from the assault paid the ultimate price.

"The parapet between the guns was manned by sharpshooters and a number of officers," Lt. Col. Strong wrote, "and men were picked off while

10.2. The footprints from the men of the 47th Ohio Infantry are still visible in the mud of the exposed beach three days after the fighting. The northwest bastion of the fort is seen as it would have appeared to the Federals as they crossed the exposed beach prior to assaulting the bastion. Courtesy, Library of Congress

struggling through the slashed timber and before the abatis was reached. . . . The enemy had neglected to construct his line of abatis to low water mark and it being ebb tide, or nearly so, there was an unobstructed passage on the beach to the river front of the fort."[66]

With the exposed beach opening an unobstructed route to the fort, the men of the 47th Ohio Infantry, advancing parallel to the river bluff, took advantage of the opportunity. They made their way down the bluff and onto the muddy beach, then ran ahead of the main assaulting column, and approached to a point quite near the fort before the garrison discovered them. Capt. J. H. Brown of Company A, 47th Ohio, remembered: "The regiment charged around to the waterfront up to the fort it being ebb tide, and at the command the 47th went up the fort and the old 47th colors were the first on the fort. Colonel [Edward A.] Parry's and Major [Thomas T.] Taylor's brave boys went on into the fort with a yell. The Confederates were somewhat panic stricken as the Yanks were coming on in the fort in a dozen places on them

10.3. The northwest bastion of Fort McAllister is the point where the men of the 47th Ohio Infantry came over the wall and engaged Confederate defenders in hand-to-hand fighting. A 6-pound gun from Capt. Nicholas Clinch's battery was located here at that time. The flag of the 47th Ohio was planted on this parapet, and the men claimed the honor of planting the first flag on the fort's wall, although several other units also claimed that honor. Courtesy, Library of Congress

with bayonets and the butt of our muskets, and the hand to hand fighting was terrible for a short time."[67]

Capt. Henry Breenfoeder of Company B, 47th Ohio, who commanded the scouts that captured the causeway that morning, wrote, "I had the pleasure, although it was not a very pleasant outlook previous to the assault, to be one of the very first to mount the fortifications of Fort McAllister, Ga., where our flag was certainly the first Union Flag planted, or rather, crossing the parapets."[68] The 47th Ohio always laid claim to having placed the first U.S. flag on the parapets of Fort McAllister but during the chaos and confusion of the battle, the 111th Illinois and the 70th Ohio Infantry would also claim this honor. Events moved so quickly as the attacking forces converged on the fort that no one could be certain who reached the wall first for they were all there within moments of one another.[69]

Lt. Col. Strong was with Gen. Sherman atop Cheves's rice mill.

And now the column, if it can be called such, nears the fort and now the colors of a regiment flutter along the ditch and hundreds of blue jackets can be seen, creeping up towards the parapet—and a daring color sergeant drives down his flag-staff upon the escarpment while the color guard group about him to protect the flag; the next instant all are cut down and swept away at one discharge from a light howitzer and the colors lie in the ditch torn to shreds and covered with blood and mangled corpses of its brave defenders. Further along towards the center another flag is planted on the enemy's works; but it too shares the fate of the first one. And now the ditch is filled with men struggling and scrambling for the parapet and one of those heavy guns commanding the ditch pours in its load of canister at forty feet and still the troops press on undaunted, undismayed—and the rebel garrison fight on, the cannoneers clinging to their pieces like grim death.[70]

Pvt. Davies of the 70th Ohio Infantry recalled the appearance of the row of abatis. "Between the row of [torpedoes] and the fort was planted a row of pine logs pointing outward, the butt end buried in the sand and every limb well sharpened. Having shed their bark, they resembled a tangle of buckhorns shining in the sun. There was no passing this barrier until a few brave men bending over their guns crawled under and thru, leaving gaps thru which the regiment rushed."[71]

Pvt. Degman, also with the 70th Ohio, describes what impediments were next. "After getting thru the torpedoes and abatis, [we] came to the ditch in the bottom of which were planted firmly a line of sharp-pointed stakes four or five feet high, set at an angle of about 30 degrees pointing outward. This was a serious obstacle, as the stakes could not be moved except in a few cases.

10.4. A line of abatis is what the men of the 111th, 90th, and 48th Illinois Infantries saw as they approached the southwest bastion of Fort McAllister. The torpedo line was located just in front of this line of abatis. Ahead of the advancing troops lay the torpedoes, abatis, a moat filled with palisades, and finally the wall of the fort itself. Courtesy, Library of Congress

Some got thru the small openings, some were held up by comrades, and fell over, others were helped over by those on the other side. Finally all were over, and then came the command from Col. Phillips: 'Forward, boys!' They fired one volley and then, with bayonet in hand, leaped forward and in only a few minutes after the torpedo line had been passed were on top of the fort."[72]

Col. John M. Oliver, 3rd Brigade commander, described what he saw. "Captain [Abner] Smith, [of the 48th Illinois Infantry] who rejoined us on the 27th of November, 1864, after escaping from Columbia, S.C., was the first man in the fort, and was killed inside of it. He was a gallant officer. The flag of the 70th Ohio was the first on the fort, though the gallant veterans of the 48th and 90th Illinois were there with them almost at the same time. Both color bearers of the 48th were killed with torpedoes. The color bearer of the 70th Ohio [John Compton] was also killed just as he handed the flag to a comrade when climbing over the abatis."[73]

"In a few moments," Pvt. Davies said, "the entire 70th Ohio had scaled the walls and were standing in line on top of the fort, with colors flying."[74] The Federals began pouring over the west wall of the fort and engaging the

10.5. The next set of obstacles was the palisades in the moat of the fort. During the assault some palisades were pulled down to open avenues through them, clearly evident in this image taken on the afternoon of 16 December 1864, three days after the attack. Courtesy, Library of Congress

defenders in hand-to-hand fighting. G. Arthur Gordon related what Maj. Anderson told him: "Hazen's troops stormed . . . over the breastworks, and the first soldier over the parapet was a huge, redheaded Irishman. Maj. Anderson was standing just inside, when he saw that Hazen's men were coming over the top, he threw away his sword, and the Irishman started to bayonet him. Maj. Anderson said quickly, 'My God, you wouldn't kill an unarmed man, would you?' whereupon, the soldier shifted his piece and knocked him down with the butt end of the gun. The [next] man over the breastworks was Gen. Hazen himself, who was so long-legged that he had kept up with the van of the assault. Gen. Hazen had been a classmate at West Point of Maj. Anderson's brother[-in-law], Gen. Robert Anderson, and he knew George Anderson quite well before the war. As he saw the soldier strike Anderson down, he said quickly, 'Get to the rear, George, and report to me later.'"[75]

Hazen described the same incident: "As I leaped upon the parapet, the first man I saw was [Maj. Anderson]. . . . He was lying on his back . . . contused by the butt of a gun. He recognized and spoke to me. He was brother-in-law of the Union Gen. Robert Anderson, and I had known him before the war."[76]

10.6. The troops of the 47th Ohio Infantry assault the northwest bastion at left, while the flag of the 111th Illinois is planted on the southwest bastion of the fort during the assault on Fort McAllister. *Harper's Weekly,* 14 January 1865

Maj. Anderson noted: "1st Lieutenant William Schirm fought his guns until the enemy had entered the fort, and notwithstanding a wound in the head, gallantly remained at his post, discharging his duties with a coolness and efficiency worthy of all commendation. . . . Among those who nobly fell was the gallant [Lt. Richard] Hazzard, whose zeal and activity were worthy of all praise. He died as a true soldier to his post, facing overwhelming odds."[77] Capt. Angus Morrison, commander of Company E, 1st Regiment, Georgia Reserves, went down when a bullet entered his left leg about six inches below his knee, bounced off the tibia, exited the leg, and then lodged in his right leg.[78]

Samuel L. Moore remembered, "The last [cannon] shot fired was a 12-pound Howitzer cannon. The man who was going to fire the cannon had hold of the lanyard and was ordered to let it go by a Yankee officer. . . . The man replied, 'I'm not taking orders from you yet.' The officer shot him with his pistol and the weight of the body, when he fell, pulled the lanyard. Some of the enemy was not three feet from the mouth of the cannon and the ball opened a space through the crowd."[79]

As Federal soldiers poured over the walls and flooded into the fort, the defenders retreated to the bombproof and magazines to continue their resistance, which Brig. Gen. Hazen describes: "The line moved on without checking . . . fighting the garrison through the fort to their bombproofs, from which they still fought, and only succumbed as each man was individually overpowered."[80]

The *New York Herald* reported, "Maj. [Thomas] Taylor and some of his command [of the 47th Ohio] engaged a squad of rebels and drove them into the magazine, from which they discharged their pistols. The Maj. decided to cage the fiends by shutting the door upon them, but in so doing had two fingers shot off."[81]

The fighting continued in chaotic confusion as the blue-coated soldiers swarmed over the walls while the Confederate defenders tried to fall back. Sgt. Saunier of the 47th Ohio recorded, "The division was now all within the Fort and for a short time were all engaged in fierce hand-to-hand encounter, fighting with the bayonet and the butt of muskets. . . . [82] As we drove them from one bomb proof to the other, Captain [J. H.] Brown seeing a fine looking Confederate officer, and thinking he was the commander of the fort, demanded his surrender, (but he was not). The officer handed his sword to the Captain, who asked the Confederate officer where the fort's flag was, it having been lowered from the flag staff; for some reason he said he did not know."[83]

Across the marsh at the Cheves rice mill, Sherman and the other officers gathered on the roof anxiously awaited the outcome. Lt. Col. Strong assessed the confrontation.

> It was indeed a grim struggle and for some time it seemed to us across the way, that the fort would win the day. It certainly deserved success for its unparalleled resistance. Soon, however, the fortunes of the day seemed to be changing in our favor. Our troops fairly swarmed about the fort and on the parapet a dozen flags could be seen and though here and there one would disappear from sight—yet there were plenty of brave fellows to hold it up again. And soon our fellows could be seen firing their guns into the fort and evidently shooting down the cannoneers, until one after another the heavy guns ceased firing and soon all were silent and nothing could be heard but the sharp crack of small arms and finally even this died away, and then the huge columns of dense black smoke that had hung so heavily about the fort, lifted and floated off towards the sea. The sun was down, McAllister was ours, and General Hazen had won his second star.[84]

Maj. Nichols recorded the day in his diary. "The firing ceased. The winds lifted the smoke. Crowds of men were visible on the parapets. . . . Then the bomb-proofs and parapets were alive with crowding swarms of our gallant men, who fired their pieces in the air. . . . Victory! The fort was won."[85]

Although the fighting ceased, some of the fort's defenders continued to resist. Capt. Nicholas B. Clinch was the last member of the garrison subdued. He received at least one gunshot wound in the left arm during the fighting but defiantly stood his ground as Federal soldiers approached him. Capt. Stephen Grimes of the 48th Illinois, who had commanded the 3rd Brigade skirmishers before the assault, demanded that Clinch surrender his sword. Clinch responded by dealing Grimes a blow to the head with the flat side of his sword blade. A sword fight immediately ensued between the two men.[86] Lt. Col. Strong continues the story: "The two fought for some minutes after the fighting had ceased. Both were good swordsmen and they were permitted to fight it out. The [Federal] officer of the line was severely wounded about the head and shoulders."[87]

Federal soldiers moved to assist Capt. Grimes, but others held them back, allowing Grimes and Clinch to proceed. Lt. Henry Wheeler of Company I, 48th Illinois, wrote, "I saw Grimes have a fight . . . with a rebel Captain by name of Clinch and tried to get to assist [Grimes] . . . but was prevented by reason of other soldiers."[88] When it became evident that Capt. Clinch was gaining the upper hand, six soldiers from Grimes's command came forward and bayoneted Clinch, bringing the contest to an abrupt halt.

George Pepper noted that "The confederate behaved very gallantly, absolutely refusing to surrender, until overpowered by wounds, when he said: 'I shall now submit to my destiny; but, as brave men should surrender only to the brave, to you, my noble antagonist, I will resign my sword.' The noble boldness, with which he expressed himself, charmed the Captain, [and] he returned the sword to him with these words: 'Take, sir, a weapon which no man better deserves to wear! Forget that you are my prisoner, but ever remember that we are friends!'"[89]

"Federal privates came to the assistance of their officer," Maj. Anderson said in his report, "but the fearless Clinch continued the unequal contest until he fell bleeding from eleven wounds, (three saber, six bayonet wounds, and two gunshot wounds), from which, after severe and protracted suffering, he . . . barely recovered. His conduct was so conspicuous, and his cool bravery so much admired as to elicit the praise of the enemy and even of General Sherman himself."[90]

When Clinch was later admitted to a hospital, the attending surgeon noted his wounds included a gunshot wound in the left arm, a bayonet wound in the left forearm, three saber wounds to his back, four saber wounds to his scalp, and a fractured skull. Although Clinch fell to his wounds, he gave as good as he got, for Capt. Grimes was not unscathed. He sustained a sword wound to his left hip, a cut across the back of his head, and a pistol shot through the left leg, about six inches above the ankle.[91] Shortly after Clinch was subdued, Brig. Gen. Hazen arrived on the scene: "I saw . . . Capt. Clinch, who commanded a light battery used for defense on the land side and temporarily thrown into the fort for that purpose. He was lying on his back, shot thru the arm, with a bayonet wound in his chest."[92]

Now the fighting ceased entirely. Col. James S. Martin of the 111th Illinois Infantry described what happened: "I entered the fort with the advance of my brigade; and being the first brigade commander in the works, the same was surrendered to me by Major Anderson, and the garrison claimed as our prisoners. No flag was found flying in the fort, and Major Anderson pledged me his word that he had none. . . . Afterwards a garrison flag was found hid in the bombproof."[93]

This flag, the fort's garrison flag, was found stuffed in the chimney of the bombproof fireplace by Capt. George E. Castle of the 111th Illinois Infantry. Capt. Castle, a native of Salem, Illinois, had farmed and raised livestock before the war interrupted his life. At the age of twenty-one he had taken command in 1862 of Company H of the 111th Illinois. The experiences he had had in the past few years would give him a lifetime of memories, but the flag he removed from the Fort McAllister bombproof would offer silent testimony in the years to come of those experiences. It remained in Capt. Castle's possession for many years to follow as a reminder of a momentous day in his life.[94]

Other flags were taken from the fort, as the individual garrison units also had unit colors, and Maj. Anderson had a personal headquarters flag. Col. William S. Oliver of the 15th Michigan reported, "A garrison flag was taken by Captain [George] Nelson, of my staff.[95] This flag was sent to the headquarters of Capt. [Gordon] Lofland, adjutant general of the 2nd Division, 15th Army Corps."[96]

Capt. J. H. Brown of Company A, 47th Ohio obtained still another flag. He questioned a Confederate soldier regarding the whereabouts of the flag that had been taken from the fort's flagstaff. The soldier said it was in the magazine, went and got it and gave it to Capt. Brown who later sent the flag north for safekeeping.[97]

Maj. Anderson in his report said, "In many instances the Confederates were disarmed by main force. The fort never surrendered. It was captured by overwhelming numbers. . . . In my endeavors to hold the fort, I was nobly seconded by the great majority of officers and men under my command. Many of them had never been under fire before, and quite a number were very young, in fact mere boys."[98]

"Major Anderson, commanding the fort," said Lt. Col. Strong, "fought his men right gallantly till the very last moment, and in fact never surrendered at all. The garrison was captured one man at a time, or in squads, after our troops had gained possession of the fort."[99]

Brig. Gen. Hazen took charge of Maj. Anderson while the garrison was gathered up and placed under guard. Then the Federal troops took stock of what they had captured, which included "24 pieces of ordnance, with their equipment, 40 tons of ammunition, a month's supply of food for the garrison, the small-arms of the command, all the animals and equipment of a light battery, the horses of the officers, and a large amount of private stores placed in the fort for safety,"[100] the private stores including "wines and cigars."[101]

The victory had not been without cost. Hazen recorded twenty-four officers and men killed and 110 officers and men wounded.[102] Lt. Col. Strong noted a puzzling fact about the Federal losses that mystified some who were involved in the fighting: "Genl. Hazen's loss was light and I cannot understand it exposed as the men were to such heavy fire."[103]

Confederate losses were proportionately a little higher. Lt. Col. Strong noted: "The loss of the rebel garrison was one officer and fifteen enlisted men killed and fifty four enlisted men wounded. Total struck, seventy. Captured: seventeen officers and one hundred and seventy eight enlisted men."[104]

With the victors and the vanquished gathered together around the fort, it was evident from the prevailing mood that each had earned the respect of the other. One act of consideration on the part of Maj. Anderson was always remembered by twenty-five-year-old 1st Lt. George W. Sylvis of the 47th Ohio, who later wrote to Maj. Anderson: "I never saw you but once and that was after the surrender[.] You was standing by the side of A[ugustus].C. Parry[,] Col of my Regmt. talking to him. I remember well in marching my Co out of the Fort in coming in front of you, you held out your hand and told me not to go out that way and you told me the way to go out and I found out afterwards that if I had went out the way I first started I would have been blown up with torpedoes Co and all."[105]

With the fort secured, the bulk of the Federal forces withdrew to points in the rear that were secure from unexploded torpedoes, where they established camps at Hardwick and at Middleton and Whitehall plantations among others. A member of the 55th Illinois Infantry wrote, "The regiment encamped on the beautiful grounds of an extensive plantation called Whitehall. The weather was charming, seeming to the Northern soldier almost summer-like; and when at night the full moon poured its refulgence upon the camp nestling under the cedars, pines, and live-oaks, whose long, spreading branches were covered with hanging moss, it presented a picture worthy to awaken ecstasy in an artist."[106]

Sgt. Saunier of the 47th Ohio described a dispute over who first planted the Stars and Stripes at the fort and which regiment entered it first.

> At about 7 P.M. we marched back up the river near one mile and encamped for the night. A contest arose between the 47th and the 70th

Ohio as to whose colors were first planted on Fort McAllister; the witnesses of the assault, while at the Fort inquired into the matter; several of General Hazen's staff who were overlooking the entire movement, decided that the colors came up first from the river front, and as the 47th Ohio alone assaulted from that front, it was its colors that first reached the Fort.

There was a dispute among the officers of the different regiments as to who went into the Fort first, and as several claimed the honor, it was decided to leave it to the Confederates. Accordingly we went down to where the prisoners were and asked them about it. The officer who surrendered said to Captain [J. H.] Brown, that, of course, they could not tell anything about the different regiments, but that the captain and the men with him were the first Yankees in the Fort. Major Anderson, the commander, confirms this decision.[107]

While the soldiers of the 2nd Division, 15th Army Corps celebrated the fall of Fort McAllister, the rest of Sherman's army remained in suspense as to events and their outcome. Along the siege lines around Savannah, Lt. William Pittenger of Company I, 39th Ohio Infantry wrote in his diary on this evening, "It is said we assaulted Ft. McAllister today but with what success we know not. Boys hungry. Only coffee, rice and beef to issue to them. Ere long something must be done."[108] But the news spread like wildfire, and the following morning Lt. Pittenger wrote, "Glorious news. I wish the world could have heard the whole souled yells pass around the lines which encircled Savannah last night when the dispatch was received announcing the capture of Ft. McAllister and joining Sherman with the fleet. No wonder, when the boys were living on rice in the hull."[109] Sherman's concerns over his supplies posed no further problem now that Fort McAllister had fallen, but Hardee's troubles had just begun. The Ogeechee River would bring more than just food and ammunition to Sherman's army. It would also bring heavy siege guns that could reach Savannah from the Federal lines west of the city.

11

THE VICTORS AND
THE VANQUISHED

The group gathered atop the Cheves rice mill rejoiced when it became obvious the fort had been taken. Gen. Sherman cried, "It's my old division, I knew they'd do it!"[1] Later, in his memoirs, he recalled: "During the progress of the assault, our little group on Cheeves' mill hardly breathed . . . [but] Fort McAllister was taken, and the good news was instantly sent by the signal-officer to our navy friends on the approaching gun-boat, for a point of timber had shut out Fort McAllister from their view, and they had not seen the action at all, but must have heard the cannonading."[2] "Flutter, flutter, right and left, up and down, goes the signal flags from the cupola above our heads," Lt. Col. Strong wrote, "and General Sherman sends his last dispatch to Admiral Dahlgren: 'Fort McAllister is captured now: You can come up.'"[3] "Look for a boat. General Sherman will come down to-night—Howard, General."[4]

Daylight was fast fading to twilight. Lt. George A. Fisher of the signal service wrote, "It was then getting dark and too dark to see a flag, and not having any torches with me, and desiring to send [a] dispatch to General Foster and Admiral Dahlgren, I turned about and returned with the tug to the Flag, where I wrote my dispatches, which were immediately sent. I then returned to the obstructions just below Fort McAllister and anchored."[5]

Even though early evening darkness was upon them, Sherman was determined to reach the fleet if possible: "I was resolved to communicate with our fleet that night, which happened to be a beautiful moonlight one. At the wharf belonging to Cheeves's mill was a small skiff, that had been used by our men in fishing or in gathering oysters. I was there in a minute, called for a volunteer crew, when several young officers, [Maj. George W.] Nichols and [Capt. Nehemiah] Merritt among the number, said they were good oarsmen, and volunteered to pull the boat down to Fort McAllister. General Howard asked to accompany me; so we took our seats in the stern of the boat and our crew of officers pulled with a will."[6]

One of the officers in the small boat with Sherman was Lt. Col. Strong.

It was nearly dark when Genl. Sherman and Genl. Howard stepped into a light skiff, which was lying at the dock near the rice mill, and two officers of General Sherman's Staff and myself were asked to accompany them down to the fort. Major George Ward Nichols was one of the officers of Sherman's Staff and he pulled one oar and I the other, while General Sherman sat in the stern and steered. It was a long pull and a hard one and some of the time it was all we could do to hold our own against the heavy tide that came sweeping up from the sea; but General Sherman was determined to reach McAllister and communicate with the navy that night, so we exerted every muscle to stem the current. It was a lively night —moonlight and starlight—and as we pulled away manfully at the oars, all the old songs were sung that we could think of and even Generals Sherman and Howard entered into the spirit of it and joined in the chorus of many an old and familiar air. I never saw General Sherman in as good spirits as that night and there were certainly good reasons for it. McAllister had fallen and he was master of the situation. Savannah would be surrendered or abandoned and the march to the sea ended.[7]

"The tide was setting in strong," Sherman recalled about that boat trip, "and they had a hard pull, for, though the distance was but three miles in an air-line, the river was so crooked that the actual distance was fully six miles. On the way down we passed the wreck of a steamer which had been sunk some years before, during a naval attack on Fort McAllister."[8]

After fighting the incoming flood tide for an hour or more, the boatload of Federal officers approached the river bluff behind the fort. Lt. Col. Strong continues his story: "It must have been half-past nine o'clock when our boat touched the shore near Genl. Hazen's Head Quarters and one and a half miles above the captured fort. My hands were blistered and my arms were weary and I was glad enough to lay down my oar."[9]

Sherman continues his narrative: "Night had fairly set in when we discovered a soldier on the beach. I hailed him, and inquired if he knew where General Hazen was. He answered that the general was at the house of the overseer of the plantation, and that he could guide me to it. We accordingly . . . tied our boat to a drift-log, and followed our guide, through bushes to a frame-house standing in a grove of live-oaks, near a row of negro quarters."[10]

Lt. Col. Strong, who accompanied Sherman to the house, wrote, "We were soon at Genl. Hazen's Head Quarters and found him just sitting down to supper and we were invited to join him which we were very glad to do, as none of us had had anything to eat since early in the morning. Major Anderson, the Commander of the fort, was a prisoner at Head Quarters and Genl. Hazen invited him to join us at the supper table, which he did."[11]

Today we can only wonder about what the conversation around the dinner table consisted of and what Maj. Anderson thought of it. Maj. Anderson told G. Arthur Gordon about the following exchange between him and Gen. Sherman.

> Major Anderson said that Gen. Sherman looked like a game rooster with all his feathers ruffled and seemed to be in a very bad humor. . . . Gen. Sherman turned to Maj. Anderson and said in a furious voice, "Were you the commanding officer at Fort McAllister?"
>
> Gen. Hazen trod on Maj. Anderson's foot to warn him that a storm was coming. . . .
>
> Maj. Anderson: "Yes Sir."
>
> Gen. Sherman: "Do you condone the use of torpedoes in civilized warfare?"
>
> Maj. Anderson: "I was sent to Fort McAllister to obey orders, not to question them."
>
> Gen Sherman: "It's inhuman. It's barbarous. And this is your Southern Chivalry."[12]

Maj. George W. Nichols wrote in his diary, "Major Anderson . . . tells me that he did not anticipate an assault to-night, and was hardly prepared for it when it came."[13]

Sherman continued his tale about that night. "Of course, I congratulated Hazen most heartily on his brilliant success, and praised its execution very highly, as it deserved, and he explained to me in detail the exact results. . . . Up to this time General Hazen did not know that a gun-boat was in the river below the fort; for it was shut off from sight by a point of timber, and I was determined to board her that night, at whatever risk or cost, as I wanted some news of what was going on in the outer world. Accordingly, after supper, we all walked down to the fort, nearly a mile from the house where we had been, entered Fort McAllister, held by a regiment of Hazen's troops, and the sentinel cautioned us to be very careful, as the ground outside the fort was full of torpedoes. Indeed, while we were there, a torpedo exploded, tearing to pieces a poor fellow who was hunting for a dead comrade."[14]

Maj. Gen. Howard described another incident that night. "Shortly after . . . we saw an ambulance, with mules hauling it, run upon a hidden torpedo.

Mules, ambulance, and men were blown to pieces. This sight indicated to us something of the dangers which our brave men had had to encounter."[15]

Sherman and his group carefully made their way through the fort, which Maj. Nichols described. "This evening we have enjoyed unrestricted opportunities of examining Fort McAllister. It is a large enclosure, with wide parapets, a deep ditch, and thickly-planted palisades, which are broken in several places where our men passed through. The dead and wounded are lying where they fell. Groups of soldiers are gathered here and there, laughing and talking of the proud deed that had been done. One said: 'If they had had embrasures for these guns,' pointing to them, 'we should have got hurt.'"[16]

Colonel Orlando Poe, Sherman's chief of engineers, wrote, "The fact that nearly all the guns of the fort were mounted in barbette rendered it much easier to carry it by assault, since our skirmish line advancing at a run readily approached within 200 yards, and by throwing themselves flat on the ground were well concealed by the high grass, and could pick off the rebel gunners at their leisure, readily silencing the fire of the fort."[17]

"Inside the fort lay the dead as they had fallen," Sherman wrote, "and they could hardly be distinguished from their living comrades, sleeping soundly side by side in the pale moonlight. In the river, close by the fort, was a good yawl tied to a stake, but the tide was high, and it required some time to get it in to the bank; the commanding officer . . . manned the boat, with a good crew of men, and with General Howard, I entered, and pulled downstream regardless of the warnings of all about torpedoes. The night was unusually bright, and we expected to find the gunboat within a mile or so; but, after pulling down the river fully three miles, and not seeing the gunboat, I began to think she had turned and gone back to the sound; but we kept on, following the bends of the river, and about six miles below McAllister we saw her lights, and soon ere hailed by the vessel at anchor."[18]

"In a short time a small boat was seen approaching," said Lt. Fisher, aboard the *Dandelion,* "which was hailed. 'What boat is that?' The answer came back: 'Sherman.' And the boat came alongside."[19]

"Pulling alongside," Sherman said, "we announced ourselves, and were received with a great warmth and enthusiasm on deck by half a dozen naval officers."[20] Lt. Fisher was there to greet them: "Generals Sherman and Howard came aboard and were welcomed with twice three cheers by those on board."[21]

Sherman wrote, "She proved to be the Dandelion, a tender of the regular gunboat Flag, posted at the mouth of the Ogeechee. All sorts of questions were made and answered, and we learned that Captain Duncan had safely reached the squadron, had communicated the good news of our approach, and they had been expecting us for some days."[22] Lt. Fisher stated, "I then told Sherman of General Foster's efforts to open communication with him and that I had sent dispatches to him."[23]

Sherman picks up the narrative.

> They explained that Admiral [John A.] Dahlgren commanded the South Atlantic Squadron . . . and was on his flagship, the <u>Harvest Moon</u>, lying in Wassaw Sound . . . and that several ships loaded with stores for the army were lying in Tybee Roads and in Port Royal Sound. From these officers I also learned that General Grant was still besieging Petersburg and Richmond, and that matters and things generally remained pretty much the same as when we left Atlanta. All thoughts seemed to have been turned to us in Georgia, cut off from all communication with our friends; and the rebel papers had reported us to be harassed, defeated, starving, and fleeing for safety to the coast. I then asked for pen and paper, and wrote several hasty notes to General [John G.] Foster, Admiral Dahlgren, General Grant, and the Secretary of War, giving in general terms the actual state of affairs, the fact of the capture of Fort McAllister, and of my desire that means should be taken to establish a line of supply from the vessels in port up the Ogeechee to the rear of the army. . . . By this time the night was well advanced, and the tide was running ebb-strong; so I asked Captain [James] Williamson to tow us up as near Fort McAllister as he would venture for the torpedoes, of which the navy officers had a wholesome dread. The <u>Dandelion</u> steamed up some three or four miles, till the lights of Fort McAllister could be seen, when she anchored, and we pulled to the fort in our own boat.[24]

Lt. Fisher wrote, "I then accompanied them back to the fort, and proceeded around the fort with them. After spending half an hour at the fort I returned to the tug and started down the river with the dispatches for General Foster and Admiral Dahlgren."[25]

By this time Sherman and Howard were ready to find some place to sleep. It had been a long and eventful day, for everyone, as Sherman relates: "General Howard and I then walked up to the McAllister [overseer's] House, where we found General Hazen and his officers asleep on the floor of one of the rooms. Lying down on the floor, I was soon fast asleep.[26]

That evening in Savannah, Lt. Gen. Hardee and the Confederate command learned of Fort McAllister's fate. The Confederate forces north of the fort, across the rivers and marshes, at the batteries on Coffee Bluff and Rose Dew Island (now Rosedew Island), had witnessed the struggle. Col. Edward C. Anderson wrote to Gen. Lafayette McLaws that night: "A telegram had been received from Beulieu announcing the fall of the fort. . . . A subsequent dispatch from the commanding officer at Rosedew states that a communication by signal had been received from Fort McAllister, without a signature, reporting the loss of the work and representing the officers unhurt with the exception of Captain [Angus] Morrison, reported wounded."[27] When Col. Anderson learned the news, he must have pondered the fate of his nephew, Maj. George Anderson.

The fall of Fort McAllister did not immediately alter the defensive posture of the Confederate forces around Savannah, although Hardee now knew they had failed to prevent Sherman from making a rendezvous with the naval forces offshore. Soon his army would be receiving fresh provisions, equipment, and heavy siege artillery that could bring Savannah under bombardment. Time was running against the Southerners, and their hold on Savannah was now tenuous at best. Hardee was forced to reevaluate his position and to look for other options, but there were only two choices: siege and capture or escape and retreat.

Lt. Fisher returned to the *Dandelion,* which proceeded downriver looking for the gunboat *Flag.*

> Had got down nearly to the mouth of the river when we met the U.S. revenue cutter Nemaha coming up. I then went aboard and reported to General Foster, and had my party transferred from the tug to the Nemaha, the general's flag-ship. We then proceeded up the river again until we arrived just below the obstructions, when I signaled to the fort.
>
> LT. FISHER: General Foster is here and would like to see General Sherman.
>
> McCLINTOCK: I will send for him. He has gone to General Howard's [Hazen's] headquarters.
>
> LT. FISHER: How far off?
>
> McCLINTOCK: Not more than a mile.
>
> McCLINTOCK: O.K., Fisher.
>
> Fisher then signaled General Foster: General Sherman will come to the fort as soon as he can, McClintock.
>
> A boat was then sent to the fort.[28]

In the early morning darkness of 14 December, an aide roused Gen. Sherman from his sleep. Sherman said he

> became conscious that someone in the room was inquiring for me among the sleepers. Calling out, I was told that an officer of General Foster's staff had just arrived from a steamboat anchored below McAllister; that the General was extremely anxious to see me on important business. . . . I was extremely weary from the incessant labor of the day and night before, but got up and again walked down the sandy road to McAllister, where I

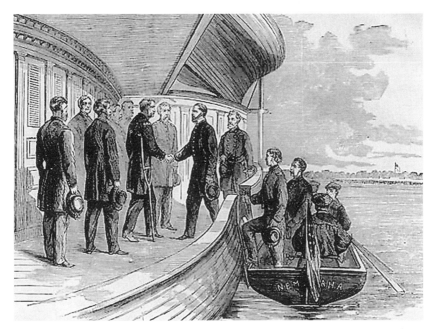

11.1. Gen. Sherman and Gen. Howard board the USS *Nemaha* and greet Gen. John Foster (on crutches), as depicted in this woodcut published 7 January 1865 in *Frank Leslie's Illustrated*. Albert G. Browne, customs agent, may be the man holding his hat who is behind Foster. The artist did an admirable job, but he was mistaken in showing the event in daylight when it actually happened at night, and Gen. Howard is shown with both arms when he was actually missing one.

found a boat awaiting us, which carried us some three miles down the river, to a steamer, [Nemaha][29] on board of which we found General [John G.] Foster.

He had just come from Port Royal, expecting to find Admiral Dahlgren in Ossabaw Sound, and, hearing of the capture of Fort Mc-Allister, he had come up to see me. . . . He explained . . . that there were at Port Royal abundant supplies of bread and provisions, as well as of clothing, designed for our use. We still had in our wagons and in camp [an] abundance of meat, but we needed bread, sugar, and coffee, and it was all-important that a route of supply should at once be opened, for which purpose the aid and assistance of the navy were indispensable. We accordingly steamed down the Ogeechee River to Ossabaw Sound, in hopes to meet Admiral Dahlgren, but he was not there, and we continued on by the inland channel to Wassaw Sound.[30]

Customs agent Albert G. Browne found himself along for the ride to witness this unfolding bit of history. In the course of the ride up to Wassaw

Sound, Browne had a chance to visit with Sherman and Howard. He noticed that both men showed the effects of many days in the saddle and exposure to the elements. He particularly noticed that Sherman's hat showed a great deal of wear and tear and commented to Sherman, "For a man of your rank and reputation, you wear a shocking bad hat." "Well what do you expect, Browne?" Sherman responded. "It's seen a lot of hard service. You've got a good hat, I'll trade you." Browne readily agreed, and the swap was made.[31]

The *Nemaha* soon entered Wassaw Sound, where, Sherman said, "We found the Harvest Moon and Admiral Dahlgren. . . . There was nothing in his power, he said, which he would not do to assist us. . . . He undertook at once to find vessels of light draught to carry our supplies from Port Royal to Cheeves' Mill or to King's Bridge, whence they could be hauled by our wagons to our several camps; he offered to return with me to Fort McAllister to superintend the removal of the torpedoes, and to relieve me of all the details of this most difficult work. General Foster then concluded to go on to Port Royal, to send back to us six hundred thousand rations, and all the rifled guns of heavy caliber and ammunition on hand with which I thought we could reach the city of Savannah from the positions already secured. Admiral Dahlgren then returned with me in the Harvest Moon to Fort McAllister."[32]

Lt. Fisher said the *Nemaha* had arrived at about 11 o'clock and Adm. Dahlgren came aboard for about an hour, then he and Gen. Sherman went aboard the *Harvest Moon,* the admiral's flagship. The general returned with the admiral to Ossabaw Sound and to his army, and the *Nemaha* returned to Hilton Head.[33]

At sunrise on 14 December, Lt. William H. Sherfy of the Signal Service moved his signal station from the area of Brig. Gen. Hazen's headquarters down to the fort itself where he established a signal station on the fort's wall. From there he could easily communicate with vessels in the river and the station at Cheves's mill.[34] With daylight, the Federal soldiers and Confederate prisoners were put to work. The dead had to be removed for temporary burial nearby. Field hospitals administered to the wounded and offered what comfort could be given to the dying. Col. Wells S. Jones, who had been wounded by the bullet that killed Capt. Groce, was eventually confined to his quarters for about a month. A physician before the war, he treated himself with the assistance of another doctor. He recovered.[35]

That morning young Charles Bateman of the 70th Ohio, who had lost both legs when he'd stepped on a torpedo, lingered between life and death. One of his comrades, Pvt. Michael Murrey, wrote, "I visited him the morning of the 14 of Dec. 1864 and found him still living but there was no hope or possibility of his living. . . . He was torn to pieces from his stomach downwards[,] all his bowels was mashed."[36]

Also injured by the explosion of a torpedo he had stepped on was 1st Sgt. Lyman Hardman, whose left foot had been badly burned and his face swollen so much that he could not open his eyes. The evening before he was brought to the field hospital and treated; however, there was little that could be done to ease his discomfort. Hardman noted in his diary, "The sufferings of that night were terrible."[37] He was, however, luckier than Charlie Bateman, for Hardman would survive, but in later years he would wonder if that survival had been a blessing or a curse.

Samuel L. Moore, now a prisoner of Hazen's forces, remembered that "General [Hazen] made the McAllister homestead his headquarters and the wounded from both sides were taken there for medical treatment. I was on the sick list and was placed on a bunk with a badly wounded Yankee boy who died before morning."[38]

Meanwhile, Brig. Gen. Hazen acknowledged "the conspicuous part taken by the 70th Ohio Volunteer Infantry in the assault on Fort McAllister" by ordering that regiment to temporarily garrison the fort. Hazen instructed them to establish their camp near the fort and to "take immediate steps to put the fort in order, cleansing it and adopting a proper system of policing."[39]

Sgt. Joseph Saunier of the 47th Ohio recorded that on the morning of 14 December, "The 47th Ohio Regiment fell into line at 8:30 A.M., and moved some fifty yards and went into camp in regular order, with orders to remain four days. We went to work and put up our tents and the camp was arranged in regular order. Some of the boys made coffee from the Ogeechee River, not knowing the tide was up and the coffee was so salty they could not drink it, and thereafter they got their water when the tide was out. We took the Confederate prisoners back to Fort McAllister to-day, and made them take up all the torpedoes placed around the fort and the road."[40]

When Gen. Sherman and Adm. Dahlgren arrived at Fort McAllister, Sherman personally ordered that the Confederate prisoners should remove the unexploded torpedoes from the area around the fort.[41] Arthur Gordon recalled in later years that Maj. Anderson told him that Sherman "ordered the prisoners at Fort McAllister to fall in. Maj. Anderson fell in separately from the men, and Gen. Sherman ordered him to fall in with the men, although he was an officer. He then ordered a guard to take them all down to the [Fort] and remove the torpedoes. This meant that there was a strong possibility that they would be blown to pieces. On the way down, an old Confederate Sergeant said to the Commander of the Guard, 'If you will give me a detail, I will . . . take the torpedoes out without anyone being hurt.' This was done and no one was hurt. The torpedoes had been attached to the end of sections of railroad rails, so that when anyone trod on the rails, a torpedo exploded. The Confederate Sergeant knew where the rails were and how deep under the surface, and by working on them from the end where there was no torpedo, he [could] extract the torpedoes without danger."[42]

Under the supervision of a naval officer from Dahlgren's staff, assisted by Capt. Thomas S. White, Maj. Anderson's chief engineer, a detail of sixteen men picked from the ranks of the Confederate prisoners removed the unexploded torpedoes.[43] Anderson protested that this was "an unwarrantable and improper treatment of prisoners of war."[44] However, his protest fell on deaf ears, and the removal of the torpedoes continued. Sherman would later declare that it was "no new thing to require prisoners to remove torpedoes buried by the enemy. Wellington did it in Spain, and history furnishes many similar instances. . . . Prisoners should be protected, but mercy is not a legitimate attribute of war. Men go to war to kill or get killed if necessary and should expect no tenderness."[45]

Yet, in later years, military lawyers and international authorities held that Sherman had gone beyond the rules of war by forcing prisoners into such dangers. Some experts agreed that the use of mines and torpedoes was "legitimate in all circumstances." The War Department, in General Order Number 100, issued on 24 April 1863, specified that prisoners must be treated with humanity.[46] But Sherman's concern was for the lives of his men: "It was, I think, a much better show of tenderness for me to have the enemy do this work than to subject my own soldiers to so frightful a risk. . . . They knew where the torpedoes were and could safely remove them while my men in hunting for them would be blown to pieces. The fact that every torpedo was safely removed showed my reasoning was right."[47]

After the fort area was secured, Federal soldiers marched the Confederate prisoners to a collection point located, ironically, at Lebanon Plantation, Maj. Anderson's home.[48] Maj. Henry Nichols tells a little about it: "After the capture of Fort McAllister, the Confederate prisoners were brought to Lebanon [Plantation] and put under guard in the yard. That night the officer on Sherman's staff who knew Major Anderson went out of the house to see his former schoolmate."[49]

This staff officer was Brig. Gen. Kilpatrick. When he learned that George Anderson was among the prisoners, he sought him out and found him tired, dirty, disgusted, and nursing a wound from having been butt-stroked in the face by a musket-wielding Federal soldier during the assault. When Anderson saw Kilpatrick, he said, "Such are the fortunes of war. Here I am sleeping on the ground in the yard of my home and you are in my bed in my father's house. . . . This is all the scoundrels left to me. . . . Its adding insult to injury to coop me up in my own pig pen."[50] Kilpatrick responded, "Don't worry about that. . . . Go clean up and you can sleep in your own bed." Kilpatrick spoke to Sherman on Anderson's behalf, and Sherman allowed Anderson to stay in his own bedroom.[51]

Shortly after his return to Fort McAllister from the conference with Foster and Dahlgren and wearing his new hat, Sherman saw his mailman, Col. A. H. Markland, appear with sacks of mail for the Army of the Tennessee. Sherman had sent him north from Atlanta to collect the mail of his soldiers.[52] After greeting Sherman, Markland said, "Before leaving Washington, I was directed to take you by the hand wherever I met you and say to you for him [Lincoln], 'God bless you and the army under your command. Since cutting loose from Atlanta, my prayers and those of the nation have been for your success.'" "'I thank the President,' said Sherman. 'Say my army is all right.'"[53]

Sherman then sent a messenger to the signal station atop the rice mill to let the army know that the mail had come—all twenty tons of it.[54] Col. Markland saw "a bewildering reception" as the sun went down that evening, "a frantic sight, men snatching letters, whooping at this first touch with home."[55]

Major Thomas T. Taylor of the 47th Ohio was recuperating at the unit headquarters from a gunshot wound to his right hand that resulted in the loss of his index finger. He was happy to receive a letter from his wife and asked the brigade surgeon, S. P. Bonner, to send her a letter about his wound.[56] Within several days Maj. Taylor himself attempted to write to her using his left hand: "At present I am at Hd Qutr. Here everyone strives to increase my comfort. One brings oysters, another sends fish and a third a buggy—calls I have innumerable. And thus my time pass[es] most pleasantly. . . . I shall not attempt a description of my wound—suffice it to say that I will esteem it a proud souvenir of the storming of Ft. McAllister. . . . My own wound is very healthy . . . yet will prove a most tedious one because it is bruised and lacsrated considerably. . . . Frank Sallyarde, William Wilson . . . and some others from the county are hurt. Frank S is wounded so high up that it is impossible to amputate it. Today he is doing much better although the chances against [him] are as zero to one."[57]

Within a few days the newly opened supply line would begin providing for the needs of Gen. Sherman's army. Until then, the Federals were very thorough in their search for provisions. Brig. Gen. Kilpatrick's cavalry ranged as far south as the Altamaha River for needed goods, and foraging parties from the infantry followed them. In the areas around Fort McAllister, the Federals made good use of the waterways to obtain abundant seafood.

Sherman's army outside Savannah still faced strong Confederate defenses armed with heavy artillery. The light field batteries his army brought could not reach Savannah and thus could only be used to engage the Confederate batteries. Heavy guns would be sent from Port Royal, but days would pass before they could be emplaced in Federal positions. Until they arrived, Sherman decided to use the heavy guns that had fallen into his hands with the capture of Fort McAllister, and he ordered the large cannon there dismounted and transported up the river to King's Bridge from where they could be carried overland or brought up the Savannah and Ogeechee Canal to the rear of the Federal lines for emplacement.[58] On 15 December Gen. Howard ordered Brig. Gen. Hazen to "Dismount two 32-lb rifled guns and have them placed on the bank ready for shipment by water to King's Bridge tomorrow."[59]

On the morning of 15 December, navy vessels removed the pilings, torpedoes, and obstructions in the river, and by that afternoon the channel had been sufficiently cleared to allow ship traffic upriver. Sherman's link to the outside world was open.[60] That afternoon, while Sherman sat in his headquarters beside the Ogeechee, completing his plans for the capture of Savannah, a steamer docked nearby, and General Grant's aide Col. Orville E. Babcock disembarked. Alerted to his arrival, Sherman met him outside his headquarters where Babcock delivered a letter Grant had written Sherman on the 6 December. Sherman anxiously opened the envelope and examined the contents. Col. Lewis M. Dayton, standing nearby, saw Sherman "make that nervous action of the left arm which characterized him when anything annoyed him. It seemed, for instance, as if he was pushing something away from him."[61]

"Come here, Dayton!" Sherman snapped as he turned and led the way into the house. Once inside, he closed the door, and began to swear and exclaimed, "Won't do it; I won't do anything of the kind!"[62] Grant had upset Sherman's plans to end the war. He had written: "I have concluded that the most important operation toward closing out the rebellion will be to close out Lee and his army. . . . My idea now is that you establish a base on the seacoast, fortify and leave in it all your artillery and cavalry and enough infantry to protect them. With the balance of your command come here by water with all dispatch. Select, yourself, the officer to leave in command, but you I want in person."[63]

Sherman disapproved of Grant's orders because he planned to march his army overland from Savannah after that city's capture to take the war to the interior of the Carolinas and then rendezvous with Grant's forces in Virginia. Besides taking time to gather the transports to move his forces, Sherman believed the western army, made up of farm boys and shop clerks and acclimated to life in the open air, would sicken and decline if cooped up in transports for a sea voyage that would require several days to accomplish. If Grant pressed the issue, Sherman also realized that he would be forced to leave

Savannah before it could be taken. Though Sherman felt that only the capture of the city would signify the successful completion of his campaign from Atlanta, he understood that orders were orders.[64]

It would take time to gather the steamers required to transport his army to Virginia, and he felt they could capture Savannah before they had to leave. If the city was not captured, then the army would need to embark from some waterway near Savannah, and the excess elements of his artillery, cavalry, and wagon trains would need to be secured somewhere. The Ogeechee River and Fort McAllister were seen as the logical points from which to move his army; the fort and its surrounding areas would be an ideal Federal stronghold on the Georgia coast. With a view toward this end, Sherman ordered his Col. Orlando M. Poe, chief of engineers, to prepare the fort for its new function and begin gathering the necessary transports.[65]

But Sherman's fears would not be realized because his logic persuaded Grant, and he was allowed to continue his overland campaign. With Fort McAllister captured and a secure supply line established, Sherman could turn his attention toward taking the city of Savannah. It was only a matter of time before it fell, and Sherman, Lt. Gen. Hardee, and the soldiers of both sides knew it.

On the morning of 16 December, another vessel from Hilton Head arrived at the dock at Fort McAllister. Among its passengers was a tall, bearded gentleman from Beaufort, South Carolina, who arrived with a team of assistants, a large camera, tripod, and equipment. He was Samuel A. Cooley, a photographer who resided in Beaufort before the war and found opportunity when

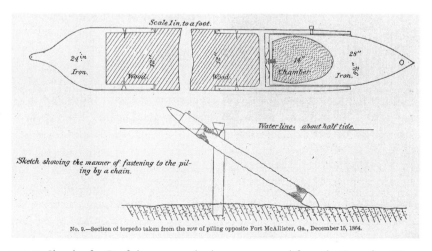

11.2. Sketch of a Confederate torpedo that was removed from the Ogeechee River on 15 December 1864. ORN, s. 1, 16:395

11.3. Samuel A. Cooley (standing third from left) with his crew of assistants, took "official" photographs of Federal operations and installations, including Fort McAllister. Cooley also photographed many of the soldiers and sailors who worked out of Hilton Head. Courtesy, Library of Congress

the U.S. military occupied Hilton Head and neighboring Beaufort early in the war. Cooley managed to stay in business and was able to perform contract work for the Federal authorities, photodocumenting the facilities at Hilton Head and Beaufort and taking on an assumed title as "official photographer to the U.S. Department of the South." In addition to this work, Cooley found a ready market for his photographic skills in the multitude of soldiers and sailors in the area who wanted to send their photographs home.[66]

Cooley had been aware of the U.S. Navy's attempts in 1862 and 1863 to reduce Fort McAllister, and the fort's reputation was well known to him. When word was received that it had been captured and the river opened, Cooley must have realized the opportunity that presented itself, and with his relationship with the army and navy authorities, he must have had the connections to arrange a ride to the Ogeechee River.

That morning, working details were in the midst of dismounting the two guns that Gen. Howard had ordered placed on the bank for transportation. Cooley documented this work and climbed all over the fort during the day setting up his camera, making adjustments, and taking images. The soldiers went about their business, casting curious glances at this man and his contraption and even posing for him while Cooley sought to capture the fort and its surroundings on fragile glass plate negatives. Cooley probably conversed with these soldiers, who wanted news from the outside world, and he could tell them all about Fort McAllister's valiant stand against the U.S. Navy a year before. Cooley spent the night but the weather changed with rain coming in, and the sunshine he'd enjoyed on December 16 was replaced by overcast skies and damp ground. He managed to capture a few more images before he packed up and departed. However, Cooley captured significant glimpses not only of Fort McAllister but of Sherman's soldiers at the end of the march, the only known images of Sherman's troops taken while on the March to the Sea.

Howard had called for two 32-pounder rifled guns to be sent to the lines but only one 32-pounder rifled gun was in the fort.[67] Cooley's photos show a 10-inch Columbiad being dismounted that morning. It makes sense that the two heaviest guns in the fort, a 10-inch Columbiad and the 32-pounder rifled gun, would be the most effective guns to move and use against Hardee's heavy guns.[68] The guns were loaded on a barge or steamer and taken up to King's Bridge late on the afternoon of 16 December.[69]

With the Ogeechee cleared of obstructions, steamer traffic had access all the way up to the landing at King's Bridge where docks had been built to receive supplies. Within a short time, navy and supply ships made regular runs up the river to Sherman's supply depot.[70] On 17 December the guns from Fort McAllister were moved overland from King's Bridge to points behind the 17th Army Corps positions from where they could be emplaced to bear on Confederate Battery Jones.[71] Also on 17 December, units of the 2nd Division, 15th Army Corps, camped in the area of Fort McAllister moved out heading south, bound for Liberty County to destroy the railroad. On 18 December elements of the 12th Illinois Infantry escorted the bulk of the Confederate prisoners from Lebanon Plantation back to Fort McAllister, where they were held in camp until transportation to Hilton Head Island arrived.[72] One of those prisoners was Samuel L. Moore of Company E: "We, the prisoners, were carried to Hilton Head, South Carolina. All of the prisoners were issued what was called 'Retaliation Rations,' which consisted of one part of rotten meat and a pickle per day. They were retaliation for Andersonville."[73]

On 18 December, Sherman issued orders for an all-out assault on Savannah to be made on 20 December, but on 19 December he countermanded these orders and issued instructions preventing any assault on the Confederate defenses until he returned from a trip to Hilton Head. There he was to confer with Adm. Dahlgren and Gen. Foster about an operation to cut the railroad link between Charleston and Savannah in order to flush Hardee out of the city.[74]

On 19 December, Maj. Gen. Frank Blair, commanding the 17th Army Corps, ordered the officer in charge of the captured ordnance stores at Fort McAllister to deliver to Lt. Samuel J. Smith, the 17th Army Corps ordnance officer, the ordnance, implements and stores "for the 32-pounder" then being mounted by 17th Army Corps elements.[75] Apparently the fort's 32-pounder rifled gun was about ready to be used against those it once defended.

As Sherman and his army prepared for the final reduction of Savannah, Lt. Gen. Hardee and his Confederate defenders were looking for a way out of the trap. They had failed to prevent Sherman's breakthrough to the coast, and now time was working against them. Sherman's army grew stronger and bolder each day, while the Confederate position became more tenuous. Hardee knew that the only logical move left was to disengage his force and retreat across the Savannah River into South Carolina. He realized that at least he could spare the city from being shelled by the heavy artillery that Sherman was expecting. Hardee's strategy was then directed at finding the quickest and most practical way to get his army out of the city without alerting the enemy.

On the night of 20 December, a week after McAllister's capture, Hardee's forces slipped away from their entrenchments and marched to Savannah where they crossed the Savannah River on makeshift pontoon bridges and escaped into South Carolina. Most of the Confederates were too preoccupied to have noted the fourth anniversary of South Carolina's secession from the Union. That event had precipitated the conflict, and it was ironic that four years before, the citizens of Savannah had cheered that act of defiance and faced the future with confidence. Four years later they were fleeing Georgia and seeking refuge in South Carolina. By sunrise on 21 December, Hardee's army was gone. Sherman's forces discovered the way to the city was open to them, and they quickly occupied it. With Savannah in Federal control, there was time for the men of Sherman's army to relax. The reputation of Fort McAllister was widely known, and many soldiers and sailors availed themselves of the opportunity to visit the earthwork that had defied the U.S. Navy for so long.[76]

While the drama of Savannah's evacuation was taking place, Sherman himself was nowhere in sight, still at Hilton Head in conference with Adm. Dahlgren and Gen. Foster and now discussing a joint movement up the Broad River to cut Hardee's escape route instead of a way to flush the Confederates out of Savannah. Early on 21 December, Sherman boarded Dahlgren's flagship, the *Harvest Moon,* and departed for the Ogeechee River. Meeting heavy weather, the ship was forced to take an inside route through the inland waterway. While navigating through Romerly Marsh opposite Wassaw Island, the ship ran aground on a mud bank.[77]

It soon became obvious that only the rising tide would free the *Harvest Moon,* so Sherman and his companions boarded a small skiff, and they were rowed toward the Ogeechee. About dusk, a tug, the *Red Legs,* came alongside with the news that Hardee had evacuated Savannah and that it was already in Federal hands. Sherman and his companions quickly boarded the tug and proceeded for the Ogeechee. So, while Sherman's troops were making their triumphant entry into Savannah, the conquering hero was stuck in the mud up a creek![78]

The steam tug returned Sherman to King's Bridge, where he retrieved his horse and headed to his headquarters. On the morning of 22 December, he traveled to Savannah. Sherman arrived as probably one of the last of the occupying soldiers to enter the city. He initially took up quarters in the Pulaski House where he had once stayed as a young lieutenant, but he would later move to the Greene Mansion, which was several blocks away, when that residence was offered to him.

While at the Greene Mansion, Albert G. Browne, the customs agent with whom he had traded hats a week earlier on the *Nemaha,* visited him. Browne told Sherman that a vessel was about to leave Savannah for Fort Monroe from where a telegraphic dispatch could be sent to President Lincoln. Acting on this suggestion, Sherman dispatched his well-known telegram to President Lincoln giving him the city of Savannah as a Christmas present.[79]

On Christmas Day, communications were opened between Fort McAllister and the abandoned Confederate battery at Rose Dew Island by way of signal stations established by Lt. William Sherfy. With the existing telegraph lines from Rose Dew to Savannah, Sherman had almost immediate communication with his forces on the Ogeechee. Within a few days additional signal stations were established from Savannah to Fort Pulaski and from there to Hilton Head, and Fort McAllister was then linked by a chain of signal stations to the Hilton Head depot.[80]

After exchanging a series of communications, Grant gave Sherman permission to pursue his campaign overland from Savannah. Fort McAllister was no longer needed as a military post. Orders instructed the Federal garrison to dismantle the fort and send all usable weapons and munitions to the depot at Hilton Head. This was accomplished by the men of the 70th Ohio Infantry, assisted by other units camped in the vicinity.[81]

A soldier of the 55th Illinois Infantry remembered, "Details from the brigade were daily sent to report to the ordnance officers in Fort McAllister, to assist in dismantling that fortification. Guns and military stores were loaded upon vessels for transportation to the North. The weather had become suddenly cold and blustering, making it disagreeable living in our slight shelters."[82]

In January of 1865, portions of Sherman's army marched out of Savannah, crossed the Savannah River, and moved into South Carolina. Once again the focus of events shifted from the Georgia coast toward the epic climax building in Virginia. Within three months the war was over, and Fort McAllister, like the Confederate cause, was abandoned.

12

A FINAL ANALYSIS

Sherman's March to the Sea illustrated that the Confederacy was a hollow shell. It brought the war home to the civilian community of Georgia and was a demoralizing influence upon Confederate soldiers fighting elsewhere. While the march was hailed in the North as a brilliant stroke of military genius, Sherman considered it merely a change of his base of operations.[1] The march from Atlanta to the Georgia coast had Savannah as one goal, but the ultimate objective was access to the sea itself. By severing his line of communication and supply, Sherman's forces had to forage off the countryside through which they passed. Once they arrived on the coast, it was necessary to open an access route to a supply fleet that was to rendezvous with his army. This supply line was necessary before an attempt could be made to take Savannah.[2]

With the arrival of Sherman's forces near the Georgia coast, Fort McAllister was thrust into the spotlight once again because its location on the Ogeechee River made it the last real obstacle to Sherman's reaching the sea. As such it became significant to Sherman as the key to the whole situation facing him. Once Fort McAllister was taken, his route to the sea was open, his line of supply and communication reestablished, and the fall of Savannah only a matter of time.[3]

But why did the Confederate forces not make a more determined effort to defend Fort McAllister and deny Sherman's access to the sea via the Ogeechee River? In later years many notable ex-Confederate officers criticized Lt. Gen. Hardee for sacrificing the fort's garrison. Why did Hardee leave this fort exposed, failing to recall the garrison in time? Or, on the other hand, if Hardee knew, as he should have, that the Ogeechee River was Sherman's most feasible line of communication, why did he fail to strengthen the garrison and make a more determined effort to hold the position? Hardee hoped that a strong defense of Savannah might lead Sherman to hesitate or even give up the idea of assaulting the city, but he apparently made little effort to ensure a strong defense for Fort McAllister.[4]

Two factors deserve consideration. First, Hardee, who had an intimate knowledge of the terrain, probably believed, as did many others, that Sherman could not maneuver a large attacking force through the supposedly impassible area around Genesis Point. In this, Hardee seriously underestimated the ability of Sherman's men to overcome natural obstacles. Second, and most important, Hardee had few options open to him. If he abandoned the fort, Sherman would have his line of communication by default; and if he reinforced the garrison, he would weaken a battle line at Savannah already bare of reserves and hardly able to withstand a determined assault.[5]

But how much of that burden of responsibility actually belonged to Maj. Anderson? While Hardee was somewhat limited in his choices pertaining to the defense of Fort McAllister, Anderson, being the commander on site, did have some control over his options. From the vantage point of well over a century later, it is possible to second-guess Anderson's decisions, for certainly a more determined and aggressive defense of Fort McAllister could have been made.

Anderson must have known that the impending arrival of Sherman's army meant Fort McAllister would be a probable objective. He prepared to put up an active defense and indicated that if the Federals came, he intended to make them take the fort as he would not surrender it. Anderson clearly had Col. Charles Olmstead on his mind, and he was determined not to bear the stigma that Olmstead had been forced to shoulder after his decision to surrender Fort Pulaski in April of 1862. At that time Southerners severely criticized Olmstead's decision, and indeed, the controversy surrounding his surrender continued for years. Olmstead obviously had other options open to him, but he appeared to have lost his nerve under the stress and viewed surrender as the only logical choice.[6]

Anderson made numerous preparations for the defense of Fort McAllister. Supplies and munitions had been stockpiled to allow the fort's garrison to hold out almost two months on their own. They pulled down the barracks and other structures, clear-cut over twenty acres of timber, constructed a line of abatis around the fort, emplaced palisades in the moat, buried 150 land mines around the fort and in the approach roads, relocated three 32-pounder guns to newly built positions on the rear wall of the fort, and built several new traverses to protect magazines that had been exposed to fire from DeGress's guns at Cheves Mill. This was no small amount of work.

Yet, by his own account, Anderson was not expecting the assault when it came, which is hard to understand. The day previous to the attack, he and a scouting party ran into Kilpatrick's cavalry coming into the county and had been hotly pursued back to the fort. But the fort would be no pushover to a cavalry assault, and Kilpatrick held back. The presence of Federal cavalry should have alerted Anderson to the proximity of the enemy. However, he must not have felt that enemy infantry forces were so near. Anderson may have assumed that he had several days before any serious threat would materialize. In this assumption he was sorely mistaken.

What exactly were Anderson's plans for the defense of the fort? He never spoke of this, and if any plan was prepared in advance of the actual assault, evidence of it has never surfaced. Apparently Anderson intended to react to developing circumstances rather than anticipate them. Clearly he could have made Hazen's men pay far more dearly for possession of Fort McAllister than the price extracted in the end. The geography at Genesis Point favored the defenders. Essentially an island, it offered extremely limited access across a narrow neck of land, the road of which had been mined. While this would have served to delay an advancing enemy force, it was no major obstacle. Indeed, it appears that the head of the causeway was merely picketed, and at that, these pickets were surprised and captured without a shot being fired.

In looking back at these events, it is clear that Anderson should have made his first line of defense there, at the head of the causeway. Surrounded by an open expanse of muddy marsh, rice fields, and the river, with the mined causeway offering the only high-ground avenue of approach, Hazen's men would have been hard pressed to cross this terrain under fire. It would have been an extremely difficult approach, and their casualties would have been high had they attempted it. If Anderson had provided for more adequate trenches and fieldworks along the western edge of Genesis Point, he could have delayed Hazen's access to Genesis Point for an extended period of time, but with Sherman's numerical superiority, Hazen could not have been denied access indefinitely. Nonetheless, it might have been sufficient to force Sherman to bypass Fort McAllister and use one of his other options for access to the supply fleet, such as at Kilkenny Bluff or Sunbury.

Had Hazen been able to force access to Genesis Point, then the Confederate defenders would merely have had to fall back to Fort McAllister under cover of the big guns there, which would have extracted another toll upon Hazen's approaching forces. As it was, Anderson was totally unaware of Hazen's approach until the Federal skirmishers opened fire on the fort. The Federal skirmish line alone probably outnumbered Anderson's garrison, and the velocity of their harassing fire was sufficient to all but suppress the artillery fire coming from the fort because the artillerists were unable to serve their guns without exposing themselves to enemy fire. This clearly negated Anderson's advantage in heavy artillery. Had Anderson made his initial stand at the head of the causeway, his artillery would have been alerted to Hazen's approach, and the Federal skirmishers would have had a more difficult time in suppressing this fire because they would not have been able to approach so close to the fort.

Fort McAllister's lack of embrasures for artillery around the rear wall of the fort also proved to be a major mistake. For all of Anderson's preparations, the addition of enough sand to build up protective embrasures for his artillery should not have been a prohibitive expenditure of time and energy. If it was an oversight, it was an unforgivable one. Any artillerist should have foreseen the dangers of trying to service artillery firing en barbette against an advancing foe. Being exposed from the waist up while trying to load and fire the guns would have been to invite instant death or injury. With embrasures, they would not have been so exposed while trying to operate the guns. Even the veterans of Hazen's division acknowledged that if the artillery had been emplaced behind embrasure, the fort would have been much harder to take.

Another question arises concerning Anderson's minimal defensive efforts when the final assault came. It is true they were overrun by an overwhelming force, but the garrison fought to the end. The actual defense when the attack came raises some questions about his motivations. Was Anderson merely trying to put up a sufficient defense to satisfy the requirements of duty and honor without sacrificing lives? His defense of the fort satisfied the requirements of duty and honor, and he did not needlessly sacrifice his men, nor did he extract as severe a toll from the attacking force as he might have. Anderson must have known the war was lost, and it must have been evident to him that within a few months they would all be countrymen again and no longer enemies. If so, then Anderson was on the horns of a dilemma. How could he put up a defense that would allow him to lose with honor and dignity without causing the garrison extensive casualties? If this was indeed Anderson's objective, then he succeeded. His final defense was never seriously questioned in later years, and he never suffered any of the stigma that Col. Olmstead had to bear. While Olmstead's surrender of Fort Pulaski marked him for the rest of his life, Southerners perceived Anderson as a hero, and his defense of Fort McAllister was seen as all it could have been in a hopeless situation.

The end of the war brought jubilation throughout the North and uncertainty in the South. The large Federal armies demobilized, and the soldiers went home to resume their lives. Displaced soldiers and civilians in the South returned to whatever the war had left them. When the McAllisters returned to their home at Strathy Hall, they were happy to see the structure still standing when so many of their neighbors had been burned out. Although the house still stood, it had been roughly handled by the Federal soldiers. The McAllisters had known many people in the North before the war, and having spent many summers at Northern resorts, Rosa McAllister Wyatt had been known as a "Newport belle." After Sherman's troops left Strathy Hall, the McAllisters found written on one wall in the house: "Had we known that this was the house of Rosa McAllister, not a thing should have been touched."[7]

In the following months, Rosa McAllister Wyatt lost the estate, receiving only $10,000 for it and that money going to her nephew Habersham Clay. In the four years following her marriage in 1861, she lost her husband, her brother, her estate, and all of her money. She later moved to Memphis, Tennessee, and in later years, filed a claim against the government for damages incurred by the Federal occupation of her property. The government delayed action on her claim for several years and then asked for contemporary evidence to support her claim. Because those people who could provide her with that evidence had died or moved away, she could not prevail in her claim and received nothing. She remained in Memphis where she died in 1914 at the age of 85.[8]

At Fort McAllister, the bodies of the dead were removed for burial elsewhere. Those who had died defending the fort were retrieved by their kin for burial in family plots and soldier's cemeteries. The dead Federal soldiers would mostly be reinterred in the Federal cemetery at Beaufort, South Carolina. The body of Capt. John Groce was disinterred in January 1865 and returned to Circleville, Ohio, for burial in Forest Cemetery. Many years later, the National Guard armory in Circleville was named for him.[9]

The events at Fort McAllister would remain vividly etched in the minds of those who were participants. All of them carried the memories; some carried scars. Maj. Thomas T. Taylor, the adjutant general of the 47th Ohio Infantry who lost an index finger in the battle, remained in the division hospital near Fort McAllister until 5 January 1865 when he was sent home on convalescent leave. He was eventually mustered out August 1865 at Little Rock, Arkansas, returned to his wife in Ohio, and resumed the practice of law. He would proudly display his withered right hand as evidence of the role he played at Fort McAllister. He died 15 February 1908 Lake Charles, Louisiana.[10]

Capt. John Foster of Company D, 111th Illinois Infantry, had been severely wounded during the assault on Fort McAllister. The bullet entered his left shoulder, passed upward through the shoulder and neck, and caused much damage to his throat and vocal chords. He suffered partial loss of his voice, and the wound never healed properly. Discharged in April 1865, he returned to Lester, Illinois, to take up his life, but the wound would always nag him. He died a slow, wasting death as a result. The wound received in the assault on McAllister that December afternoon in 1864 finally killed him on 5 December 1874, almost exactly ten years after the event.[11]

1st Sgt. Lyman Hardman of Company I, 30th Ohio, who had been injured when he stepped on a torpedo, had been evacuated to a hospital at David's Island in New York harbor. He was furloughed home and discharged from the service in June 1865. There had been some question as to whether or not to amputate his foot, but it was not removed. The foot healed improperly and shriveled up.[12]

Hardman returned to New Philadelphia, Ohio, to resume his civilian life. He married in September 1868, and he and his wife had three children. He claimed a pension for his service and worked hard to make a living for his family. However, his foot was a constant source of discomfort for him.[13] John Milone noted in 1892, "He suffers constantly from pain in the left foot. . . . Some of the bones were broken in the foot, it is deformed, weak and stiff in the ankle, and the leg between the ankle and knee is much smaller than that of the right. . . . Being crippled and suffering constantly is a great detriment to his business, and that at times he is not really capable of attending to business. . . . That he has not been free from pain in the foot at any time since the 13th day of December 1864."[14] Hardman's condition dogged him throughout the remainder of his life, and he died 26 January 1919 at his home.[15]

After Capt. William Duncan arrived in Hilton Head with Maj. Gen. Howard's dispatches, he was taken to Washington, D.C., to personally deliver them to the secretary of war. For a few weeks he was wined and dined and honored among his countrymen but he finally returned to his command in Savannah in early January 1865. On 13 March 1865 Duncan was breveted a major for conspicuous gallantry. At the war's end, he returned to Elgin, Illinois, to marry his sweetheart and lived out his days as a farmer in Minnesota.[16]

Pvt. George W. Quinn of the 31st Illinois Infantry, who accompanied Capt. Duncan on his harrowing trip down the Ogeechee, was mustered out in July 1865. He went to Missouri where he settled down to farming and raising a family. He died November 1914 at Gibson, Missouri.[17]

Duncan and Quinn's companion on that trip down the Ogeechee, Sgt. Myron J. Amick of the 15th Illinois Cavalry, was captured in March 1865 at Bentonville, North Carolina, but easily survived the war. He returned to Illinois after the war and eventually settled in Portland, Oregon. He developed a condition of weak lungs, which he believed to be due to exposure from his service during the war. His condition caused him to seek different climates with the hope of healing his ailment. He died of pneumonia in January 1906 in New York City.[18]

Lt. George W. Sylvis of the 47th Ohio Infantry, was discharged in late March of 1865 due to deafness caused from being too close to supporting artillery at Vicksburg, Mississippi, and Bentonville, North Carolina. He returned to his wife in Ohio and through the years traveled to New York and eventually Colorado seeking a climate that was better suited to his health.[19] In January 1890 he penned the following letter to Maj. George W. Anderson Jr.

> About twenty-five years ago you and I met at Fort McAllister, Ga. under circumstances of which this generation knows but little about. You of course do not remember me as I was only one who took a very small part in the conflict we had at Fort [McAllister] in which you was in command and in such . . . commanded well. But we had too many for your little brave band and of course came out on top. But it was not your fa[u]lt. I have often thought of you and would like to see you and have a talk with you. I was in Cincinnati last Sept. and there I learnt from Henry Beckman, a member of my regt. that you was in Savannah and I want to here state that I am glad you are still on top of the ground and in the land of the living. I never saw you but once and that was after the surrender . . . do you remember it[?] Now then I want to ask you this[,] why you did not punish our left more than you did[?] My regt. the 47th Ohio Vol. was on our left and as my Co. "B" was on the extreme left of the regt. it brought us at the waters edge[.] we only lost one man killed and three or four wounded[.] Major [Thomas] Taylor had two fingers shot off[.] I have a piece of your flag. I was in command of my Co in the fight. Pls excuse me for writing you hoping you will think enough of it to ans it.[20]

The piece of flag that Lt. Sylvis speaks of may have been a part of Anderson's headquarters flag. Probably this was the flag taken by Capt. J. H. Brown of Company A, 47th Ohio. Brown had sent the flag to Cincinnati, Ohio, where it remained until the men of the 47th Ohio were mustered out in August of 1865. The flag was then sent to Columbus, Ohio.[21] It may have been cut into pieces for each man to have a small souvenir of the event. Lt. Sylvis settled in Ohio and died November 1916 at the Soldier's Home in Lafayette, Indiana.[22]

Capt. Stephen F. Grimes, who fought the sword duel with Capt. Nicholas Clinch in the closing minutes of the final assault, recovered from his wounds and returned to his wife and child in Xenia, Illinois. He later opened a dry goods business in Bement, Illinois, and later moved to Spring Garden, Illinois, where he and his growing family spent many years. In later years, Grimes was troubled by the wound he received at Shiloh. The bullet had passed through his right shoulder and lung and lodged in his back between the shoulder and spine. Even twenty years later, one could feel the bullet under the skin. It caused partial paralysis of his right side and frequent hemorrhaging of his lung. These problems caused him to seek relief in other climates, and he spent three years traveling in Colorado and California seeking conditions that would, he hoped, bring about a healing or a remedy to his problems. In the end it was to no avail. Grimes's Shiloh wound would eventually kill him, and on 20 October 1917 he died at Belle Rive, Illinois, and is buried in New Hope Cemetery.[23]

Capt. George E. Castle of the 111th Illinois Infantry returned to Salem, Illinois, after the war and carried the Fort McAllister garrison flag home with him as a war trophy. He resumed his former occupation of farming and raising livestock but with difficulty due to his unstable health. His condition was caused by an infection received after an improper vaccination during his military service, and his health continued to decline. On 23 March, 1883 he married Julia T. Badolett, but they had no children. Castle filed for divorce in February 1887 but died at the age of forty-six in November 1887 before the case was settled. A short time later, Julia Castle was declared insane and placed in the custody of her sister. Julia died in 1896.[24] Fort McAllister's garrison flag remained in Capt. Castle's possession and was eventually given to his nephew George W. Castle of St. Louis because there were no other living descendants. Thus Fort McAllister's flag remained in St. Louis for over forty years.[25]

The men who fought to defend that flag picked up the pieces of their lives and went about trying to put together their individual worlds. Some did not survive to see the end of the war. Lt. Col. Joseph L. McAllister lead the Hardwick Mounted Rifles to Virginia in April 1864 where they found the war to be a different experience from that on the Georgia coast. In Virginia, the 7th Georgia Cavalry had been part of a Confederate force sent out in pursuit of Federal cavalry who were on a raiding expedition toward Lynchburg, Virginia. On 10 June, the 7th Georgia arrived near Louisa Courthouse, where they went into camp. The following morning they awoke to find the Federals preparing to attack them. In the ensuing battle the men of the Hardwick Mounted Rifles fought bravely and held their own against an overwhelming enemy force. Lt. Col. McAllister remained at the forefront of his men.[26] One member of the Mounted Rifles described the leader: "Throughout that bloody day he was the Bayard of the field, the very impersonification of lofty daring. . . . He was too invincible to surrender to his foes until he became a lifeless corpse."[27]

The Federal cavalry soon prevailed against the Confederates, and the men of the Hardwick Mounted Rifles found themselves surrounded with little hope of escape. One of the Confederate troopers wrote, "Colonel McAllister fired every shot he had and after he fell with four balls in his body threw his pistol into the face of the foe."[28] Edward W. Wyatt, McAllister's nephew, said, "Uncle Joe was a Harvard man. He and Neil Habersham swore never to surrender. Eleven days out of Louisa Court House, Va., they were surrounded by some regiments of Northerners. All surrendered but Uncle Joe. Some of his college mates begged him to surrender, he replied by backing into a fence corner and firing his pistols. They shot him down. . . . Habersham was cut to pieces with swords."[29] Telegrams were sent to notify the family of Lt. Col. McAllister's death, and his sword was later returned to them. However he was never to be returned to Georgia, and his remains were buried at Louisa Courthouse with his men near where he fell.[30]

Lt. Elijah A. Ellarbee, who had commanded the sharpshooters who had hidden in the marsh opposite the fort during the 3 March 1863 attack by the three ironclads, was captured June 1864 with the Hardwick Mounted Rifles at Louisa Courthouse, Virginia, when Lt. Col. McAllister was killed. Ellarbee was sent to Point Lookout Prison in Maryland and later transferred to Elmira Prison, Elmira, New York, where he died of chronic diarrhea in October 1864 and is buried in the prison cemetery.[31]

Of Lt. Ellarbee's detachment that had been in the marsh with him on that 3 March 1862, Brittain Cobb was wounded at the Battle of Haw's Shop on 22 June 1864 and died of that wound in August 1864.[32] Sgt. Stoughton Haymans was also captured that June of 1864 at Louisa Courthouse and sent to Point Lookout Prison. That October he was exchanged but died at Fort Monroe, Virginia, before reaching the exchange point.[33] Pvt. J. C. Proctor survived the attrition rate in Virginia and surrendered with Lee's army at Appomattox Courthouse. He returned to Georgia to pick up the pieces of his life.[34]

For the captured garrison of Fort McAllister, their war was over but their struggle to survive was not. They had been sent to Hilton Head before going to prisons in the north, primarily to Fort Delaware. The wounded and sick were hospitalized at Hilton Head until they could be sent on. Young Samuel L. Moore, who was fifteen in 1864, remembered not only his prison experience but also the ordeal to get back home after the war ended.

So we were carried . . . to Fort Delaware, a downcast, disappointed lot of boys. . . . [We survived] on six [hardtack] crackers a day and an occasional rat stew. . . . On July 18, 1865, I took the amnesty oath and was sent, with 500 other prisoners of war, to New York to be transported South. We went by way of Philadelphia and were marched up into the city and halted by an open square and children were sent among us with baskets of sandwiches and pitchers of lemonade. . . . It was like a change from purgatory to the Seventh Heaven. I was ashamed of my personal appearance, but I was not ashamed of the cause that put me there. Finally, we reached New York and while eating at Castle Garden, awaiting orders, I sold the cotton that was between my quilted blankets, and my woolen socks to an Irish woman for $1.50. This dollar was the first green back I saw and I felt rich. After a few weeks in New York, I was sent South. We had some bad times on the boat, for five hundred men were crowded into the hold of the boat, with 'built-in-bunks.' . . .

My shoes were lost over board, but I did not feel the loss of them until I reached Jacksonville, Florida and had to walk twelve miles, barefooted, where the railroad bridge was torn up. The train took us up, finally, and when we got to Madison, Florida, I had to walk sixteen miles with Mr. Jim Barrs to his home where I spent the night. . . . Barrs' family . . . had given him up for dead, when . . . lice and vermin ridden he reached home. . . . He stripped off all of his clothing outside, bathed, put on clean clothes and burned his old clothing before going into their home. . . . Mr. Barrs was very kind to me and sent me to . . . my home, next day with his boy on a mule.

When I reached home, my mother did not know me and I was indeed a sad looking spectacle. I had on a blue United States Military shirt, a pair of pants . . . one leg . . . torn off halfway to the knee, and the other leg rolled up to match it. I had on a Confederate gray cap, the visor torn off. I was barefooted and my hair was down to my shoulders. My appearance did not dampen the joy of my mother and the home folks, however, when they finally realized I was home at last.[35]

Lt. William P. Schirm of Clinch's Light Battery, whose bravery and devotion to duty in the final attack elicited prominent mention in Maj. Anderson's report, was imprisoned at Point Lookout, Maryland, transferred to Old Capitol Prison in Washington, D.C., and then sent to Fort Delaware. He was released in June of 1865 and returned to Savannah, where he eventually became director of the Chatham Real Estate and Improvement Company.[36]

Maj. George Anderson Jr. survived his imprisonment at Fort Delaware and returned to Savannah where he became a cotton classer for the W. W. Gordon Company of Savannah. There he often related numerous war stories for his young assistant Arthur Gordon. Anderson died in Savannah in 1906 and is buried in Laurel Grove Cemetery, not far from the grave of Maj. Gallie.[37]

From Fort McAllister, Capt. William D. Dixon followed the Republican Blues to Kennesaw, Georgia, in May of 1864 where they were engaged in the battles around Atlanta. These soldiers, who had given out after two miles of a ten-mile march from Way's Station to Fort McAllister in August of 1862, were by late 1864, consistently making daily marches of fifteen, twenty, and twenty-five miles. It was a different war, and they were different soldiers from what they had been while serving in the garrison at Fort McAllister.[38]

Capt. Dixon followed the Army of Tennessee on its ill-fated invasion of Tennessee and the subsequent retreat into Alabama and Mississippi. After taking a short furlough in Columbus and Macon, Georgia, he rejoined the Blues in South Carolina where they participated in the campaign through the Carolinas, finally surrendering with Johnston's army near Durham, North Carolina. From there he marched back to Augusta with his unit, where it disbanded, and they made their way home. Dixon took a boat from there back to Savannah.[39]

Dixon would marry twice. He became a partner in a Savannah funeral home and was active with the local volunteer fire department. In later years he did not participate with the Confederate veterans in Savannah parades because he knew that many had been deserters, and he did not wish to march with deserters. He kept the Republican Blues daybook rather than turning it over to the Blues, because it identified those who had deserted and those who had not.[40] He died in Savannah on 20 March 1914 and is buried in Bonaventure Cemetery.

In the postwar years the people of Georgia were too concerned with the problems of Reconstruction to consider the fate of the earthen defenses that once protected them or the events that occurred there. Immediately after the war, many former Federal soldiers saw opportunities in rebuilding the war-ravaged South. Cheap land, a more temperate climate, and a large labor force of freedmen, all served to attract some Northerners to the South. Orville B. Seagrave, who had served as an officer aboard the gunboat *Dandelion* when that vessel established contact with Gen. Sherman on 13 December 1864, returned to Genesis Point in 1866 and arranged to rent the old plantation complex there that had been part of the McAllister's property. Seagrave hired many of the local freedmen and spent two years raising cotton, one of the first attempts in the area to grow cotton after the war's end. But as with most of these efforts, the lack of reliable labor and markets doomed them to failure.[41]

The forest gradually reclaimed the earthen parapets of Fort McAllister. Erosion softened its contours while the large timbers supporting the bombproofs and magazines rotted out, and the weight of the earth over them collapsed them. The land upon which the fort's garrison lived and across which Hazen's forces had charged was sporadically used for agriculture, and cattle grazed upon the grass that grew over the walls of the old fort. For almost eighty years the fort stood empty, its usefulness passed and the memory of its struggle all but forgotten.

In 1912 Arthur Seagrave and his new bride visited the ruins of Fort McAllister on their honeymoon trip. Although Arthur's father, Orville Seagrave, died when Arthur was very young, he had often listened to his uncle relate the story of his father's service aboard the *Dandelion* and how they made contact with Sherman shortly before Fort McAllister's capture. This, added to his father's later efforts to grow cotton on the land near the old fort, all served to bring Arthur to visit the site. During his visit, he met a local black man who remembered his father very well. It would be twenty-seven years before Arthur and his wife had the opportunity to revisit the old fort, and at that time they would notice tremendous changes due to the efforts of one man— Henry Ford.[42]

In the mid-1920s, Ford purchased large quantities of property in Bryan County to develop a winter resort for his family and friends as well as a working plantation to experiment with agricultural projects, among other things. He made his first purchase of land at Ways, Georgia, after inspecting the properties in 1925. At this time, Ways, Georgia, consisted of two railroad stations, a consolidated school, a general store in which the post office was located, and a few scattered farmhouses. The chief occupations were farming, shad fishing, timber, and turpentine.

The majority of Ford's holdings comprised several antebellum estates that had been grouped together, which included Richmond, Cherry Hill, Strathy Hall, Whitehall, Valambrosia, Cottonham, Rabbit Hill, Fancy Hall, and several smaller tracts. It was at this time the old Genesis Point property came into Ford's possession.[43] He purchased the Cape Hardwick property and the Genesis Point property from a Mrs. Sasser through R. L. Cooper, a real estate broker. The Genesis Point property comprised 2,850 acres, 685 of which was high ground, while the Cape property totaled 500 acres, 200 of which was high ground. The Cape property sold for about $7,000; the Genesis Point property sold for about $25,000. Cooper recommended the purchase of this property, which he considered "a good buy" and "unusually attractive water front property."[44]

For his personal residence, Ford chose the site of the old Clay Plantation, known as Richmond, which had been burned by Sherman's men. He later purchased the Hermitage, an antebellum mansion on the Savannah River, and had it dismantled and rebuilt on the site of the former Clay home. An old rice mill, also destroyed by Sherman's men, was rebuilt to house the electrical and heating plant for his residence. It is an interesting irony that Northern soldiers all but destroyed much of Bryan County during the war, and real prosperity never fully returned until sixty years later when a man from Michigan brought a certain measure of economic recovery to the area.[45]

While Ford was occupied building his complex of shops, sawmills, trade schools, experimental laboratories, and expanding the tiny community of Ways, Georgia, he was apparently uninterested in the old fort that was a part of his land holdings. But others were interested to learn that Ford now owned Fort McAllister. In late June of 1930, eighty-four-year-old George W. Harmony, living in San Bernardino, California, noted a four-line paragraph in the *Los Angeles Examiner* that told of Ford's purchase of old Fort McAllister. It had

12.1. Will Donaldson, Henry Ford, and George Gregory, superintendent of Ford's Richmond Hill Plantation, dig out the hot shot furnace in the spring of 1935. Courtesy, Georgia Department of Natural Resources, Fort McAllister State Historic Park

been sixty-five years since Harmony participated in the assault on the fort with his comrades of the 6th Missouri Infantry. A short time later, Harmony wrote a letter to Ford in order to express his approval of the purchase: "I read in a paper recently here you had purchased . . . Fort McAllister. . . . It brought back memories of the battle that I was in on that afternoon. . . . I want to congratulate you on buying this property. . . . I hope you will keep this land mark for some time to come."[46] Ford replied to the letter, and Harmony forwarded a copy of the newspaper clipping and a photograph of himself.

It was not until 1935 that Ford took steps to renovate the fort. At that time, Will Donaldson and Bob Bryan, students of Greenfield Village School in Dearborn, Michigan, were visiting the Fords. While exploring along the river, they located the ruins of the fort. Ford's interest grew when he recognized its significance, and he took steps to renovate and preserve it. Workmen opened up a road to the site and cleared the underbrush and second-growth pine from the fort. He had the bombproof and magazines excavated and carefully rebuilt so that gradually the fort began to take shape once again. When complete, the renovation cost $14,636.48. Ironically, Fort McAllister, long neglected by the Southern people, was renovated by a son of the North to serve as a monument to all Americans who fought in that conflict.[47]

12.2. Henry Ford (left) walks with Charles Sorenson on the exposed flooring timbers of the original bombproof at Fort McAllister. By 1935 all of the magazines
and the bombproof had collapsed. Ford had them excavated and reconstructed.
The chimney of the bombproof's fireplace is clearly visible. Courtesy, Georgia
Department of Natural Resources, Fort McAllister State Historic Park

Ford's renovation of the fort focused new attention on its history and significance, and it soon became the scene of various group visits and Confederate observances. In 1938 Phoebe H. Elliott, president of the Savannah
chapter of the United Daughters of the Confederacy, acquired the fort's garrison flag from George W. Castle of St. Louis, the nephew of Capt. George
Castle. On 7 December 1939, a meeting of the Liberty County chapter of the
United Daughters of the Confederacy and the Colonial Dames was held at
the fort to mark the seventy-fifth anniversary of its capture. The garrison flag
was once again unfurled over the earthen parapet for the first time since that
December day in 1864.[48]

On 3 June 1941, the Georgia Historical Society hosted a meeting and picnic at the fort to mark the birthday of Jefferson Davis. Numerous descendants
of those who had served at the fort attended, including Clarence G. Anderson
and Capt. George Drummond, a descendant of Capt. William D. Dixon.
The keynote address was given by Walter Hartridge, a descendant of Alfred
Hartridge, one of the first commanders of the Genesis Point Battery in 1861.[49]

After the fort's initial renovation, the annual cost of upkeep and maintenance averaged about $440, and because it had not been intended to be operated as a public attraction, there came a time when the further expenditure of funds was questioned. On 1 May 1946, it was decided that Fort McAllister was of no material importance to the operation of the Ford Plantation, and it was suggested that upkeep be discontinued. The magazines and bombproof had been closed by this time, due to the deterioration of the timbers, and by 20 July 1946 it was estimated that it would cost $4,000 to replace the rotted timbers. Plans were made to rebuild the fort in late May of 1947 using concrete and steel instead of wooden timbers, but Ford's death prevented this from being undertaken.[50]

During the winter of 1947, Williard T. S. Jones visited the Savannah area and learned of Ford's renovation of the fort, which aroused his interest. Jones was the son of Col. Wells S. Jones, who had been wounded at the time Capt. John Groce was killed during the final assault on the fort. In August of 1948, Williard Jones wrote to the Ford Foundation with an offer to donate his father's sword and personal effects for a museum at Fort McAllister. The Ford Foundation referred him to H. R. Waddell at Richmond Hill Plantation. Waddell declined the offer because there was no museum at the fort, there were no plans to build one, and there were no means of securing the objects offered.[51]

Ford's landholdings in Bryan County were sold after his death in 1947, and once again the fort was forgotten. The property became part of the International Paper Company holdings until March of 1958 when they deeded the immediate thirty acres with the fort and surrounding lands to the Georgia Historical Commission. Land clearing and stabilization work began in the early 1960s, and a museum building and workshop constructed. The central bombproof was rebuilt as was one magazine. The remaining collapsed magazines were filled in, and false doors constructed to show where the entrances had been.[52]

In 1960 the U.S. Army Corps of Engineers recovered several large machinery parts from the wreck of the *Nashville* that were brought to the fort for display. Through the spring and summer of 1963, restoration of the parapets and gun positions was accomplished under the guidance of Col. Allen P. Julian of the Georgia Historical Commission. On 14 November 1963, almost one hundred years after the great naval bombardments, Fort McAllister was opened to the public as a state historic site, with Alston C. Waylor as its first superintendent. In 1972 the State of Georgia purchased a large block of land directly behind the fort, and a state park was developed. Children now play, and families enjoy picnic outings along the scenic river bluff where men once fought and died.

12.3. After Henry Ford completed his renovation of Fort McAllister, the entrance to the hot shot furnace had extensive brickwork installed, and the number-one position, where the hot shot gun was located, was totally removed for an access road to enter the parade ground. When the State of Georgia renovated the fort in the early 1960s, reconstruction of the position for the number-one gun was attempted, but the work did not resemble the original position. Courtesy, Georgia Department of Natural Resources, Fort McAllister State Historic Park

Today Fort McAllister looks similar to photographs of over a century ago. Only the growth of trees alters its appearance. Shell craters are still visible in front of the fort and give silent testimony of the savage bombardments to which the fort was once subjected and echo the words written by Charles C. Jones Jr. over a century before: "The scars caused by the shot and shell . . . are still numerous in and about the fort, and will continue for many days to come."[53] Fort McAllister still stands at its post, guarding the entrance to the Great Ogeechee River. Pleasure boaters, water skiers, and fishermen travel the river past the fort where once heavy ironclads and wooden gunboats fought to gain that privilege.

Thousands of visitors come to the site each year to ponder the events that occurred there. The sea breezes whispering through the trees, scenic beauty, and natural surroundings are in sharp contrast to the blazing fire of battle that

12.4. The foundation is being put down for the museum during the State of Georgia's development of the fort as a historic site. The fort is just out of the picture on the right side. Courtesy, Georgia Department of Natural Resources, Fort McAllister State Historic Park

once engulfed the fort. The navy ironclads that bombarded the fort with impunity no longer exist. Only sketches and old photographs remain to stir our imaginations with their images. Fort McAllister has outlived them all. It remains the Guardian of the Ogeechee, still at its post even though its usefulness has passed, the people it once protected gone, and its importance long diminished. Memories of the events that occurred there have dimmed over the years, just as erosion and the effects of time have softened and settled the earth of the old fort.

As one surveys the scenic beauty that is Genesis Point today, it is difficult to comprehend that such violent events happened there. The peaceful surroundings seem to contradict that reality. But if one pauses to look beyond the picnic tables and playground, the new homes and docks, a glimpse in the mind's eye might be caught of what it once looked like when the monitors bombarded the fort or when Brig. Gen. Hazen's thousands swarmed across the ground to overwhelm the fort's defenders. If one concentrates, one might hear the roar of big cannons and the explosions of shells or the bugle notes sounding on the evening air before Hazen's men raised the cheer and charged

12.5. The completed museum building is seen from the fort in 1962. The renovation of the fort's walls is evident; the southwest bastion wall is devoid of any grass or ground cover. Courtesy Georgia Department of Natural Resources, Fort McAllister State Historic Park

into history amid the crackling, rolling sound of musketry and the crash of cannons. The victories and defeats of that tragic war are now the common property of our national heritage. The fort stands today as a monument to the grit and determination of all the Americans of that conflict who fought for what they believed in against seemingly insurmountable odds. The time has come when we must no longer look back upon that conflict as Yankees or Rebels, Northerners or Southerners, but as Americans, for the men of both sides were Americans.

APPENDIX 1

An Analysis of Fort McAllister's Evolution

Throughout the four years of the Civil War, Fort McAllister evolved to meet the demands placed upon it. Today, the specific steps through which this occurred cannot be identified with certainty, but enough information exists to develop a conjectural sequence. Using information contained in records, period documents, and sketch maps as reference points, we can "connect the dots" to see a picture of the process. Through this can come some insight into how the four-gun battery built in the summer of 1861 became the massive fortification mounting twenty-two guns when it was finally captured in 1864.

In the summer of 1861, the primary line of defense had been placed upon the barrier islands of Georgia's coast, so the battery at Genesis Point was a secondary work (see fig. A1.1). Its initial armament consisted of four 32-pounder smoothbore cannon.[1] In October of 1861, with an impending Federal invasion expected to strike somewhere on the southeast coast, a fifth 32-pound smoothbore cannon was sent to Genesis Point, where it was probably emplaced in a position to the right of the existing battery (see fig. A1.2). It is possible that the hot shot furnace was initially constructed at this time or very shortly after the fall of Hilton Head in November 1861.

Charles C. Jones Jr., in his book *A Historical Sketch of the Chatham Artillery during the Confederate Struggle for Independence*, states that by late July of 1862, the fort had five 32-pound smoothbores and a 42-pound gun (see fig. A1.3).[2] Just when the 42-pounder gun was sent to the battery cannot be determined exactly, but it was sometime after the Confederates abandoned the barrier islands between November 1861 to February 1862. This abandonment of these islands would have freed up cannons that were reutilized in the Savannah defenses. The abandonment of the barrier islands also placed the Genesis Point battery on the front line, so that it was no longer a secondary work and would have been reinforced due to the importance of its location. The forty-two-pounder gun was probably located in a new position constructed on the far right of the battery. On 29 July 1862, the U.S. gunboat *Potomska,* commanded by Lt. Cmdr. Pendleton G. Watmough, was the

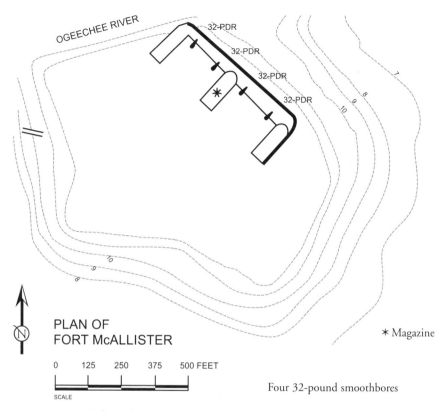

PLAN OF
FORT McALLISTER

* Magazine

0   125   250   375   500 FEET

Four 32-pound smoothbores

SCALE

FIG. A1.1. July 1861

first to engage the battery. Watmough's report of the action states that the battery mounted six guns, which would corroborate Jones's statement, written in 1867.[3]

On 30 July, the day following the *Potomska*'s exchange of fire with the battery, Capt. Alfred Hartridge of the DeKalb Riflemen stated in a letter to his mother that they were due to receive an 8-inch Columbiad, which he would have mounted by morning (see fig. A1.4).[4] This gun was received and mounted within two weeks of this date. It is hard to determine specifically where the 8-inch was emplaced but it is conjectured that a position was constructed on the far right to accommodate it.

Following his visit to the post in October of 1862, Gen. P. G. T. Beauregard recommended that a 32-pounder gun be moved to a position from where it could rake the pilings in the river, that the hotshot furnace be rebuilt, and that a mortar be sent to the battery to protect against enfilade fire.[5] This may have been accomplished by moving the 32-pounder on the right to a newly built position on the far left (see fig. A1.5). Its vacated position would

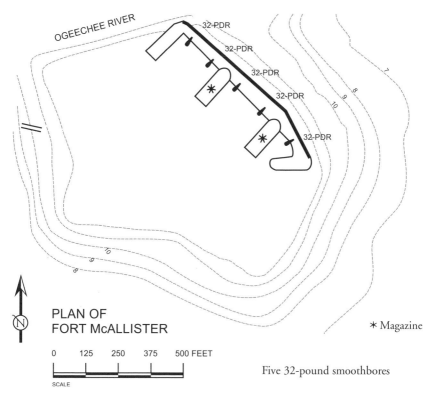

PLAN OF
FORT McALLISTER

0   125   250   375   500 FEET

SCALE

✳ Magazine

Five 32-pound smoothbores

FIG. A1.2. October 1861

then be taken up by relocating the 8-inch Columbiad there. On 19 November 1862, following a naval attack on the battery, the 10-inch mortar arrived at the fort and was more than likely emplaced in the position constructed on the far right. This would have put the mortar in a position to protect the battery from enfilade fire as recommended by Gen. Beauregard. He also recommended raising and lengthening the traverses, and this probably resulted in the right "double-chamber" being separated, as well as changes in the traverses around other emplacements.[6]

On 20 November 1862, Lt. William Daniel Dixon recorded in his journal that they had over one hundred slaves working on the battery, strengthening a magazine, and building a bombproof, which was probably the central bombproof located in the center of the fort today (see fig. A1.6).[7]

On 27 December 1862, Maj. John Barnwell inspected the fort and listed the armament: five 32-pounder smoothbores, a 10-inch mortar, an 8-inch Columbiad, and a 42-pounder gun.[8] He also recommended moving the mortar away from the battery and placing it in its own work due to damage it

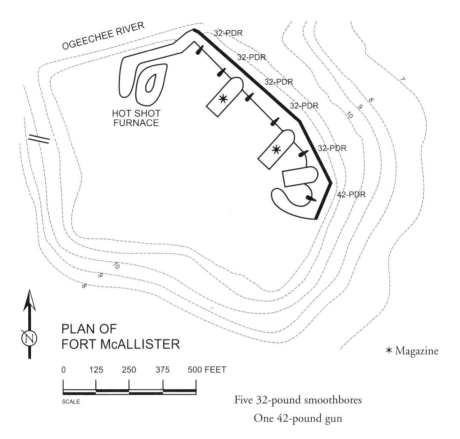

PLAN OF
FORT McALLISTER

0   125   250   375   500 FEET

SCALE

* Magazine

Five 32-pound smoothbores
One 42-pound gun

FIG. A1.3. July 1862

caused to the fort by the concussion of firing the piece.[9] This was probably accomplished fairly soon after Barnwell's visit.

On 3 January 1863, a 10-inch Columbiad and a 32-pounder rifled gun arrived at the post (see fig. A1.7).[10] The 32-pounder rifle was placed in the position vacated by the 42-pounder gun on the far right of the battery and the 10-inch Columbiad was put in a position vacated for it by removing the 32-pounder next to the 42-pound gun. This would have left two 32-pounder smoothbores unused.

During the 1 February 1863 attack by the *Montauk,* Maj. John B. Gallie was killed when a 32-pound cannon in the double chamber was struck by a shell. One of the cannon's trunnions was broken off, and either the trunnion or a fragment of the exploding shell decapitated Gallie (or at the least the back of his head was taken off, leaving his face). The damage to the trunnion would have effectively rendered the 32-pounder useless because it could never

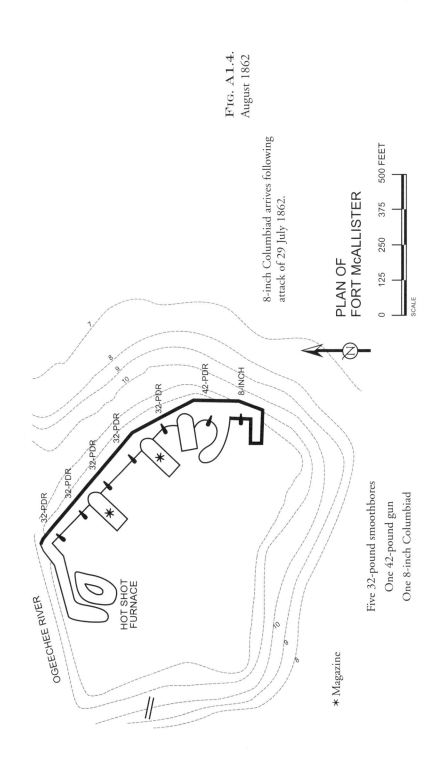

FIG. A1.4.
August 1862

8-inch Columbiad arrives following
attack of 29 July 1862.

PLAN OF
FORT McALLISTER

0   125   250   375   500 FEET

SCALE

Five 32-pound smoothbores
One 42-pound gun
One 8-inch Columbiad

* Magazine

OGEECHEE RIVER

HOT SHOT
FURNACE

32-PDR
32-PDR
32-PDR
32-PDR
32-PDR
42-PDR
8-INCH

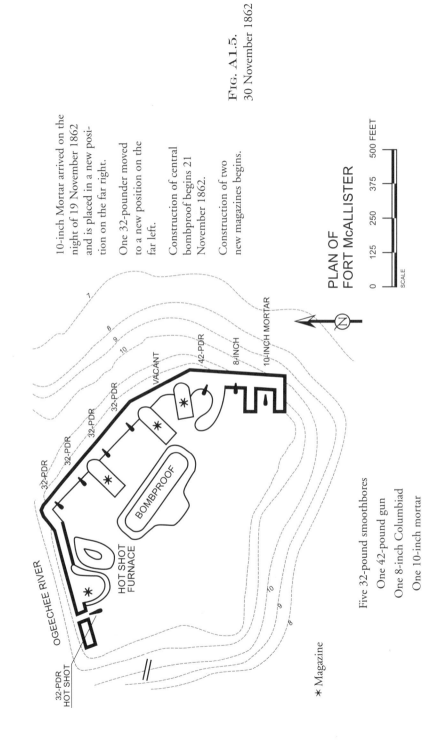

10-inch Mortar arrived on the night of 19 November 1862 and is placed in a new position on the far right.

One 32-pounder moved to a new position on the far left.

Construction of central bombproof begins 21 November 1862.

Construction of two new magazines begins.

FIG. A1.5.
30 November 1862

PLAN OF
FORT McALLISTER

SCALE

0   125   250   375   500 FEET

OGEECHEE RIVER

32-PDR
HOT SHOT

32-PDR

32-PDR

32-PDR

32-PDR

VACANT

42-PDR

8-INCH

10-INCH MORTAR

HOT SHOT
FURNACE

BOMBPROOF

Five 32-pound smoothbores
One 42-pound gun
One 8-inch Columbiad
One 10-inch mortar

* Magazine

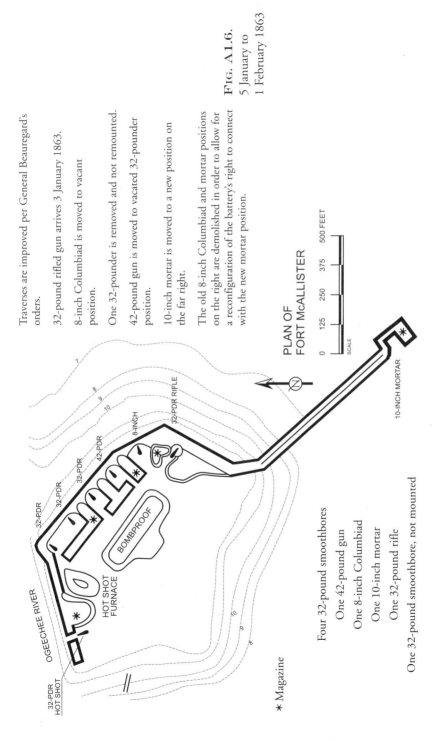

Traverses are improved per General Beauregard's orders.

32-pound rifled gun arrives 3 January 1863.

8-inch Columbiad is moved to vacant position.

One 32-pounder is removed and not remounted.

42-pound gun is moved to vacated 32-pounder position.

10-inch mortar is moved to a new position on the far right.

The old 8-inch Columbiad and mortar positions on the right are demolished in order to allow for a reconfiguration of the battery's right to connect with the new mortar position.

PLAN OF
FORT McALLISTER

N

SCALE

0   125   250   375   500 FEET

OGEECHEE RIVER

32-PDR
HOT SHOT

32-PDR

32-PDR

32-PDR

42-PDR

8-INCH

32-PDR RIFLE

HOT SHOT
FURNACE

BOMBPROOF

10-INCH MORTAR

* Magazine

Four 32-pound smoothbores
One 42-pound gun
One 8-inch Columbiad
One 10-inch mortar
One 32-pound rifle
One 32-pound smoothbore, not mounted

FIG. A1.6.
5 January to
1 February 1863

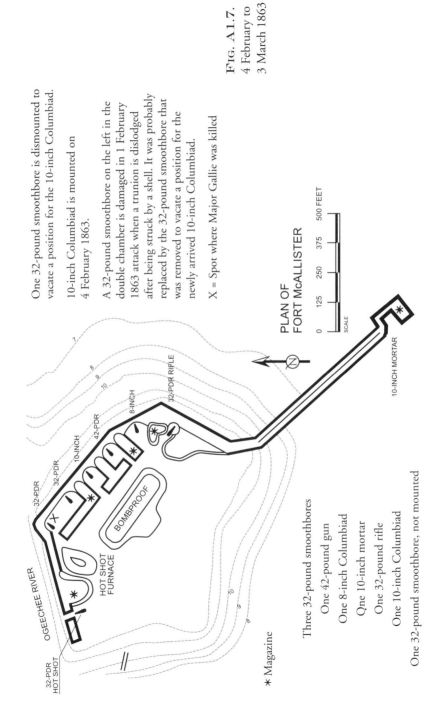

One 32-pound smoothbore is dismounted to vacate a position for the 10-inch Columbiad.

10-inch Columbiad is mounted on 4 February 1863.

A 32-pound smoothbore on the left in the double chamber is damaged in 1 February 1863 attack when a trunion is dislodged after being struck by a shell. It was probably replaced by the 32-pound smoothbore that was removed to vacate a position for the newly arrived 10-inch Columbiad.

X = Spot where Major Gallie was killed

PLAN OF
FORT McALLISTER

SCALE

0   125   250   375   500 FEET

Fɪɢ. A1.7.
4 February to
3 March 1863

OGEECHEE RIVER

32-PDR
HOT SHOT

32-PDR

X

10-INCH

32-PDR

42-PDR

8-INCH

32-PDR RIFLE

HOT SHOT
FURNACE

BOMBPROOF

10-INCH MORTAR

N

✱ Magazine

Three 32-pound smoothbores

One 42-pound gun

One 8-inch Columbiad

One 10-inch mortar

One 32-pound rifle

One 10-inch Columbiad

One 32-pound smoothbore, not mounted

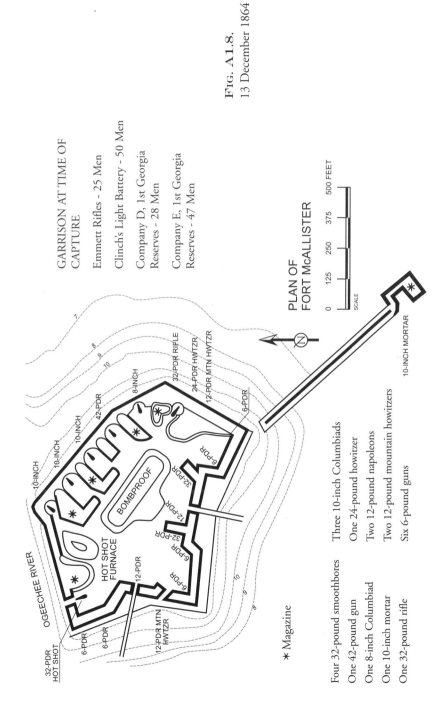

OGEECHEE RIVER

32-PDR
HOT SHOT

6-PDR

6-PDR

12-PDR MTN
HWTZR

HOT SHOT
FURNACE

12-PDR

6-PDR

6-PDR

32-PDR

12-PDR

BOMBPROOF

32-PDR

12-PDR

6-PDR

6-PDR

10-INCH

10-INCH

10-INCH

42-PDR

8-INCH

32-PDR RIFLE

24-PDR HWTZR

12-PDR MTN HWTZR

6-PDR

10-INCH MORTAR

* Magazine

Four 32-pound smoothbores
One 42-pound gun
One 8-inch Columbiad
One 10-inch mortar
One 32-pound rifle

Three 10-inch Columbiads
One 24-pound howitzer
Two 12-pound napoleons
Two 12-pound mountain howitzers
Six 6-pound guns

GARRISON AT TIME OF
CAPTURE

Emmett Rifles - 25 Men

Clinch's Light Battery - 50 Men

Company D, 1st Georgia
Reserves - 28 Men

Company E, 1st Georgia
Reserves - 47 Men

N

PLAN OF
FORT McALLISTER

SCALE

0   125   250   375   500 FEET

Fig. A1.8.
13 December 1864

be remounted without considerable repair. It is reasonable to assume that one of the spare 32-pounders that had not been remounted was used to replace this damaged 32-pounder.

After the last naval attack on 3 March 1863, there is a gap in the developmental sequence of the fort. Sometime between 4 March 1863 and 13 December 1864, the fort underwent additional changes in design and armament. The rear defenses, which consisted of a trench work system, were changed in February and March 1864 by the construction of a more compact, bastioned wall, complete with moat and glacis.[11]

By mid-1863 only a few 10-inch Columbiads were available to the Confederates in Savannah. A board of inquiry convened in Savannah in March of 1863 to discuss the city's defenses[12] recommended adding several 10-inch Columbiads to the armament at Fort McAllister. The Republican Blues were ordered to north Georgia in May of 1864. Prior to that time, Capt. William Dixon's journal gives a good accounting of when the 10-inch mortar, 10-inch Columbiad, and 32-pound rifle arrived, however he makes no mention of receiving additional 10-inch Columbiads. It stands to reason that the two additional 10-inch Columbiads located on the front face of the fort when it was captured in December 1864 were probably received after May 1864. When Gen. Sherman arrived in December 1864, the fort bristled with guns (see fig. A1.8). The rear defense was augmented by emplacing the three dismounted 32-pounder smoothbores in positions along the rear wall, and the added field guns belonging to Clinch's Light Battery helped provide a varied array of armament. When the fort fell, the inventory of artillery was as follows: three 10-inch Columbiads, a 42-pounder gun, an 8-inch Columbiad, a 32-pounder rifle, a 10-inch mortar, four 32-pounder smoothbores, a 24-pounder howitzer, two 12-pound Napoleon fieldpieces, two 12-pound Mountain Howitzers, and six 6-pound fieldpieces.[13]

Figure 9 is a view of an 1863 sketch map of Fort McAllister that gives a reference point to build on. It was drawn by an unidentified member of the Republican Blues and identifies what guns are in what positions at that point in time. It shows the four Monitors in the river, which would date the sketch at just after the 3 March 1863 attack.

The fort that one visits today is representative of its appearance when it was captured. The original four-gun battery built in the summer of 1861 is still there, although greatly altered. In looking at the fort today, it is easy to forget that it went through a long, evolutionary process to arrive at the configuration of today. Regardless, the story of how the Genesis Point Battery became Fort McAllister is every bit as important as the story of the events that occurred there.

Fig. A1.9. 1863 sketch map

APPENDIX 2

An Analysis of the Fort McAllister Photographs
Taken by Samuel Cooley

Samuel A. Cooley was a resident of Beaufort, South Carolina, where he operated a photography studio. For a time he was employed by the Federal forces
on Hilton Head Island, and he provided many views not only of Hilton Head
but also wartime Beaufort. Having been in the Hilton Head–Beaufort areas
throughout the war, Cooley was familiar with the reputation of Fort Mc-
Allister and how it had withstood the navy's attempts to reduce it. With the
capture of the fort in December 1864, Cooley availed himself of the opportunity to visit and photograph it. Fortunately many of these photographs survive and allow views of Fort McAllister as it appeared to the soldiers of both
sides during the final assault.

One of the significant features of these photographs is that they portray
Sherman's soldiers in the field after the completion of the March to the Sea.
It is known that the 70th Ohio Infantry was ordered to garrison the fort and
later to dismantle it and that the 55th Illinois Infantry assisted, so the soldiers
in Cooley's views are from these units.

One question about these images is the date on which they were taken.
The key to the answer lies in the big guns in the fort and the tide. Analysis
indicates that Cooley's images were taken on 16 and 17 December 1864. This
determination is made based on two factors: on 15 December 1864 Gen.
Oliver Otis Howard ordered Brig. Gen. William Hazen to have his men
dismount two 32-pounder rifled guns and to "have them placed on the bank
ready for shipment by water to King's Bridge to-morrow,"[1] and on 19 December Maj. Gen. Frank Blair requested the officer in charge of ordnance
stores captured at Fort McAllister to release to the 17th Army Corps ordnance
officer "such ordnance stores as he may require for the 32-pounder now being
mounted by his corps."[2]

This would indicate that between 16 and 19 December, the requested
guns were removed from Fort McAllister and sent to the 17th Army Corps
lines west of Savannah. Because all of the big guns in the fort are accounted

for in Cooley's photographs, the images could only have been taken 16 and 17 December. Indeed, in one image, a 10-inch Columbiad is being dismounted; the shadows indicate that the time is early morning, which would coincide with the time this work would have begun. Gen. Howard issued his initial orders on 15 December, and allowing for time for this order to reach Fort McAllister, work probably did not begin until the morning of 16 December.

Another piece of evidence to corroborate this time frame is the tide. The photograph of the fort taken from the exposed beach during low tide appears to be an early-morning image, based on the prevailing shadows. The tide rises and falls within a fairly consistent period of time that can be calculated and projected forward; thus, it is a simple matter to calculate the tide tables for December 1864 to see when Cooley would have found an early-morning low tide. It is well documented that when the fort was assaulted on 13 December, the tide was low between 4:30 to 5:30 P.M. Tide tables indicate that morning low tides on 14 and 15 December were before daylight. The first low tide in morning daylight would have been on the morning of 16 December, sometime between 6:30 to 7:30 A.M. This also matches the date that Federal troops would have begun dismounting the two guns Gen. Howard requested. The next tidal opportunity for taking the marsh image in morning sunlight would not have been until 31 December, and by that time, the two guns ordered moved to the Federal lines were long gone, leaving two empty gun chambers behind. At no other time can all of these factors of the presence of the big guns and the tide match.

Gen. Howard requested two 32-pounder rifled guns. However, only one 32-pounder rifled gun was in the fort. The next largest gun available would have been the 10-inch Columbiads, and one of these is being dismounted in two of Cooley's images. The 32-pounder rifled gun was moved to Sherman's lines, as archeological evidence indicates in the 1969 recovery of twenty unfired 6.4-inch Mullane shells from a gun position in the 17th Army Corps area. These unfired Confederate shells were out of place in the Federal lines, and their presence there was only explained recently through these details. Savannah was still in Confederate hands when Cooley's images of Fort McAllister were taken on 16 and 17 December, 1864.

It is fortunate to have Cooley's photographs of Fort McAllister. They provide a multifaceted view of the fort and its surroundings as it looked in December of 1864. This appendix next takes an in-depth look at each of Cooley's photographs of Fort McAllister, analyzing each view and what is evident in that view.

FIG. A2.1. During their assault, the soldiers of the 47th Ohio Infantry would have looked up at the northwest bastion of Fort McAllister. Their footprints are still visible in the mud. The signal station is on the wall of the fort to the left, where a signalman is reclining on a chair in front of a wedge tent. This view from the beach at morning low tide was probably one of Samuel A. Cooley's first images taken on 16 December 1864. The shadows and the tide level indicate the time. Courtesy, Library of Congress

FIG. A2.2. (*Overleaf*) Photographer Samuel A. Cooley crossed the footbridge to enter the fort and moved along the firing step on the inside of the wall to capture this view of the hot shot gun from the northwest bastion. The shadows under the folding stool in the foreground indicate this is a morning view. The wedge tent of the signal station on the wall is at far left, and the top of a gun gin in gun position number three is beyond the base of the flagpole to the far right. Courtesy, Library of Congress

FIG. A2.3. (*Overleaf*) A wheelbarrow detail is in the process of removing 10-inch shells from the magazine that served the number-three gun position. Cooley asked the line to stop long enough for him to expose an image. This is one of the best images of Sherman's troops in the field at the end of the March to the Sea. The entrance to the hot shot furnace is behind the two soldiers at the left. Behind the traverse at the right, the gun gin used to dismount the 10-inch Columbiad in position number three is behind the base of the flagpole. Courtesy, Library of Congress

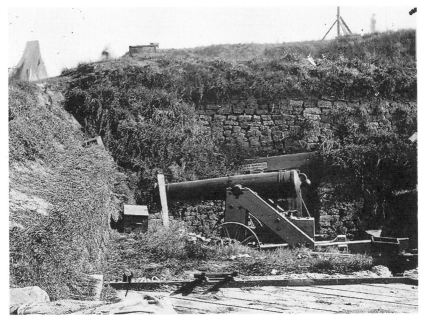

FIG. A2.2

FIG. A2.3

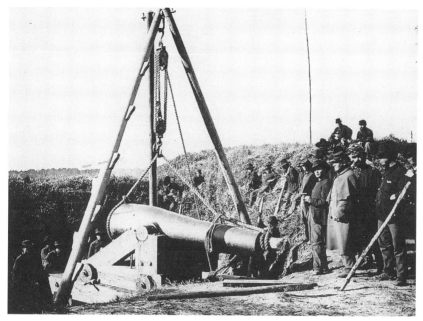

FIG. A2.4. In early morning, Cooley placed his camera on the fort's front wall to capture the 10-inch Columbiad trussed up on a gun gin in preparation for dismounting. A glimpse once again is provided of Sherman's men in the field. The flagpole is at the right. Courtesy, Library of Congress

FIG. A2.5. Cooley relocated his camera atop the traverse behind the 10-inch Columbiad to capture the tube being lifted on the gin in early morning. Courtesy, Library of Congress

FIG. A2.6. Maj. John B. Gallie was killed at position number two at lower right. Upstream is the fort's dock. To the left is the open ground across which the final assault had crossed three days earlier. Obstructions are being piled up for burning. This morning view is from atop the traverse looking upstream. Courtesy, Library of Congress

FIG. A2.7. (*facing*) Cooley then took his camera to the traverse at the left in fig. A2.6 and looked back at the 10-inch Columbiad and the signal station on the wall. The signalmen are apparently waiting for the side-wheel steamer to come up. The length of railroad rail propped up at left may have come from one of the torpedoes removed from behind the fort. Its purpose on the wall is open to conjecture, although it may have been used in dismounting the Columbiad seen in earlier views. The dirt wall at lower right was built on 12 December to cover the entrance to the magazine that served the 10-inch gun; the wall was meant as a protective barrier from the fire of Capt. Francis DeGress's section at Cheves Mill. Courtesy, Library of Congress

FIG. A2.8. (*facing*) At the opposite end of the fort is 32-pound rifled gun in position number seven in the late morning. The traverse at left is where fig. A2.14 was taken; the bombproof, at rear center, is where figures A2.15 and A2.16 were taken. Courtesy, Library of Congress

FIG. A2.7

FIG. A2.8

FIG. A2.9. Four soldiers pose behind a 32-pound rifled gun at the opposite side of the emplacement. Courtesy, Library of Congress

FIG. A2.10. (*facing*) The individual beside the gun is believed to be Brig. Gen. William B. Hazen, who would have been in the area. The camera has not moved since the taking of fig. A2.9, but the sun has, as clearly shown by the sun shining on the breech of the gun, which had been in shadow. Courtesy, Library of Congress

FIG. A2.11. (*facing*) The southeast bastion looking across the rear of the fort is Cooley's next subject after he reversed his camera perspective and moved slightly to the left. In the foreground is his portable darkroom, a funnel and bottles sitting on the overturned sentry box next to it. Courtesy, Library of Congress

FIG. A2.10

FIG. A2.11

FIG. A2.12. The bombproof as seen from behind the 32-pound rifled-gun position was next in the lens after the Cooley turned camera to his right and moved it forward. The flagpole is atop the traverse at right, as is the top of the gun gin in the number-three gun position. Courtesy, Library of Congress

FIG. A2.13. (*facing*) The large hole in the ground in the foreground is a shell crater surviving from the naval bombardment of a year and a half earlier. The two men on the wall, which shows signs of erosion from rain, give a good sense of its scale and the size. They stand in front of the number-six gun position where Capt. William Daniel Dixon's Pet Gun was located. Apparently, photographer Cooley climbed down the wall and carried the camera out front for a late-morning exposure. The wall of the original battery with the gun gin in the number-three gun position is at right; the 32-pound rifled gun is at far left. Courtesy, Library of Congress

FIG. A2.14. (*facing*) Cooley climbed across a traverse to obtain this elevated view of the parade ground. The gun platform at left is one that was constructed in preparation for the final assault as evidenced by the fresh dirt; a 12-pound Napoleon was emplaced here. The gun carriage and truck stacked against the bombproof at center are apparently spares, because they cannot be matched to any gun in the Cooley images. The parade ground shows stacked muskets and wheelbarrows remaining after the ammunition-removal detail. The steamer approaching in fig. A2.7 is now at anchor. The northwest bastion is at upper right. For this elevated view of the parade ground, Cooley returned to the interior of the fort and climbed atop a traverse. The shadows indicate that the sun is directly overhead. Courtesy, Library of Congress

FIG. A2.13

FIG. A2.14

FIG. A2.15. From atop the bombproof, the camera looks southwest across the southwest bastion and the rear of the fort. The soldiers reclining in the shade of the traverse are also seen in fig. A2.14. The footbridge entrance to the fort is at far right; just to the left is a barbette carriage, minus the 32-pounder tube, upended on the truck. The sun is directly overhead, so the image was taken at about the same time as fig. A2.14. Courtesy, Library of Congress

FIG. A2.16. (*facing*) In midafternoon, the camera turns around for the view across the front wall toward the river beyond. A 10-inch Columbiad at left is in the number-four gun position, a 42-pounder gun is at right in the number-five gun position. At center, gun carriage and truck parts lie at the base of the traverse. Courtesy, Library of Congress

FIG. A2.17. (*facing*) The "6" on the cascabel indicates this is the Pet Gun, the 8-inch Columbiad served by Capt. William Daniel Dixon and his gun crew. On the breech of the gun in an arch over the cascabel is "John B. Gallie." This gun was named to honor Gallie and is so noted on an 1863 sketch map of the fort drawn by a member of the Republican Blues (see appendix 1, fig. A1.9). The decorative pinstriping on the carriage and truck is not seen on any other gun documented by Cooley. The long shadows show this photograph was taken in the late-afternoon sun. Courtesy, Library of Congress

FIG. A2.16

FIG. A2.17

FIG. A2.18. A Federal soldier leans on a broom in the late afternoon and casts a curious glance at photographer Cooley. The northwest bastion shows the side-wheeler either coming up to the dock or departing from it. The number-one gun, the hot shot gun, is in its emplacement. The equipment on the racks to the left appears to be horse harnesses and tack; the horses for the Confederate officers and two light batteries were housed in the fort during the final assault. fig. A2.2 was taken from a point just behind the soldier; the camera was taken off the tripod and placed on the sandbags. Courtesy, Library of Congress

FIG. A2.19. (*facing*) To the rear of the fort, the camp of the 70th Ohio Infantry is on the ground they charged across three days before. Gen. Hazen ordered the 70th Ohio to garrison the fort. The fresh dirt of the gun emplacement at center indicates that it had been built just prior to the final assault to position heavier guns across the rear wall. Blankets are hung on the gun carriage to air out; on the parade ground are two stands of arms and a wheelbarrow. Three muskets are stuck in the ground muzzle down. It was common practice to do this: stretch a line between the trigger guards, and hang a tent over the line. Where the two shovels are propped up at center is where Cooley took the image of the wheelbarrow detail removing the 10-inch ammunition (see fig. A2.2). The heavy cloud cover seen building up in fig. A2.18 allows no shadows. For this photography, Cooley turned his camera ninety degrees to his left from fig. A2.18 to look southeast across the rear of the fort. Courtesy, Library of Congress

FIG. A2.20. (*facing*) The 10-inch mortar is in its position outside the fort in late afternoon. Courtesy, Library of Congress

FIG. A2.19

FIG. A2.20

FIG. A2.21. A 32-pounder tube sits on the wall of the southeast bastion; the truck from its carriage is on the front of the wall below the tube. Cooley climbed atop the magazine that served the mortar to capture this image of the fort from the mortar battery. Courtesy, Library of Congress

FIG. A2.22. (*facing*) The last line of abatis across the rear of the fort is how the Federal soldiers saw it during the final assault. Cooley took this shot on his way back from the mortar battery. Courtesy, Library of Congress

FIG. A2.23. (*facing*) A gun-sling cart, behind the man standing at right, is used to transport the heavy artillery tubes once dismounted. A soldier is apparently sitting on the 32-pounder tube. The traverse at upper left center is the vantage point for fig. A2.14. In late afternoon of 16 December, Cooley moved his camera up through the abatis for this image of the palisades in the moat, looking across the rear of the fort toward the southeast bastion. Courtesy, Library of Congress

FIG. A2.22

FIG. A2.23

FIG. A2.24. A working party, the fort behind them, stands around a dismantled gun gin. Moving to his left in the very late afternoon, Cooley captured this image (possibly his last photograph of 16 December) from outside the abatis line, looking back toward the head of the footbridge. Courtesy, Library of Congress

FIG. A2.25. (*facing*) The Confederate signal tower constructed at Fort McAllister in June of 1864 is part of a chain of signal stations connecting Fort McAllister to the railroad bridge upstream and hence to the telegraph relay at Ways Station. The fort also has contact with Coffee Bluff, across the river from where another telegraph connects to Savannah. The exact location of the tower is unknown today. It was on the river bluff; the presence of the downed tree indicates that it is within the area cleared for a Confederate field of fire prior to the assault. Other photographs show that many trees were left standing along this bluff. This image was taken in late afternoon. Courtesy, National Archives

FIG. A2.26. (*facing*) The muskets and the soldiers are gone, and a large puddle of water rests where they had been sitting. This Cooley photo shows the bombproof at left and a traverse at right, but it is not in the sequence of the other images, which show soldiers lounging at the base of the traverse on the right and two stands of muskets stacked in the foreground. The gun carriage in fig. A2.14 is still in place here. How this image fits the sequence is uncertain, but it was obviously taken on a different day, possibly 17 December 1864. Courtesy, Library of Congress

Fig. A2.25

Fig. A2.26

ABBREVIATIONS

Sources

BCC-60	Bryan County Census, 1860
CCC-60	Chatham County Census, 1860
ORA	*Official Records of the Union and Confederate Armies*
ORN	*Official Records of the Union and Confederate Navies*
RBD	*Republican Blues Daybook*
RCS	Roster of Confederate Soldiers from Georgia
SCD-70	*Savannah City Directory,* 1870

NOTES

Chapter 1: A Time of Change

1. Ralston B. Lattimore, *Fort Pulaski National Monument, Georgia* (Washington, D.C.: GPO, 1954), 12–14; E. B. Long, *The Civil War Day by Day: An Almanac 1861–1865* (Garden City, N.Y.: Doubleday, 1971), 27.

2. John M. Sheftall, *Sunbury on the Medway* (Atlanta: Georgia Department of Natural Resources, 1971), 71.

3. Charles C. Jones Jr., *Historical Sketch of the Chatham Artillery during the Confederate Struggle for Independence* (Albany, N.Y.: Joel Munsell, 1867), 51.

4. Lattimore, 17.

5. Alexander A. Lawrence, *Storm over Savannah* (Athens: University of Georgia Press, 1951), 17.

6. William Harden, *Recollections of a Long and Satisfactory Life* (Savannah, Ga., 1934), 96–97.

7. John Barnwell, Report of Inspection, 27 December 1862, records group 109, box 47, entry 76, National Archives, Washington, D.C.

8. Edward W. Wyatt to Henry Ford, 5 May 1825, Henry Ford Library, Dearborn, Mich.

9. Augustus P. Wetter, a native of Mainz, Germany, was thirty-two in 1862 and formerly employed as a planter (CCC-60:395).

10. Alfred L. Hartridge to his mother, 2 July 1861, W. C. Hartridge Collection 1349, Georgia Historical Society, Savannah; J. L. Agnew and F. D. Lee, *Historical Record of the City of Savannah* (Savannah: Estill, 1869), 115. Alfred L. Hartridge, a native of Savannah, was twenty-four in 1861 and formerly employed as a bank clerk (CCC-60:389). Joseph L. McAllister, a native of Bryan County, born at Strathy Hall, his father's plantation, was forty-two in 1862 and educated at Amherst College but returned to Georgia following his father's death to operate the plantation he inherited. In 1861 he organized and commanded the Hardwick Mounted Rifles. They served on the coast of Bryan County and in January 1864 became part of the 24th Battalion Georgia Cavalry. McAllister was promoted to colonel. That spring the unit was transferred in spring 1864 to Virginia where Col. McAllister was killed 11 June 1864 in his first engagement at Trevilian's Station near Louisa Courthouse. He is buried at Louisa Courthouse (Robert Manson Myers, *The Children of Pride* [New Haven, Conn.: Yale University Press, 1972], 1601; BCC-60:3).

11. James W. McAlpin was a native of Savannah, twenty-nine in 1861, and employed as a brick and lumber manufacturer before the war (CCC-60:228).

12. Jones, *Historical Sketch,* 134–35; *Official Records of the Union and Confederate Armies in the War of the Rebellion,* 4th series (Washington, D.C: GPO, 1893), 2:35.

13. David Herbert Donald, ed., *Gone for a Soldier, the Civil War Memoirs of Private Alfred Bellard* (Boston: Little, Brown, 1975), 162.

14. Ibid.

15. Hartridge, 2 July 1861.

16. James Leonard, pension records, Georgia Department of Archives and History, Atlanta, Ga.; Gordon B. Smith, "DeKalb Riflemen," collection 169, box 11, folder 10, Georgia Historical Society, Savannah; ORA s. 1, 6:304.

17. Philip Van Doren Sterns, *The Confederate Navy, a Pictorial History* (Garden City, N.Y.: Doubleday, 1962), 62.

18. Jones, *Historical Sketch*, 50; Roger S. Durham, *The Blues in Gray: The Civil War Journal of William Daniel Dixon and the Republican Blues Daybook* (Knoxville: University of Tennessee Press, 2000), 45–47.

19. Robert Carse, *Hilton Head Island in the Civil War* (Columbia, S.C.: State Printing, 1961), 5–6; Daniel Ammen, "Du Pont and the Port Royal Expedition," in *Battles and Leaders of the Civil War* (reprint, New York: Thomas Yoseloff, 1956), 1:687.

20. Carse, 8–9, 18–19, 71–94.

21. Jones, *Historical Sketch*, 51, 63. Also, a review of cavalry inspection reports in the National Archives, records group 109, verifies the locations of cavalry units and picket stations on the lower coast throughout the war.

22. Allen P. Julian, "Historic Fort McAllister," *Georgia Magazine* (June–July 1960): 11.

23. Myers, 846–47.

24. Thomas Gamble, "The McAllisters, Leaders in Three Great States," *Savannah Morning News,* 5 October 1930.

25. Hartridge, 25 January 1862.

26. Carse, 121; John D. Hayes, ed., *Samuel Francis Du Pont, a Selection from His Civil War Letters* (Ithaca, N.Y.: Cornell University Press, 1969), 1:347–50.

27. ORA s. 1, 6:304.

28. R. Jervis Cooke, *Sand and Grit: The Story of Fort McAllister: A Confederate Earthwork on the Great Ogeechee River, Genesis Point* (Washington, D.C.: U.S. Department of the Interior, National Park Service, 1938), 6. NOTE: The Republican Blues sketch map (fig. ap1.9) of the fort also shows two rows of pilings.

29. Lattimore, 25, 28–29.

30. Ibid., 29; Jack Coggins, *Arms and Equipment of the Civil War* (Garden City, N.Y.: Doubleday, 1962), 76–80.

31. Quincy A. Gillmore, "Siege and Capture of Fort Pulaski," in *Battles and Leaders of the Civil War* (reprint, New York: Thomas Yoseloff, 1956) 2:8–11, 32–35.

32. Ibid., 2:7–9.

33. Myers, 877.

34. Ibid., 881.

35. *Official Records of the Union and Confederate Navies in the War of the Rebellion,* series 1 (Washington, D.C.: GPO, 1897), 12:772–73.

36. S. Dana Greene, "In the 'Monitor' Turret," in *Battles and Leaders of the Civil War* (reprint, New York: Thomas Yoseloff, 1956), 1:727.

37. Jones, *Historical Sketch,* 114.

38. Hartridge to his mother, 16 April 1862.

39. ORA s. 1, 13:161–62.

40. Henry Bryan, Report of Inspection for Hardwick Mounted Rifles, 3 January 1862; L. DuBose, Report of Inspection for Hardwick Mounted Rifles, 13 January 1863; D. B. Harris, Report of Inspection for Hardwick Mounted Rifles, 26 March 1863, records group 109, box 34, entry F-76, National Archives, Washington, D.C. The Hardwick Mounted Rifles established their headquarters at Camp Rogers, located about four miles from Fort McAllister at Cottonham Plantation owned by Rev. William Charles Rogers. They maintained picket posts at Cottonham Plantation, Kilkenny Bluff, and Tivoli on the Medway River. A daily scouting party of twelve men patrolled the area between St. Catherine's Sound and Ossabaw Sound, remaining out twenty-four hours before returning to camp, after which another party was sent out in their place.

41. Hartridge, 18 June 1862.

42. Isaac Hermann, *Memoirs of a Veteran* (Atlanta: Byrd Printing, 1911), 79.

43. Ibid., 80.

Chapter 2: Baptism by Fire

1. ORN s. 2, 1:161–62. USS *Potomska,* logbook, 30 June–1 July 1862, National Archives, Washington, D.C.

2. ORN s. 2, 1:183. Pendleton Gaines Watmough was a thirty-three-year-old native of Montgomery County, Pennsylvania, who entered the navy at the age of thirteen in 1841 and served on the coast of South America, the Mediterranean, the Pacific coast of the United States, and aboard the frigate *Savannah.* Watmough participated in Mexican War operations in California in 1846 and in 1847 entered the Naval Academy. He served aboard the USS *Mississippi* in Commodore Matthew Calbraith Perry's expedition to Japan in 1853. Watmough, commissioned a lieutenant in 1855, served in the Pacific. In June 1858 he was ordered to the USS *Michigan* to cruise the Great Lakes. He resigned his commission in April 1859 and entered private life. With the outbreak of war, he offered his services to the secretary of the navy and served in the Chesapeake Bay area during the early weeks of the war. Assigned to duty on the southeast coast, he participated in the attack on Hilton Head in November 1861 and the capture of Beaufort, South Carolina. Ordered to the Brooklyn Navy Yard in December 1861, he took command of the gunboat *Potomska* and returned to the southeast coast in January 1862 (*Genealogies of Old Philadelphia,* vol. 3; military service and pension records, National Archives, Washington, D.C.).

3. ORN s. 1, 13:161.

4. USS *Potomska,* logbook, 1 July 1862.

5. ORN s. 1, 13:161–62.

6. Ibid., 186.

7. Ibid., 221.

8. Frank Chance, Paul Chance, and David Topper, *Tangled Machinery and Charred Relics* (Orangeburg, S.C.: Sun Printing, 1985), 19, 23, 77; *New York Times,* 19, 22, 25 October 1861.

9. Chance, Chance, and Topper, 19–23.

10. Ibid., 61, 76–78, 80.

11. ORN s. 1, 13:21.

12. ORN s. 2, 1:105, 131, 171, 228.

13. *Savannah Republican,* 30 July 1862.

14. Hartridge, 30 July 1862.

15. Ibid.

16. Ibid.

17. ORN s. 1, 13:221.

18. Hartridge, 30 July 1862.

19. Ibid.

20. Ibid.

21. Barnwell, Report of Inspection, 27 December 1862.

22. Agnew and Lee, *Historical Record,* 117.

23. Agnew and Lee, *Historical Record,* 117; Mary H. Bonaud, interview by author and correspondence with author, 15 September 15 and 28 October 1981.

24. Agnew and Lee, *Historical Record,* 117. John Wayne Anderson (1805–1866), a graduate of Union College, Schenectady, New York, was also a director of the Central of Georgia Railroad. Anderson died in Macon, Georgia, on 22 August 1866 and is buried in Laurel Grove Cemetery, Savannah (Myers, 1453).

25. Durham, 96–98.

26. The *Blues' Daybook* confirms this: "The road was very bad and a continued rain did not improve matters" (RBD entry, 21 August 1862, Georgia Historical Society, Savannah).

27. The *Blues' Daybook* notes, "The Emmett Rifles have been assigned to quarters inside of the battery, the Blues to an old barn outside until other arrangements can be made" (RBD entry, 23 August 1862, Georgia Historical Society, Savannah).

28. Durham, 98–99.

29. Ibid., 99–100.

30. Ibid., 101

31. RBD entry, 23, 26 August 1862.

32. RBD entry, 23, 26 August 1862.

33. George Washington Dickerson, a native of Savannah and twenty in 1862, had been an engineer apprentice. He enlisted as a private in Company B, 8th Georgia Infantry on 21 May 1861 and was elected second lieutenant of the Emmett Rifles. He resigned on 6 January 1863 as a result of disability from a beating he received at Fort Jackson, Georgia. He died in Savannah on 14 February 1869 at the age of twenty-six and is buried in Laurel Grove Cemetery (CCC-60, 99; RCS 1:926).

34. George A. Nicoll, a native of Savannah, was thirty in 1862 and a former bookkeeper. He enlisted with the Blues on 25 April 1861 and served successive reenlistments rising to the rank of first lieutenant at Fort McAllister. He was elected captain of the Emmett Rifles on 8 November 1863, was captured at Fort McAllister on 13 December 1864, and was imprisoned at Fort Delaware. He was released on 4 June 1865 (CCC-60, 277; RCS 1:138).

35. Durham, 102.

36. Ibid., 107.

37. Ibid.

38. Ibid.

39. Ibid., 108.

40. ORN s. 1, 12:206, 348; C. R. P. Rodgers, "Du Pont's Attack on Charleston," in *Battles and Leaders of the Civil War* (reprint, N.Y.: Thomas Yoseloff, 1956), 4:33; Durham, 109.

41. Durham, 109.

42. ORA s. 1, 14:658.

43. Ibid.

44. ORN s. 1, 13:427.

45. Ibid.

46. RBD, 2 November 1862.

47. Durham, 111.

48. Ibid., 113–14.

49. Augustus Bonaud, service records, Georgia Department of Archives and History, Atlanta; Mary H. Bonaud, interview by author and correspondence, May 1983.

50. Durham, 109–10.

51. Ibid., 113–14.

52. Ibid., 114–15.

53. George Wayne Anderson Jr. (1839–1906), a native of Savannah, was twenty-three in 1862 and had been a clerk in his uncle John W. Anderson's commission house. He enlisted with the Blues in April 1861 and served successive enlistments as lieutenant. Anderson was elected captain of the Blues in August 1862, appointed major of artillery on 30 April 1863, and captured at Fort McAllister 13 December 1864. He was released 4 June 1865 from Fort Delaware (CCC-60, 4; RCS 1:132).

54. Ibid., 121–25.

55. USS *Wissahickon,* logbook, 10 November 1862, National Archives, Washington, D.C.

56. Ibid.; ORN s. 1, 13:440–41.

57. Jim Dan Hill, ed., *The Civil War Sketchbook of Charles Ellery Stedman, Surgeon, United States Navy* (San Rafael, Calif.: Presidio, 1976), 131–32.

58. Robert Pierce, diary entry, 17 November 1862, item 793, Manuscript Collection, Special Collections, University of Georgia Library, Athens, Ga.

59. Ibid., 18 November 1862.

60. Jones, *Historical Sketch,* 115; Durham, 139–43.

61. RBD, 19 November 1862.

62. Pierce, 19 November 1862.

63. Durham, 115–16.

64. ORN s. 1, 13:454.

65. Ibid.

66. Pierce, 19 November 1862.

67. ORN s. 1, 13:454; USS *Wissahickon,* logbook, 19 November 1862; Pierce, 19 November 1862.

68. Pierce, 19 November 1862.

69. Jones, *Historical Sketch,* 115.

70. Pierce, 19 November 1862.

71. William Jeffers enlisted 18 May 1862 in the Blues at Fort Jackson, Savannah, Georgia and is noted present at Fort McAllister on the 1 September and 31 December 1863 muster rolls. He deserted from Fort McAllister with seven other soldiers in a picket boat on the night of 15 January 1864 (RCS 1:144; RBD).

72. Durham, 116–17.

73. Ibid.

74. John B. Gallie, Report of Inspection, 1 January 1863, records group 109, entry 76, box 47, National Archives, Washington, D.C.

75. Robert Houston Anderson (1835–1888) was a native of Savannah, a son of John W. Anderson, twenty-six or twenty-seven in 1862, and a graduate of the U.S. Military Academy. He resigned his commission with the U.S. Army and entered Confederate service as a first lieutenant. He raised the 1st Battalion, Georgia Sharpshooters, and was promoted to major. In 1863 he was promoted to colonel and commanded the 5th Regiment, Georgia Cavalry and in 1864 was promoted to brigadier general. After the war he entered his father's commission business, later opened his own insurance firm, and was elected chief of police. He died in Savannah on 8 February 1888 and is buried in Bonaventure Cemetery (Myers, 1453–54; CCC-60, 4).

76. Durham, 116–17.

77. James Leonard, letter of 15 September 1919, Georgia Department of Archives and History, Atlanta; James Leonard, pension records, Georgia Department of Archives and History, Atlanta, Ga.

78. Durham, 117–18.

79. John B. Gallie (1806–1863) migrated to Nova Scotia, then to New Orleans, and eventually to Savannah. He organized several artillery units when the war broke out, was eventually elected major of the 22nd Battalion, Georgia Artillery, and was assigned to Fort McAllister. He was killed there during a naval attack on 1 February 1863 and is buried in Laurel Grove Cemetery in Savannah (Myers, 1526).

80. Myers, 1526.

81. Durham, 118.

82. Ibid.

83. Ibid., 120.

84. Ibid., 119–20.

85. Ibid., 120.

86. Ibid., 102; Chance, Chance, and Topper, 81.

87. Sterns, 78.

88. Ibid.

89. Barnwell, Report of Inspection, 27 December 1862. According to Barnwell's report, the armament of the fort at this time consisted of: one 10-inch mortar, dated 1862, serial number 1666, marked "JRA & Co. T.F."; one 8-inch Columbiad, dated 1861, serial number 7941, marked "JRA & Co. T.F."; one 42-pound gun, dated 1862, serial number 7143, marked "JRA & Co. T.F."; and five 32-pound naval smoothbore cannons. The mortar, 8-inch gun, and 42-pound gun were products of the Tredegar Foundry of Richmond, Virginia, owned and operated by James Reid Anderson, hence the "JRA" is Anderson's initials, and the "TF" stands for "Tredegar Foundry" (Warren Ripley, *Artillery and Ammunition of the Civil War* [N.Y.: Van Nostrand Reinhold, 1970], 77, 127).

90. Gallie, Report of Inspection, 1 January 1863.

91. USS *Seneca* logbook, 28 December 1862, National Archives, Washington, D.C.

92. Durham, 125.

93. Ripley, 38–40.

94. ORN s. 1, 14:507–8.

Chapter 3. Sand and Grit

1. Hayes, 1:31.
2. Samuel T. Browne, *First Cruise of the Montauk* (Providence, R.I.: Bangs William, 1880), 10, 12, 28; ORN s. 2, 1:149.
3. Browne, 10–13, 34.
4. ORN s. 1, 13:520.
5. Browne, 53.
6. Ibid., 31–33.
7. Pierce, 24 January 1863.
8. ORN s. 1, 13:544.
9. Browne, 33.
10. ORN s. 1, 13:544.
11. Ibid., 548.
12. The deserter was probably from the Emmett Rifles as records for the period indicate they had three soldiers absent without leave, while the Republican Blues had none. The deserter may have been Thomas Murphy, twenty-nine, a native of Baltimore, Maryland, and employed as a coasting-vessel mariner before the war. The 1860 Savannah Census shows he was the only Murphy in the city employed in an occupation that would have prepared him with knowledge of the coastal waterways (CCC-60, 360).
13. Browne, 33–34.
14. ORN s. 1, 13:544.
15. Browne, 34–35.
16. ORN s. 1, 13:544.
17. Browne, 35–36.
18. ORN s. 1, 13:545.
19. Ibid.
20. Browne, 34.
21. Bradley S. Osbon, *New York Herald,* 13 February 1863; ORN s.1, 13:549.
22. Browne, 37–38.
23. ORN s. 1, 13:544.
24. Osbon, *New York Herald,* 13 February 1863.
25. Browne used the term *pet gun,* the name Lt. William Dixon had given the 8-inch Columbiad. Browne's account was written twenty years after the war. Was this a coincidence? Although Dixon's journal calls the gun by that name, Browne does not offer any information on how the name came about.
26. Browne, 38–40.
27. Durham, 129–30.
28. ORN s. 1, 13:545–46.
29. Bradley S. Osbon, *Harpers Weekly,* 28 March 1863. It is known that Osbon was the only newspaper correspondent present aboard the *Montauk.* Although his accounts appeared in the *New York Herald,* they were also quoted in other papers, as it was a common for newspapers to reprint articles from other newspapers to provide news of interest to its readers. This would explain Osbon's accounts in other newspapers.
30. ORN s. 1, 13:544.
31. Ibid., 627.

32. Osbon, *New York Herald,* 13 February 1863.

33. Charles C. Jones Jr., "Chickamauga Address," *Speeches Given to Confederate Survivors Association, April 1866, 1888, 1890, 1896* (Savannah: Georgia Historical Society, 1900), 12–13.

34. ORN s. 1, 13:627.

35. Browne, 41.

36. Osborn, *New York Herald,* 13 February 1863.

37. Pierce, 28 January 1863.

38. Browne, 42.

39. ORN s. 1, 13:627.

40. Browne, 43–44.

41. Osbon, *New York Herald,* 13 February 1863.

42. Pierce, 28 January 1863.

43. ORN s. 1, 13:547.

44. Browne, 42–44.

45. Osborn, *New York Herald,* 13 February 1863. Please note that there were no 10-inch guns in place at this time.

46. USS *Dawn* logbook, 28 January 1863, National Archives, Washington, D.C.; USS *Montauk,* logbook, 28 January 1863, National Archives, Washington, D.C.

47. Jones, *Historical Sketch,* 116.

48. Ibid.

49. Osbon, *New York Herald,* 13 February 1863.

50. ORN s. 1, 13:628.

51. Browne, 44–45.

52. Samuel Francis Du Pont to his wife, 28 January 1862, W9–2797, Hagley Museum and Library, Wilmington, Delaware; Hayes, 2:390–91.

53. Hayes, 2:401.

54. ORN s. 1, 13:546–47.

55. Ibid., 543.

56. Ibid.

57. Ibid., 549.

58. Osbon, *New York Herald,* 13 February 1863.

Chapter 4. The Noise Rolls Like Distant Thunder

1. ORA s. 1, 14:213–14.

2. USS *Dawn,* logbook, 31 January 1863.

3. ORN s. 1, 13:628.

4. ORA s. 1, 14:214.

5. ORN s. 1, 13:680.

6. ORN s. 1, 13:628–29.

7. ORA s. 1, 14:214.

8. Durham, 130–32. Francis Willis, twenty-four in 1863, had been an engineer on the Central of Georgia Railroad. He enlisted in the Blues in April 1861 and served with them through the war (CCC-60, 68, 402; RBD).

9. ORA s. 1, 14:216.

10. Ibid.

11. John Mahon, a native of Ireland, was thirty-three in 1863 and formerly employed as a laborer. He enlisted in the Blues in April 1861 and the last notation was absent, sick, 30 November 1863 (CCC-60, 244; RCS 1:147; RBD).

12. Anthony L. Robider, a native of Paris, France, was twenty-five in 1863 and a carpenter. He enlisted in the Blues in March 1862 and was wounded 5 July 1864 in a skirmish at Smyrna, Georgia (CCC-60, 320; RCS 1:147; RBD).

13. James Barbour, a native of England, was twenty-two in 1863 and a black-smith. He enlisted in the Blues in March 1862 and was wounded on 16 June 1864 near Pine Mountain, Georgia (CCC-60, 11; RCS 1:140; RBD).

14. Durham, 130–32.

15. ORA s. 1, 14:214.

16. Durham, 130–32.

17. RBD, 1 February 1863.

18. ORA s. 1, 14:214.

19. John Grey was twenty-one in 1863 and had been a printer. He enlisted in the Blues 12 July 1862 and was wounded 31 August 1864 at Jonesboro, Georgia (CCC-60, 156; RCS 1:143; RBD).

20. Charles F. Blancho, a native of Florida, was twenty-eight in 1863 and a brick-layer. He enlisted in the Blues in April 1861 and was transferred to Sappers and Miners Company of Confederate Engineer Corps 12 September 1863 (CCC-60, 24; RCS 1:140; RBD).

21. Mark Masters, from St. Augustine, Florida, was twenty-two in 1863 and a plumber's apprentice. He enlisted in the Blues 20 August 1861, and the last note says that he was present at Fort McAllister on 1 September 1863 muster roll (CCC-60, 366; RCS 1:145; RBD).

22. William J. Ballie, of Savannah, Georgia, was twenty in 1863 and a mariner. He enlisted with the Blues in May 1862, was wounded 20 July 1864 at the Battle of Peachtree Creek, and surrendered and was paroled 27 April 1865 at Greensboro, North Carolina (CCC-60, 183; RCS 1:139; RBD).

23. Timothy S. Flood, of Savannah, was twenty-six in 1863 and a wheelwright and painter. He enlisted with the Blues in April 1861 and surrendered and was paroled 26 April 1865 at Greensboro, North Carolina (CCC-60, 50; RCS 1:143; RBD).

24. Durham, 130–32.

25. Osbon, *Harpers Weekly,* 28 March 1863.

26. Osbon, *New York Herald,* 13 February 1863.

27. ORN s. 1, 13:628.

28. Jones, *Historical Sketch,* 117.

29. John Ash, diary, 1 February 1863, Special Collections, Manuscript, Archives and Rare Book Library, Emory University Library, Decatur, Georgia.

30. William Tappan Thompson (1812–1882) was a Ohio native who began his career in journalism in Philadelphia in 1823. In 1835 he moved to Augusta, Georgia, and established a newspaper there. He moved to Savannah in 1850 and the *Savannah Morning News,* where he was editor for thirty-two years. He died in Savannah 24 March 1882 and is buried in Laurel Grove Cemetery (Myers, 1701).

31. *Savannah Republican,* 2 February 1863.

32. Hermann, 82–83.
33. ORA s. 1, 14:216, 633; Hermann, 82–83.
34. Hermann, 82–83.
35. ORA s. 1, 14:216.
36. Osbon, *Harpers Weekly,* 28 March 1863.
37. Pierce, 1 February 1863.
38. ORA s. 1, 14:217.
39. Hermann, 84.
40. ORN s. 1, 13:628.
41. Ibid., 680.
42. ORA s. 1, 14:215.
43. ORN s. 1, 13:680.
44. Osbon, *New York Herald,* 13 February 1863.
45. ORA s. 1, 13:217.
46. Hermann, 84.
47. ORN s. 1, 13:735.
48. ORA s. 1, 14:635.
49. *Savannah Republican,* 2 February 1863.
50. Hermann, 84.
51. Durham, 130–32; RBD, 1 February 1863.
52. Durham, 132.
53. Ibid., 133.
54. ORN s. 1, 13:637.
55. Milton F. Perry, *Infernal Machines* (Baton Rouge: University of Louisiana Press, 1965), 37–38.
56. ORA s. 1, 14:757.
57. Ibid., 212.
58. Durham, 135.
59. Myers, 1027.
60. Durham, 136.
61. Ibid., 132.
62. The correspondent was James Roddey Sneed (1818–1891). A native of Richmond County, Georgia, he came to Savannah in 1855, where he entered a partnership and operated the *Savannah Republican* newspaper until Savannah fell in 1864. After the war he relocated to Macon where he was associated with the *Macon Telegraph* before returning to Savannah. In 1872 he moved to Atlanta and eventually to Washington, D.C. Sneed died in Chicago in 1891, and his remains returned to Savannah (Myers, 1681).
63. Peter E. Judenna served with the Blues through the war and was wounded by friendly fire in June 1864 near Pine Mountain. He was one of fourteen members of the Blues to surrender in North Carolina at the end of the war (RCS, 1:144).
64. *Savannah Republican,* 27 February 1863; Emmett Rifles, muster and payroll records, Collection 169, Box 9, Folder 48, Georgia Historical Society, Savannah, Ga.
65. ORN s. 1, 13:692.

Chapter 5. Tangled Machinery and Charred Relics

1. *Savannah Republican,* 2 March 1863.
2. Ibid., 17 and 21 February 1863.

3. ORN s. 1, 13:342, 768; *Savannah Republican,* 2 March 1863.

4. Browne, 46–47; Chance, Chance and Topper, 79; Hartridge, 30 July 1862.

5. *Savannah Republican,* 2 March 1863.

6. Myers, 1034.

7. William Morrison Robinson, *The Confederate Privateers* (New Haven, Conn.: Yale University Press, 1928), 131.

8. Browne, 48; Emmett Rifles, muster and payroll records.

9. Durham, 136–37.

10. Browne, 47–50.

11. Ibid., 50. Paymaster Browne speaks of witnessing the *Nashville* run aground about 4:00 P.M. on the afternoon of Friday 27 February, but Savannah newspapers indicate that the vessel ran aground about 4:00 A.M. on the morning of 27 February. Which is correct? One might expect the Savannah newspapers to have had access to correct information, and it must be remembered that Browne wrote his account twenty years later, possibly getting the A.M. and P.M. confused. 1st Lt. Dixon states that the vessel ran aground opposite the battery "today." There is nothing in his journal that would shed any light on exactly when the grounding occurred. Depending on the tides, if the vessel grounded at 4:00 A.M., then by 4:00 P.M. the tides would have been right for an attempt to free the ship. The steam tug *Columbus* is known to have been operating in the Ogeechee and was used to try to free the *Nashville.* The movements Browne witnessed were probably those of the *Columbus* made during this attempt.

12. ORN s. 1, 13:697.

13. Browne, 51, 52, 54.

14. Durham, 137–38.

15. Osbon, *Harpers Weekly,* 2 March and 28 March 1863.

16. Ibid.

17. Durham, 137–38.

18. ORN s. 1, 13:698.

19. Durham, 137–38.

20. Browne, 55–57.

21. ORN s. 1, 13:700–701.

22. Ibid.

23. Ibid., 701.

24. Browne, 57–58.

25. ORN s. 1, 13:701–2.

26. USS *Montauk,* logbook, 28 February1863.

27. ORN s. 1, 13:702.

28. Ibid., 709.

29. Ibid., 708.

30. Durham, 137–38.

31. William Patrick Hunt, a native of New York, was twenty-eight in 1862 and formerly employed as a caulker (CCC-60:84).

32. Daniel Clancy was a native of Clare, Ireland, twenty-three in 1862, and formerly employed as a laborer (CCC-60:327).

33. Durham, 137–38.

34. Ibid., 138.

35. Hayes, 2:458–60.

36. Myers, 1034.

Chapter 6. A Terrible Storm of Iron

1. ORN s. 1, 13:692.
2. Ibid., 694.
3. Durham, 139.
4. ORN s. 1, 13:692, 695; Hayes, 2:472.
5. ORN s. 1, 13:692, 695; Hayes, 2:472.
6. USS *Wissahickon,* logbook, 28 February 1863 and 1 March 1863; Hill, 132–33.
7. Ibid.
8. ORN s. 1, 13:727; Jones, *Historical Sketch of Chatham Artillery,* 126.
9. ORN s. 1, 13:727. This pilot would have been from the Emmett Rifles, as the Blues Daybook records no deserters or AWOLs from that unit in this time frame. This was not the pilot Murphy to whom Capt. Worden referred in earlier reports.
10. No information has been found relating to Stoughton Hayman and J. C. Proctor. Wyatt Harper, thirty-one in 1863, resided in Savannah with his wife and daughter and was a carpenter before the war (CCC-60:168). Brittain Cobb was thirty-nine in 1863, resided in Bryan County, and was a farmer before the war. He became a lieutenant in Company B of the Hardwick Mounted Rifles when it reorganized (BCC-60:1).
11. Elijah A. Ellarbee was thirty-five in 1863, a resident of Bryan County, and a merchant before the war (BCC-60:20).
12. *Savannah Republican,* 11 March 1863.
13. ORN s. 1, 13:719; USS *Seneca,* logbook, 2 March 1863.
14. ORN s. 1, 13:720–24; Hill, 132.
15. RBD, 3 March 1863.
16. Robert J. Smith, a twenty-nine-year-old native of Ireland, was a corporal but reduced to the ranks for disobedience of orders (CCC-60, 347; RCS 1:140; RBD).
17. James Madison Theus, a native of Beaufort, South Carolina, was twenty-eight in 1863 and formerly employed as a blacksmith. He enlisted with the Blues in April 1861, rising to the rank of second lieutenant. He was wounded in the arms on 22 July 1864 at the Battle of Atlanta and sent to Savannah to recover. He returned to duty 19 January 1865 and was paroled 18 May 1865 at Thomasville, Georgia (CCC-60:54; RCS 1:148; RBD).
18. William S. Rockwell Jr., a native of Savannah, was nineteen in 1863. His father, Col. William S. Rockwell, was a Savannah attorney and served as executive officer of the 1st Regiment Georgia Infantry. In May 1861 William Jr. enlisted as a private in Company B, 8th Regiment Georgia Volunteer Infantry, the Oglethorpe Light Infantry. In February 1862 he was elected second lieutenant of Company F, 22nd Battalion Georgia Artillery (Emmett Rifles). He was captured at Fort McAllister on 13 December 1864 and imprisoned at Hilton Head, South Carolina, Old Capitol Prison, Washington, D.C., and Fort Delaware, Delaware. He was released on 17 June 1863 (CCC-60:32; RCS 1:195).
19. Jones, *Historical Sketch of Chatham Artillery,* 134. Durham, 139–43, 146–47; Emmett Rifles, muster and payroll. Sylvester McGrath enlisted in the Blues in April 1861 and served with them throughout the war. In Savannah when Gen. Sherman took the city, McGrath is recorded as having deserted at that time (RCS 1:146; RBD).

John H. O'Bryne, a native of Savannah, was twenty-five in 1863 and formerly employed as a grocery store clerk. After enlisting in the Blues in April 1861, he served with them until he transferred sometime after October 1863 to Company B, 1st Regiment Georgia Infantry. He was wounded on 15 August 1864, deserted on 7 March 1865, and returned to Savannah after the war and was employed there as a grocer in 1870 (CCC-60:281; CCC-70; RCS 1:146; RBD).

20. *New York Herald* 28 March 1863; Osbon, *Harpers Weekly,* 28 March 1863.

21. ORN s. 1, 13:721–24; Jones, *Historical Sketch of Chatham Artillery,* 129.

22. Jones, *Historical Sketch of Chatham Artillery,* 126–27.

23. ORN s. 1, 13:727.

24. Osbon, *New York Herald,* 28 March 1863; Osbon, *Harpers Weekly,* 28 March 1863.

25. *Savannah Republican,* 6 March 1863.

26. ORN s. 1, 13:726–27.

27. Ibid., 718.

28. Durham, 139–43.

29. ORN s 1, 13:720–21.

30. Ibid., 722.

31. Ibid., 721.

32. Osbon, *New York Herald,* 28 March 1863; Osbon, *Harpers Weekly* 28 March 1863.

33. Jones, *Historical Sketch of Chatham Artillery,* 132–33.

34. Osbon, *New York Herald;* 28 March 1863; Osbon, *Harpers Weekly,* 28 March 1863.

35. ORA s. 1, 14:220. Jones, 132–33.

36. Durham, 139–43.

37. RBD, 3 March 1863.

38. Jones, *Historical Sketch of Chatham Artillery,* 130; Emmett Rifles, muster and payroll records.

39. Jones, *Historical Sketch of Chatham Artillery,*133.

40. Durham, 139–43.

41. *Savannah Republican,* 11 March 1863.

42. Durham, 139–43.

43. Jones, *Historical Sketch of Chatham Artillery,*133.

44. Ash, Robert Epps, "Born to Lose," *Savannah Morning Press, Sunday Magazine,* 11 January 1959, 5.

45. ORA s. 1, 14:221.

46. Osbon, *New York Herald,* 28 March 1863; Osbon, *Harpers Weekly,* 28 March 1863.

47. Jones, *Historical Sketch of Chatham Artillery,* 131–32.

48. Osbon, *New York Herald,* 28 March 1863; Osbon, *Harpers Weekly,* 28 March 1863.

49. Jones, *Historical Sketch of Chatham Artillery,* 131–32.

50. ORN s. 1, 13:720, 721, 729, 731.

51. Osbon, *New York Herald,* 28 March 1863; Osbon, *Harpers Weekly,* 28 March 1863.

52. ORA s.1, 14:220.

53. ORN s. 1, 13:727.

54. Ibid., 720.

55. Ibid., 718.

56. Ibid., 720.

57. Ibid., 727.

58. ORA s. 1, 14:221.

59. ORN s. 1, 13:717.

60. *Savannah Republican,* 6 March 1863; Jones, *Historical Sketch of Chatham Artillery,* 132.

61. ORA s, 1, 6:223; Jones, *Historical Sketch of Chatham Artillery,* 132.

62. *Savannah Republican,* 11 March 1863.

63. Ibid.

64. Durham, 139–43.

65. ORN s. 1, 13:719, 720, 728.

66. Ibid., 718, 719, 717, 718, 727.

67. Ibid., 727.

68. Durham, 139–43.

69. ORA s. 1, 14:221–2.

70. *Savannah Republican,* 3 March 1863; Durham, 146.

71. ORA s. 1, 14:222.

72. Jones, *Historical Sketch of Chatham Artillery,* 132; *Savannah Republican,* 6 March 1863. Mims was a member of Company D, 1st Battalion Georgia Sharpshooters (*Savannah Republican,* 11 March 1863).

73. ORN s. 1, 13:720.

74. Durham, 143–44; ORN s. 1, 13:720.

75. RBD, 4 March 1863.

76. ORA s. 1, 14:220.

77. Ibid., 219.

78. Durham, 145–46. RBD, 7 March 1863.

79. RBD, 9 March 1863.

80. USS *Dawn,* logbook, 4 March to 6 March 1863; USS *Seneca,* logbook, 4 March to 6 March 1863; Charles W. Waage, "Ossabaw Island, Ga. A Chapter from the Experiences of the 47th N.Y.," *National Tribune,* 25 July 1907.

81. Durham, 146–47.

82. USS *Dawn,* logbook, 2 April 1863.

Chapter 7: Lessons Lost and Lessons Learned

1. ORN series 1, 13:672–73.

2. Ibid., 14:427.

3. Ibid., 13:716.

4. Du Pont to his wife, 4 March 1863, W9–2822; Hayes, 2:467. Gustavus Fox was assistant secretary of the navy.

5. Ibid.

6. Du Pont to William W. McKean, April 1863; Hayes, 3:66.

7. Du Pont to James S. Biddle, 25 March 1863, W9–2836, Hagley Museum and Library, Wilmington, Delaware; Hayes, 2:510.

8. Du Pont to his wife, 1 March 1863, W9–2819; Hayes, 2:453.

9. Rodgers, 4:37–39.

10. Ibid., 325.

11. Ibid., 10.

12. Ibid.

13. Ibid., 4:45.

14. Jones, *Historical Sketch of Chatham Artillery,* 54–55.

15. John McCrady to his father, 3 November 1864, transcript in collection of Fort McAllister State Historic Park, Georgia.

Chapter 8. A Post of Honor

1. RBD, 20 March 1863.

2. ORA s. 1, 53:290.

3. Durham, 154; RBD, 12 April 1863.

4. Durham, 155.

5. Ibid.

6. Ibid.

7. Ibid. J. J. Newsome enlisted 18 March 1861 in the Washington Rifles, Company E, 1st Regiment, Georgia Infantry, and was mustered out 18 March 1862 at Augusta, Georgia. On 1 May 1862, he was elected first lieutenant of the 3rd Company B, 12th Battalion, Georgia Light Artillery, and promoted 17 May 1863 to corporal (RCS, 1:262).

8. Durham, 155; RBD, 18 and 20 April 1863.

9. RBD, 18 and 20 April 1863.

10. Durham, 155.

11. Ibid., 156.

12. RBD, 4 May 1863.

13. Durham, 157.

14. Ibid.; RBD, 7 May 1863.

15. Order Book, Special Order No. 2, 4 July 1864, Fort McAllister, Georgia, photocopy, archives, Fort McAllister State Historical Park.

16. Engineer manual. Photocopied pages from the manual were provided in 1980 to Fort McAllister State Historic Park by Scott Smith, director, Coastal Heritage Society. The manual outlines duties and procedures for maintaining and garrisoning earthwork fortifications.

17. Ibid.

18. Ibid.

19. Durham, 126, 153, 163, 206, 211; Order Book, Special Order No. 2, 4 July 1864. In her 1866 reminiscences of the war, "War Memories," William Dixon's sister Mary Ann Dixon Drummond said, "My Brother, Capt. Dixon, had been in command of Fort McAllister so long that he had a small farm down there. When he was ordered to the front, he sent all of his live stock to us." The original is in the possession of her great granddaughter Mrs. Charles Youngblood Jr.; a copy is in Alexander Lawrence Papers, Georgia Historical Society, Savannah.

20. Durham, 158. Charles William Rogers Jr. was the son of Rev. Charles William Rogers, a Presbyterian clergyman and wealthy planter who resided in Savannah but kept the plantation at Kilkenny as a summer home. The son maintained Cottonham

Plantation to the north of Kilkenny. When the elder Rogers died in Savannah on 9 May 1861, the son inherited the Kilkenny house (Myers, 1662).

21. Durham, 163.

22. Ibid.

23. Ibid., 205.

24. Ibid., 171–72.

25. Ibid., 172.

26. Ibid, 173. James Barbour and Anthony Robider had served with Dixon's gun crew on the 8-inch Columbiad during the naval bombardments of Fort McAllister.

27. Durham, 171–72.

28. Ibid., 183.

29. RBD, 31 October 1863.

30. Durham, 183–84; RBD, 3 November 1863.

31. Durham, 184; RBD, 14 November 1863.

32. Anna Patterson was twenty-one in 1863 and the oldest child of William Patterson of Bryan County, Georgia. Their plantation was located on the Ogeechee River, just west of Fort McAllister (BCC-60:2). The woman who accompanied Anna Patterson was probably Martha Rowland, who was sixty-one in 1863 and the mother of William Henry Rowland, who was serving with the Blues at Fort McAllister (CCC-60:325; RCS 1:147; RBD).

33. Dr. Harris was either Dr. Raymond Harris, a native of Liberty County, Georgia, who also resided in Savannah, or Dr. Juriah Harriss, a native of Columbia County, Georgia, who was a faculty member of the Savannah Medical College at this time (Myers, 1545).

34. Maj. Hartridge was Alfred Hartridge, former commander of Fort McAllister, who was at this time in command of the defenses of Rosedew Island, across the rivers and marshes to the north of Fort McAllister.

35. Capt. Anderson who accompanied Maj. Hartridge may have been John W. Anderson, former commander of the Blues.

36. Durham, 184; RBD, 17 November 1863.

37. Durham, 186.

38. Miss Turner is probably Sally D. Turner, who was twenty-one in 1863 and was the daughter of L. T. Turner, who was forty in 1863 and a physician in lower Bryan County, Georgia (BCC-60:3). Miss White was probably Mary A. White, who was twenty-five in 1863 and resided in lower Bryan County with her mother and father, Paul White, who was a slave catcher (BCC-60:5). For biographical information on Brittain Cobb, see note 10, chapter 6. Raymond M. Demere (pronounced *Dem*-aree) was a native of Bryan County, Georgia, twenty-one in 1863, and formerly employed in Savannah as a commission house clerk. He enlisted in the Hardwick Mounted Rifles and at this time was third lieutenant of Company A of the Hardwick Mounted Rifles (CCC-60:97).

39. Durham, 186.

40. Durham, 187; RBD, 23 November 1863; RCS 6:406.

41. Durham, 189.

42. Edward J. Purse, a former member of the Blues, was a native of Charleston, South Carolina, age forty-six, and employed as a printer and dealer in stationery. He served in the Blues with his two sons, Benjamin and William, but he did not pursue

further military service after his term expired in March 1862. However, he did not forget his former comrades and his two sons at Fort McAllister on Christmas of 1863 (CCC-60:305; RCS 1:136; RBD).

43. Durham, 191.

44. William W. Gordon (1834–1912) was a native of Savannah and graduate of Yale University, became a commission merchant in Savannah. He served as a company commander in the 1st Regiment, Georgia Infantry, during the war and resumed his commission business after the war, served in state house of representatives, and was president of the Georgia Central Railroad and Banking Co. During the Spanish-American War, he served as a brigadier general in the U.S. Army. He died at White Sulphur Springs, Virginia, in September 1912 and is buried in Laurel Grove Cemetery (Myers, 1531).

45. Durham, 191–92.

46. Ibid., 192. Thomas C. Arnold (1836–1875) was born at Whitehall, his father's plantation, three miles west of the fort. His father was a native of Rhode Island. Thomas attended Brown University but did not graduate. When the war came, he and his brother stayed in Georgia, and his parents moved to Rhode Island. He served briefly in the Confederate States Army and was captured at Fort McAllister 13 December 1864. Thomas died at Whitehall in December 1875 and is buried in Laurel Grove Cemetery (Myers, 1455; RBD, 1 January 1864).

47. Durham, 193–94.

48. Dixon's journal and the Daybook contradict each other about the identity of one man who deserted. Dixon's journal says "[Lawrence J.] Connell" was in the group of deserters. The Daybook says he was "P[atrick] Carliss," not "Connell." There could have been confusion because of the similarities of the names. Apparently Patrick Carliss, Lawrence J. Connell, and Livingston J. Cornell were all at Fort McAllister at this time. The men who deserted on the night of 15 January 1864 are:

—Cpl. Simon Jackson. He was a native of Prussia, twenty-eight in 1863, and a former clothing-store clerk. He enlisted with the Blues in April 1861 and served with them until he deserted at Fort McAllister (CCC-60:45; RCS 1:144; RBD).

—Pvt. Patrick Carliss (or Carlos). A native of Roscommon, Ireland, Carliss was thirty-five in 1863.He served with several units before enlisting with the Blues and being discharged the same day as the records indicate he provided Morris Cohen as a substitute. The daybook shows Cohen as having enlisted at Fort Jackson on 11 June 1862. Apparently, Carliss was called back to service when the conscript law went into effect, and those who had furnished substitutes had to report to their units or face the draft. When he deserted, he left a wife and three daughters in Savannah, Georgia (CCC-60:50; RCS 1:140; RBD).

—Pvt. Isadore C. Cohen (also Israel). A native of Prussia, Cohen was twenty-seven in 1863 and a former clerk in a dry-goods store. Records indicate he was a private with the Blues on 20 August 1861, reenlisted March 1862 at Fort Jackson, Savannah, Georgia, and was carried as present at Fort McAllister on the 1 September and 31 December 1863 muster rolls (CC-60:67; RCS 1:141; RBD).

—Pvt. Isaac S. Davidson. He was twenty-four in 1863 and a former cigar maker. Davidson enlisted in march 1862 with the Blues and was present at Fort

McAllister on the 1 September and 31 December 1863 muster rolls (CCC-60:181; RCS 1:142; RBD).

—Pvt. James Dunbar. He enlisted in March 1862 with the Blues and is shown present at Fort McAllister on the 1 September 1863 muster roll (RCS 1:142; RBD).

—Pvt. Raiford Jackson. He enlisted in August 1861 with the Blues and is noted as present at Fort McAllister on the 1 September and 31 December 1863 muster rolls (RCS 1:144; RBD).

—Pvt. William Jeffers. See chapter 2, note 71.

—Pvt. Aaron Mitchell. A native of Prussia, Mitchell, a former clothing-store clerk, was twenty-four in 1863. He enlisted with the Blues in April 1861 and served with them until he deserted from Fort McAllister. He returned to Savannah after the war and in 1870 was a farm laborer (CCC-60:181; CCC-70; RCS 1:146; RBD).

49. Durham, 193–94.

50. RBD, 16 January 1864.

51. RBD, 23 January 1864.

52. RBD, 26 January 1864; Durham, 194.

53. RBD, 28 January 1864; RCS 6:425.

54. RBD, 29 January 1864.

55. William H. Harden to his wife, 28 January 1864, "The Collected Civil War Correspondence of William Harmon Harden, Corporal, 63rd Infantry Regiment, Georgia Volunteers, C.S.A., January 30, 1845 to August 28, 1895," Collection 462, Manuscript, Archives, and Rare Book Library, Emory University, Decatur, Georgia.

56. Ibid., 31 January 1864.

57. Ibid., 8 February 1864.

58. James S. Williams, a native of Savannah, was 52 in 1864 and had been a civil engineer (CCC-60:400).

59. James S. Williams, Report of Inspection, 18 February 1864, records group 109, item F-76, National Archives, Washington, D.C.

60. Ibid.

61. Ibid.

62. Ibid.

63. Durham, 198.

64. Ibid., 200.

65. Harden, 10 March 1864.

66. RBD, 6 April 1864.

67. Durham, 205; RBD, 11 April 1864. Miss Theus was Ann Caroline Theus, who later became the wife of Capt. William D. Dixon. Miss Miscally was Sarah Miscally, who would marry Blues member James M. Theus, brother of Ann Caroline Theus. Mrs. Calvert is Ellen Calvert of Savannah.

68. Durham, 206. Jane E. Ferguson was the sister of Dougald Ferguson, a friend and business partner of William Dixon. Ferguson had served in the Republican Blues with Dixon but had transferred to Company I, 5th Georgia Cavalry. Miss Posey was Jane H. Posey, who boarded at the Ferguson house in Savannah. Miss White was Mary A. White, who resided in lower Bryan County with her mother and father (see also chapter 8, note 38).

69. Durham, 207.

70. RBD, 25 April 1864.

71. Durham, 207.

72. Jeremy Francis Gilmer (1818 to 1883) was a native of North Carolina, a graduate of the U.S. Military Academy, worked as an engineer on projects at New York City and Washington, D.C., and served in the Mexican War as chief engineer for the Army of the West. Sent to Savannah, he supervised construction on Fort Jackson and Fort Pulaski. He was in California when the Civil War came, resigned his commission, and entered Confederate service as a lieutenant colonel, serving in engineer duties. Appointed chief of Confederate Engineer Corps, he was assigned in August 1863 to the Department of South Carolina, Georgia, and Florida and served around Charleston and Atlanta before being sent to Virginia. After the war he returned to Savannah and served as president and engineer of the Savannah Gas and Light Company and as a director of the Georgia Central Railroad and Banking Company. Gilmer died in Savannah in December 1883 and is buried in Laurel Grove Cemetery. (Myers, 1529–30).

73. Durham, 207.

74. RBD, 25 April 1864.

75. RBD, 27 April 1864.

76. RBD, 30 April 1864.

77. Ibid.

78. Ibid., 5 May 1864.

79. Ibid., 18 May 1864.

80. Emanuel Williams, who was thirty-two in 1864, was a native of Madeira, Spain, and a former deputy lighthouse keeper (CCC-60:399).

81. Stephen Phillips was probably William S. Phillips, who was thirty-six in 1864 and a farmer in Effingham County, married with a young son (CCC-60:298).

82. Carl Hanson, a member of the Emmett Rifles, performed noble service during the naval bombardments of the fort, risking his life to pass through incoming artillery fire in order to obtain a replacement traverse wheel for a damaged gun carriage. He rolled the wheel back through the heavy artillery fire, taking it to the damaged gun, which was repaired and put back into service. Jones, *Historical Sketch of Chatham Artillery,* 130.

83. RBD, 23 May 1864.

84. Durham, 213; RBD, 25 May 1864.

85. Durham, 213.

86. Ibid.; RBD, 26 May 1864.

87. Order Book, Special Order 136, 24 June 1864, Headquarters Military District of Georgia; Special Order 2, 4 July 1864, Fort McAllister; Special Order 199, 29 August 1864, Headquarters Military District of Georgia; Special Order 211, 12 September 1864, and Special Order 212, 12 September 1864, Headquarters Military District of Georgia.

88. CCC-60, 364.

89. 1st (Symons) Regiment, Infantry Reserves, records, microfilm drawer 254, boxes 94 and 95, Georgia Department of Archives and History, Atlanta, Georgia.

90. Edith Clarke Barrows and Mary Oakley McRory, *History of Jefferson County, Florida* (Monticello, Florida, Kiwanis Club, 1935), 79–80.

91. Ibid.; Special Order 220, paragraph 23, 23 September 1864, Headquarters Savannah. Photocopy. Archives, Fort McAllister State Historic Park.

92. Agnew and Lee, 94.

Chapter 9: A Time of Reckoning

1. Lt. Col. William Strong to Gen. Sherman, 30 December 1864, Report on Operations of U.S. Army of the Tennessee, Sherman Papers, Library of Congress, Washington, D.C.

2. John McCrady to Charles C. Jones Jr., 1 October 1874, transcript, Archives, Fort McAllister State Historic Park, Georgia.

3. ORN s. 2, 1:320.

4. ORN, s. 1, 13:622 and s. 2, 1:283.

5. ORN, s. 1, 14:427 and 15:18–22.

6. Ibid.

7. ORN, s. 1, 15:334–35.

8. ORA s. 1, 44:880.

9. Ibid., 885.

10. Charles C. Jones Jr., *Historical Sketch of Chatham Artillery,* 138.

11. Order Book, Special Order 247, 20 October 1864, Headquarters Military District of Georgia. Nicholas Barnard Clinch, a native of Louisiana, was 32 in 1864 and was a planter before the war (CCC-60:66).

12. Jones, *The Siege of Savannah in December 1864 and the Confederate Operations in Georgia and the Third Military District of South Carolina during General Sherman's March from Atlanta to the Sea* (Albany, N.Y.: Joel Munsell, 1874), 128.

13. Emmett Rifles, muster and payroll records.

14. Jones, *Historical Sketch of Chatham Artillery,* 139.

15. Ibid., 142. An outer trench work across the rear of the fort may have been the remnant of an earlier rear defense. This exterior trench work is documented in period photographs. It is doubtful the outer trench across the rear was part of the preparations for the final defense because it would be too long to be defended and too easily overrun by an attacking force. Also, the torpedoes were located directly in the rear of this trench so it makes little sense to place defenders in advance of the torpedo line.

16. Order Book, Special Order 2, 12 November 1864, Headquarters Savannah.

17. A number of bases, or culottes, from 10-inch mortar shells have been recovered from the Fort McAllister area, which lends validity to historic accounts that identify 10-inch shells as having been utilized as torpedoes, and the ammunition from the fort's mortar magazine would have been used.

18. Jones, *Siege of Savannah,* 139, 140, 142; G. Arthur Gordon to Henry Ford, 23 February 1938, Henry Ford Library, Dearborn, Mich. Gordon says Anderson told him that railroad rails were used, which seems unusual; however, a Cooley photograph of the signal station on the fort's wall clearly shows a railroad rail propped up adjacent to the tent.

19. Jones, *Siege of Savannah,* 126.

20. Order Book, John K. Jackson, 21 November 1864, Military HQ Savannah; ORA s. 1, 44:61; Lloyd Lewis, *Sherman—Fighting Prophet* (New York: Harcourt, Brace, 1932), 461; and Henry Hitchcock, *Marching to the Sea with Sherman* (New Haven, Conn.: Yale University Press, 1927), 161–62.

21. Jones, *Siege of Savannah,* 140.

22. Ibid.

23. ORA, s. 1, 44:61.

24. George W. Pepper, *Personal Recollections of Sherman's Campaign in Georgia and the Carolinas* (Zanesville, Ohio: Hugh Dunn, 1866), 259.

25. ORN s. 1, 16:127; ORA s. 1, 44:61; William Duncan, service records, National Archives, Washington, D.C.

26. Strong Report.

27. Ibid.

28. Oliver O. Howard, "General Howard's Memoirs," *National Tribune,* 30 January 1896.

29. Ibid.

30. ORN s. 1, 16:122.

31. Ibid., 127; Strong Report.

32. Myron J. Amick, service and pension records, National Archives, Washington, D.C.

33. George W. Quinn, service and pension records, National Archives, Washington, D.C.

34. Pepper, 257.

35. Strong Report.

36. Pepper, 257–58.

37. Ibid.

38. Strong Report.

39. ORA s. 1, 44:77.

40. Lewis, 463.

41. Ibid.; Jones, *Siege of Savannah,* 117; William B. Hazen, "General Hazen's Memoirs," *National Tribune,* 29 October 1914; George Ward Nichols, *The Story of the Great March: From the Diary of a Staff Officer* (New York: Harper & Brothers, 1866), 92.

42. Pepper, 258.

43. Ibid.

44. USS *Flag,* logbook, 10–11 December 1864, National Archives, Washington, D.C.

45. Pepper, 258–59.

46. USS *Flag,* logbook, 11 December 1864; USS *Dandelion,* logbook, 12 December 1864, National Archives, Washington, D.C.; William Duncan, service records, National Archives, Washington, D.C.

47. Strong Report.

48. William H. Pittenger, diary, 12 December 1864 entry, Manuscript Collection, vol. 395, Ohio Historical Society, Columbus, Ohio.

49. Howard.

50. Ibid.

51. Ibid.

52. ORA s. 1, 44:61.

53. Ibid., 367; Jones, *Siege of Savannah,* 140–41.

54. Ibid.

55. ORA s. 1, 44:103, 367, 368, 706.

56. Ibid., 367.

57. Ada Warnell to J. R. Gregory, 13 December 1939, Henry Ford Library, Dearborn, Michigan; Julia King to Henry Ford, 3 September 1926, Henry Ford Library, Dearborn, Michigan; USS *Fernandina,* logbook, 12–13 December 1864, National Archives, Washington, D.C.; ORA, s. 1, 44:709.

58. Edward W. Wyatt to Henry Ford, 5 May 1925, Henry Ford Library, Dearborn, Mich.

59. ORA s. 1, 44:72, 103.

60. Jones, *Siege of Savannah,* 141.

61. Barrows, 79–80.

62. USS *Flag,* logbook, 12 December 1864.

63. ORA s. 1, 44:751.

64. Ibid.

65. USS *Flag,* logbook, 12 December 1864.

66. Howard, *National Tribune,* 30 January 1896. Atlas to accompany the *Official Record of the Union and Confederate Armies in the War of the Rebellion,* plate 69, no. 4.

67. William T. Sherman, *Official Account of His Great March through Georgia and the Carolinas* (New York: Bunce and Huntington, 1865), 196; Nichols, 92.

68. John M. Groce, service records, National Archives, Washington, D.C.

69. Ibid.; Charles G. Will, *Captain John Groce,* unpublished biography, private collection, Karl R. Eby.

70. James Horner, service and pension records, National Archives, Washington, D.C.

71. Lyman Hardman, service and pension records, National Archives, Washington, D.C.

72. Abner B. Smith, service and pension records, National Archives, Washington, D.C.

73. Stephen F. Grimes, service and pension records, National Archives, Washington, D.C.

74. Ibid.

75. Ibid.

76. Charles Bateman, service and pension records, National Archives, Washington, D.C.

77. Ibid.

78. Sherman, *Official Account,* 196.

79. Ibid.

Chapter 10. A Perfect Chaos

1. ORA s. 1, 44:396–99.

2. Sherman, *Official Account,* 196–97.

3. Nichols, 90.

4. Strong Report.

5. Hazen.

6. ORA s. 1, 44:97.

7. George W. Anderson Jr., "General Outline of the Fall of Fort McAllister," Anderson Papers, Georgia Historical Society, Savannah, Ga.; Strong Report.

8. Ibid.

9. Anderson Report.

10. Hazen.

11. ORA s. 1, 44:110.

12. Ibid.

13. Joseph A. Saunier, *History of the 47th Ohio Volunteer Infantry* (Hillsboro, Ohio: Press of the Lyle Printing, 1903), 363.

14. ORA s. 1, 44:97.

15. Gordon.

16. 1st (Symons) Regiment.

17. Saunier, 363.

18. Ibid., 367.

19. Jones, *Siege of Savannah,* 142.

20. Barrows and McRory, 79–80.

21. Ibid., 122.

22. Sherman, *Official Account,* 199.

23. Saunier, 366.

24. Ibid.

25. ORA s. 1, 44:398–99.

26. Ibid., 709; USS *Fernandina,* logbook, 12 December 1864.

27. ORA s. 1, 44:398–99. USS *Fernandina,* logbook, 13 December 1864.

28. ORA s.1, 44:705–6.

29. Sherman, *Official Account,* 197.

30. William R. Scaife, *The March to the Sea* (Atlanta: Washington Printing, 1989), 77–78. Strong Report.

31. USS *Dandelion,* logbook, 13 December 1864.

32. According to the *Dandelion'*s logbook, this was Rockfish Creek; however, chart analysis indicates that Fisher was probably in Harvey's Cut.

33. ORA s. 1, 44:751–52.

34. USS *Dandelion,* logbook, 13 December 1864.

35. ORA s.1, 44:751–52.

36. Ibid., 114–15; Wells S. Jones, service records, National Archives, Washington, D.C.

37. ORA s. 1, 44:115.

38. Strong Report.

39. Sherman, *Official Account,* 197.

40. ORA s.1, 44:752.

41. Strong Report; ORA s. 1, 44:751–52.

42. Hazen.

43. Nichols, 89–90.

44. ORA s.1, 44:752; Nichols, 89–90.

45. Sherman, *Official Account,* 197.

46. Strong Report.

47. Nichols, 90.

48. Sherman, *Official Account,* 197.

49. Yerby Davies, service records, National Archives, Washington, D.C.

50. Yerby Davies, letter to *National Tribune,* 20 February 1913.

51. John Compton, service and pension records, National Archives, Washington, D.C.

52. Strong Report.
53. Hazen.
54. Saunier, 364.
55. Strong Report.
56. Nichols, 90.
57. Lewis, 462.
58. Nichols, 90.
59. Lewis, 462.
60. Strong Report.
61. James S. Horner, letter to the *National Tribune,* 11 July 1907.
62. Hardman, service and pension records.
63. Lyman Hardman, diary entry, 14 December 1864, Hardman Papers, Western Reserve Historical Society, Cleveland, Ohio.
64. Charles C. Degman, letter to the *National Tribune,* 20 June 1907.
65. Davies, letter.
66. Strong Report.
67. Saunier, 365.
68. Ibid., ORA s. 1, 44:97.
69. Thomas T. Taylor, diary entry, 13 December 1864, Taylor Papers, Ohio Historical Society, Columbus, Ohio; S. P. Bonner to Mrs. Taylor, 15 December 1864, Maj. Taylor's service records, National Archives, Washington, D.C.
70. Strong Report.
71. Davies, *National Tribune.*
72. Degman, *National Tribune.*
73. ORA s. 1, 44:122.
74. Davies, *National Tribune.*
75. Gordon.
76. Hazen.
77. Jones, *Siege of Savannah,* 142.
78. 1st (Symons) Regiment.
79. Barrows and McRory, 79–80.
80. ORA s.1, 44:110.
81. *New York Herald,* 26 December 1864.
82. Saunier, 364.
83. Ibid., 372.
84. Strong Report.
85. Nichols, 90–91.
86. Nicholas Clinch, service records, microfilm, drawer 254, box 50, Georgia Department of Archives and History, Atlanta, Georgia; Strong Report; Jones, *Siege of Savannah,* 142; Pepper, 255. Accounts vary about the number and type of wounds Clinch received in the final assault on Fort McAllister. William P. Schirm was sent to the Old Capitol Prison in Washington, D.C., arriving on 2 February 1865. He was then sent to Fort Delaware, arriving on 8 February 1865, and was released on 5 June 1865 (Clinch's Battery, Microfilm, drawer 254, box 50, Georgia Department of Archives and History).
87. Strong Report.
88. Grimes.

89. Pepper, 255. Whether Clinch actually said this to Grimes is a matter of speculation, for the exchange sounds more like a romanticized version, if it happened at all.

90. Jones, *Siege of Savannah,* 142.

91. Scaife, 80. It is possible some of the saber wounds to Clinch's back were actually bayonet wounds, hence the discrepancy between the surgeon's report and Maj. Anderson's report. Clinch was treated at a field hospital and on 24 December 1864 sent aboard the U.S. hospital steamer *SR Spaulding.* He was admitted on 25 December 1864 to the U.S. General Hospital at Beaufort, South Carolina (Clinch).

92. Hazen.

93. ORA, s. 1, 44:115.

94. George E. Castle, service records, National Archives, Washington, D.C.

95. ORA s. 1, 44:122.

96. Ibid.

97. Ibid., 101; Saunier, 372.

98. Jones, *Siege of Savannah,* 142.

99. Strong Report.

100. ORA s. 1, 44:111.

101. Strong Report.

102. ORA s. 1, 44:111.

103. Strong Report.

104. Ibid.

105. Anderson Report.

106. *The Story of the 55th Regiment Illinois Volunteer Infantry in the Civil War* (Clinton, Mass.: Coulter, 1887), 398.

107. Saunier, 365.

108. Pittenger, diary entry, 13 December 1864.

109. Ibid., 14 December 1864.

Chapter 11. The Victors and the Vanquished

1. Lewis, 463.

2. Sherman, *Official Account,* 198.

3. Strong Report.

4. ORA s. 1, 44:753.

5. Ibid.

6. Sherman, *Official Account,* 198.

7. Strong Report.

8. Sherman, *Official Account,* 198.

9. Strong Report.

10. Sherman, *Official Account,* 198.

11. Strong Report.

12. Gordon.

13. Nichols, 92.

14. Sherman, *Official Account,* 199.

15. Howard.

16. Nichols, 91.

17. ORA s.1, 44:61.

18. Sherman, *Official Account,* 199–202.

19. ORA s.1, 44:753.

20. Sherman, *Official Account,* 199.

21. ORA s.1, 44:753.

22. Sherman, *Official Account,* 199.

23. ORA s.1, 44:753.

24. Sherman, *Official Account,* 200.

25. ORA s.1, 44:753.

26. Sherman, *Official Account,* 201. Hazen moved his headquarters from the Middleton House to the McAllister overseer's house closer to the fort.

27. ORA s. 1, 44:955.

28. Ibid., 753.

29. This vessel was actually the Revenue Cutter USS *Nemaha.* Sherman relates in his memoirs that it was the *W. W. Coit,* which is incorrect.

30. Sherman, *Official Account,* 202.

31. The hat is in the collection of the U.S. Army Heritage Museum's Massachusetts Military Order of the Loyal Legion of the United States (MOLLUS) collection. Provenance was provided by Browne's nephew, James Browne Gardner.

32. Sherman, *Official Account,* 202.

33. ORA s.1, 44:754.

34. ORA s. 1, 44:97.

35. Will; Wells S. Jones, service and pension records, National Archives, Washington, D.C.

36. Bateman.

37. Hardman, diary entry, 14 December 1864.

38. Barrows and McRory, 79–80. Moore says that Sherman made his headquarters at the McAllister homestead but actually Hazen did. Sherman did use it briefly.

39. ORA s. 1, 44:711.

40. Saunier, 372–73.

41. Lewis, 462.

42. Gordon.

43. Lewis, 462.

44. Jones, *Siege of Savannah,* 142.

45. Lewis, 462.

46. Ibid.

47. Ibid.

48. Hitchcock, 192.

49. Ibid.

50. Nichols, 92.

51. Ibid.

52. Lewis, 465.

53. Ibid.

54. Ibid.

55. Ibid.

56. Taylor, service and pension records, National Archives, Washington, D.C.; Taylor, diary entry, 14 December 1864.

57. Thomas T. Taylor to his wife, 20 December 1864, Taylor Papers.

58. ORA s. 1, 44:13, 62, 63, 717.

59. Ibid.

60. Ibid., 61.

61. Lewis, 467.

62. Ibid.

63. Ibid.

64. Sherman, *Official Account,* 203–4.

65. Lewis, 408; Sherman, *Official Account,* 205.

66. William C. Davis, *The Image of War* (Garden City, N.Y.: Doubleday, 1966), 2:86–87.

67. ORA s.1, 44:717.

68. The 32-pound rifle was probably moved to Sherman's line. This supposition is supported by archeological evidence in the 1969 recovery of twenty unfired 6.4-inch Mullane shells from Federal positions opposite Confederate positions at Piney Point Battery and Battery Jones.

69. This is based on the author's analysis of photographs and tide tables for the Ossabaw Sound area in 1864.

70. J. B. Kilbourne to the *National Tribune,* 24 May 1883.

71. ORA s.1, 44:757–58.

72. Saunier, 373; ORA s. 1, 44:79, 141. On 23 December 1864, Confederate prisoners held near Fort McAllister were sent aboard the steamer *Ashland* for transportation to Hilton Head, South Carolina. The wounded were cared for at hospitals in Beaufort, South Carolina, the remainder sent to prisons in the north, primarily at Fort Delaware.

73. Barrows and McRory, 79–80.

74. Ibid.

75. ORA s.1, 44:757–58.

76. Williamson D. Ward, diary entry, 21 December 1864, Indiana Historical Library, Indianapolis, Indiana.

77. Mills B. Lane, *War Is Hell* (Savannah, Ga.: Beehive, 1974), 177.

78. Ibid., 178.

79. Ibid., 178–81.

80. ORA s. 1, 44:97.

81. *Story of the 55th Regiment Illinois Volunteer Infantry,* 400.

82. Ibid.

Chapter 12: A Final Analysis

1. Lane, *War Is Hell,* 142.

2. Strong Report.

3. Ibid.

4. Jones, *Siege of Savannah,* 7.

5. N. C. Hughes Jr., "Sherman at Savannah," *Georgia Historical Quarterly,* 47 (March 1963), 60.

6. Myers, 877.

7. Edward W. Wyatt to Henry Ford, 5 May 1925 and 31 August 1925, Henry Ford Library, Dearborn, Mich.

8. Ibid., 5 May 1925 and 20 July 1925.

9. Will; Karl R. Eby to author, 5 May 1983 and 23 June 1983; Wells S. Jones.

10. Taylor, service and pension records.

11. John Foster, service and pension records, National Archives, Washington, D.C.

12 Hardman, service and pension records.

13. Ibid.

14. Ibid., pension records, 1892 and 1893 requests.

15. Ibid.

16. Duncan, pension records.

17. George W. Quinn, service and pension records, National Archives, Washington, D.C.

18. Amick, pension records.

19. George W. Sylvis, service records and pension records, National Archives, Washington, D.C.

20. George W. Sylvis to George W. Anderson Jr., January 1890, Anderson Papers, Georgia Historical Society, Savannah.

21. Saunier, 372.

22. Sylvis, pension records.

23. Grimes.

24. Castle.

25. "McAllister Flag Is Returned Home," *Savannah Evening Press,* 24 January 1936; "Confederate Flag Flies over Fort McAllister after 76 Years," *Savannah Morning News,* 8 December 1940.

26. *Savannah Republican,* 8 July 1864.

27. Ibid.

28. Gamble, "The McAllisters."

29. Wyatt to Henry Ford, 20 July 1925.

30. Ibid.; Myers, 1601.

31. Elijah A. Ellarbee, service records, drawer 23, box 109, item 112, Georgia Department of Archives and History, Atlanta.

32. Brittain Cobb, service records, box 109, drawer 23, Georgia Department of Archives and History, Atlanta.

33. Stoughton Haymans, service records, drawer 23, box 109, Georgia Department of Archives and History, Atlanta.

34. J. C. Proctor, service records, drawer 23, box 109, Georgia Department of Archives and History, Atlanta.

35. Barrows and McRory, 79–80.

36. William Harden, *A History of Savannah and South Georgia* (Chicago and New York: Lewis, 1913), 2:944–45.

37. Gordon.

38. Durham, 242.

39. Ibid., 286–87.

40. Caroline T. Bosbyshell to the author, 13 November 1990.

41. Arthur F. Seagrave to Henry Ford, 8 May 1939, Henry Ford Library, Dearborn, Mich.

42. Ibid.

43. Mills B. Lane, "Ford at Way's, Georgia," *Savannah Morning News Press,* 20 April 1940.

44. R. L. Cooper to Frank Campsall, 22 July 1927 and 30 July 1927, Henry Ford Library, Dearborn, Mich.

45. Lane, "Ford at Way's, Georgia."

46. George Harmony to Henry Ford, 11 July 1930 and 7 August 1930, acc-292, box 30, Henry Ford Library, Dearborn, Mich.

47. Tommy Darieng to the author, interview, 1980; J. R. Gregory to Frank Campsall, 15 April 1940, Henry Ford Library, Dearborn, Mich.

48. "Confederate Flag Flies."

49. "Tribute Paid to Heroic Defenders," *Savannah Morning News,* 4 June 1941.

50. H. R. Waddell to Henry Ford Foundation, 1 May 1946 and 20 July 1946, Henry Ford Library, Dearborn, Mich.; *McGraw-Hill Encyclopedia of World Biography* (New York: McGraw-Hill Book, 1973), 4:152.

51. Williard T. S. Jones to Henry Ford Foundation, 24 August 1948, Henry Ford Library, Dearborn, Mich.; H. R. Waddell to Williard T. S. Jones, 1 September 1948, Henry Ford Library, Dearborn, Mich.

52. Allen P. Julian, "Historic Fort McAllister," *Georgia Magazine,* June–July 1960.

53. Myers, 1027.

Appendix 1. An Analysis of Fort McAllister's Evolution

1. ORA s.1, 6:304.

2. Jones, *Historical Sketch of the Chatham Artillery,* 114.

3. ORN s. 1, 13:161.

4. Hartridge, to his mother, 30 July 1862.

5. ORA s.1, 14:658.

6. Ibid.

7. Durham, 116–17.

8. Barnwell, report of inspection, 27 December 1862.

9. Ibid.

10. Durham, 125.

11. Ibid., 133.

12. ORA s.1, 14:867–70.

13. Jones, *Siege of Savannah,* 139.

Appendix 2. An Analysis of Samuel A. Cooley's Fort McAllister Photographs

1. ORA s.1, 44:717.

2. Ibid., 757–58.

BIBLIOGRAPHY

Manuscripts

Amick, Myron J. Service and pension records. National Archives, Washington, D.C.

Anderson, George W., Jr. "General Outline of the Fall of Fort McAllister." Anderson Papers, Georgia Historical Society, Savannah, Ga.

Ash, John. Diary. Special Collections, Manuscript, Archives and Rare Book Library, Emory University Library, Emory University, Decatur, Ga.

Barnwell, John. Report of Inspection, 27 December 1862. Records group 109, entry 76, box 47, National Archives, Washington, D.C.

Bateman, Charles. Service and pension records. National Archives, Washington, D.C.

Bonaud, Augustus. Service and pension records. Georgia Department of Archives and History, Atlanta, Ga.

Bonner, S. P. To Mrs. Taylor. 15 December 1864. Maj. Thomas Taylor service records, National Archives, Washington, D.C.

Bryan, Henry. Inspection reports, 17 December 1862, 3 January 1863, and 26 March 1863. Records group 109, entry 76, box 34. National Archives, Washington, D.C.

Castle, George E. Service and pension records. National Archives, Washington, D.C.

Clinch, Nicholas. Service records. Microfilm, drawer 254, box 50, Georgia Department of Archives and History, Atlanta, Georgia.

Cobb, Brittain. Service records. Box 109, microfilm, drawer 23, Georgia Department of Archives and History, Atlanta, Ga.

Compton, John. Service and pension records. National Archives, Washington, D.C.

Cooper, R. L. To Frank Campsall. 22 July 1927 and 30 July 1927. Henry Ford Library, Dearborn, Mich.

Davies, Yerby. Letter to *National Tribune,* 20 February 1913.

———. Service and pension records. National Archives, Washington, D.C.

Degman, Charles C. Letter to the *National Tribune,* 20 June 1907.

———. Service and pension records. National Archives, Washington, D.C.

Dixon, William D. Journal. Dixon Papers. Georgia Historical Society, Savannah, Ga.

Drummond, Mary Ann Dixon. "War Memories." 1866. Private collection, Mrs. Charles Youngblood Jr.; photocopy, Alexander Lawrence Papers, Georgia Historical Society, Savannah, Ga.

DuBose, L. Report of inspection, 13 January 1863, Records group 109, entry 76, box 47. National Archives, Washington, D.C.

Duncan, William. Service and pension records. National Archives, Washington, D.C.

Du Pont, Samuel Francis. To his wife, 28 January 1862, 1 March 1863, and 4 March 1863. W9-2797, (W9–2819), (W9–2822), Hagley Museum and Library, Wilmington, Delaware.

———. To James S. Biddle, 25 March 1863. (W9–2836), Hagley Museum and Library, Wilmington, Delaware.

———. To William W. McKean, April 1863, National Archives, Washington, D.C.

Dye, Isaac. Letter transcript. Archives, Fort McAllister State Historic Park, Ga.

Ellarbee, Elijah A. Service records. Item 112, box 109, drawer 23, Georgia Department of Archives and History, Atlanta, Ga.

Emmett Rifles. Muster and payroll records. Collection 169, box 9, folder 48. Georgia Historical Society, Savannah, Ga.

First (Symons) Regiment, Infantry Reserves. Records. Microfilm drawer 254, boxes 94 and 95, Georgia Department of Archives and History, Atlanta, Ga.

Foster, John. Service and pension records. National Archives, Washington, D.C.

Gallie, John B. Service records. Georgia Department of Archives and History, Atlanta, Ga.

———. Report of Inspection, 1 January 1863. Records group 109, entry 76, box 47, National Archives, Washington, D.C.

Gordon, G. Arthur. To Henry Ford, 23 February 1938. Henry Ford Library, Dearborn, Mich.

Grant, Robert. Report of inspection, 28 January 1864. Museum of the Confederacy, Richmond, Va.

Gregory, J. F. To Frank Campsall, 15 April 1940. Henry Ford Library, Dearborn, Mich.

Grimes, Stephen F. Service and pension records. National Archives, Washington, D.C.

Groce, John M. Service records. National Archives, Washington, D.C.

Harden, William Harmon. "The Collected Civil War Correspondence of William Harmon Harden, Corporal, 63rd Infantry Regiment, Georgia Volunteers, C.S.A., January 30, 1845 to August 28, 1895." Collection 462, Manuscript, Archives, and Rare Book Library, Emory University, Decatur, Ga.

———. To his wife, 28 January 1864. William Harmon Harden Papers, Collection 462, Manuscript, Archives, and Rare Book Library, Emory University, Decatur, Georgia.

Hardman, Lyman. Diary and papers. Western Reserve Historical Society, Cleveland, Ohio.

———. Service and pension records. National Archives, Washington, D.C.

Harmony, George W. To Henry Ford, 11 July 1930 and 7 August 1930, acc-292, box 30, Henry Ford Library, Dearborn, Mich.

Harris, D. B. Report of inspection, 26 March 1863. Records group 109, National Archives, Washington, D.C.

Hartridge, Alfred L. Letters 2 July 1861, 25 January 1862, 16 April 1862, 18 June 1862, and 30 July 1862. W. C. Hartridge Collection 1349. Georgia Historical Society, Savannah, Ga.

Haymans, Stoughton. Service records. Drawer 23, box 109, Georgia Department of Archives and History, Atlanta, Ga.

Hendry, George N. Service records. Georgia Department of Archives and History, Atlanta, Ga.

———. To Henry Ford, 11 July 1930 and 7 August 1930. Acc. 292, box 30, Henry Ford Library, Dearborn, Mich.

Horner, James. Service and pension records. National Archives, Washington, D.C.

Ingram, D. P. 25 December 1864. Bentley Historical Library, Ann Arbor, Mich.

Jones, Wells S. Service and pension records. National Archives, Washington, D.C.

Jones, Williard T. S. To Henry Ford Foundation, 24 August 1948. Henry Ford Library, Dearborn, Mich.

Kilbourne, J. B. To the *National Tribune,* 24 May 1883.

King, Julia. To Henry Ford, 3 September 1926. Henry Ford Library, Dearborn, Mich.

Land, Lewis J. Service records. National Archives, Washington, D.C.

LeBey, Andrew. Service records. Georgia Department of Archives and History, Atlanta, Ga.

Leonard, James. Pension records. Georgia Department of Archives and History, Atlanta, Ga.

McCrady, John. To Charles C. Jones Jr., 1 October 1874. Transcript. Archives, Fort McAllister State Historic Park, Ga.

———. To his father, 3 November 1864. Transcript. Archives, Fort McAllister State Historic Park, Ga.

Morse, Mrs. Charles F. (Ellen). To Henry Ford, 17 March 1938. Henry Ford Library, Dearborn, Mich.

Order Book, Fort McAllister. 24 June 1864 to 2 December 1864. Photocopy. Archives, Fort McAllister State Historic Park, Ga.

Phillips, Stephen. Service records. Georgia Department of Archives and History, Atlanta, Ga.

Pierce, Robert. Diary. Item 793, Manuscript Collection, Special Collections, University of Georgia Library, Athens, Ga.

Pittenger, William H. Diary. Vol. 395, Manuscript Collection, Ohio Historical Society, Columbus, Ohio.

Proctor, J. C. Service records. Drawer 23, box 109, Georgia Department of Archives and History, Atlanta, Ga.

Quinn, George W. Service and pension records. National Archives, Washington, D.C.

Republican Blues Daybook. January 1860–June 1866. William Dixon Papers, Georgia Historical Society, Savannah, Ga.

Seagrave, Arthur E. To Henry Ford, 8 May 1939. Henry Ford Library, Dearborn, Mich.

Schirm, William P. Service records. Microfilm, drawer 254, box 50, Georgia Department of Archives and History, Atlanta, Ga.

Smith, Abner B. Service records. National Archives, Washington, D.C.

Smith, Gordon B. "DeKalb Riflemen." Collection 169, box 11, folder 10, Georgia Historical Society, Savannah, Ga.

Stevens, William. Letters, November 1864–January 1865. Stevens Collection, Bentley Historical Library, Ann Arbor, Mich.

Strong, William. Report on Operations of U.S. Army of the Tennessee to General William Tecumseh Sherman, 30 December 1864. Sherman Papers, Library of Congress, Washington, D.C.

Sylvis, George W. Service and pension records. National Archives, Washington, D.C.

———. To George W. Anderson Jr., January 1890. Anderson Papers, Georgia Historical Society, Savannah, Ga.

Symons, William R. Service records. Georgia Department of Archives and History, Atlanta, Ga.

Taylor, Thomas T. Diary and letters. Taylor Papers, Ohio Historical Society, Columbus, Ohio.

———. Service and pension records. National Archives, Washington, D.C.

USS *Dandelion.* Logbook. National Archives, Washington, D.C.

USS *Dawn.* Logbook. National Archives, Washington, D.C.

USS *Fernandina.* Logbook. National Archives, Washington, D.C.

USS *Flag.* Logbook. National Archives, Washington, D.C.

USS *Montauk.* Logbook. National Archives, Washington, D.C.

USS *Potomska.* Logbook. National Archives, Washington, D.C.

USS *Seneca.* Logbook. National Archives, Washington, D.C.

USS *Sonoma.* Logbook. National Archives, Washington, D.C.

USS *Winona.* Logbook. National Archives, Washington, D.C.

USS *Wissahickon.* Logbook. National Archives, Washington, D.C.

Waddell, H. R. To Henry Ford Foundation, 1 May 1946 and 20 July 1946, Henry Ford Library, Dearborn, Mich.

———. To Williard T. S. Jones, 1 September 1948. Henry Ford Library, Dearborn, Mich.

Ward, Williamson D. Diary. 21 December entry. Indiana Society Library, Indianapolis, Ind.

Warnell, Mrs. W. F. (Ada). To Henry Ford, 13 December 1939. Henry Ford Library, Dearborn, Mich.

———. To J. F. Gregory, 13 December 1939. Henry Ford Library, Dearborn, Mich.

Watmough, Pendleton G. Service and pension records. National Archives, Washington, D.C.

Williams, James S. Report of Inspection, 18 February 1864. Records group 109, item F-76. National Archives, Washington, D.C.

Wyatt, Edward W. To Henry Ford, 5 May 1925, 20 July 1925, and 31 August 1925. Henry Ford Library, Dearborn, Mich.

Books and Articles

Agnew, J. L., and F. D. Lee. *Historical Record of the City of Savannah.* Savannah, Ga.: Estill, 1869.

Ammen, Daniel. "The Atlantic Coast." *In the Navies in the Civil War.* Vol. 2. New York: Scribner's Sons, 1883.

———. "The Civil War Story of Fort McAllister." *Savannah Morning News,* 18 February 1924.

———. "Confederate Flag Flies over Fort McAllister after 76 Years." *Savannah Morning News,* 8 December 1940.

———. "Du Pont and the Port Royal Expedition." In *Battles and Leaders of the Civil War.* Vol. 1. Reprint, New York: Thomas Yoseloff, 1956. 671–90.

———. "Heroic, Inspiring Is the Story of Fort McAllister." *Savannah Evening Press,* 19 February 1938.

————. "McAllister Flag Is Returned Home." *Savannah Evening Press,* 24 January 1936.

————. "Meet June 3 at Fort M'Allister." *Savannah Morning News,* 1 June 1941.

————. "Tells Valiant Story of Fort." *Savannah Evening Press,* 4 June 1941.

————. "Tribute Paid to Heroic Defenders." *Savannah Morning News,* 4 June 1941.

Barrow, David C. "Says M'Allister Never Surrendered." *Savannah Daily News,* 15 November 1929.

Barrows, Edith Clarke, and Mary Oakley McRory. *History of Jefferson County, Florida.* Monticello, Fla.: Kiwanis Club, 1935.

Browne, Samuel T. *First Cruise of the Montauk.* Providence, R.I.: Bangs William, 1880.

Butler, Frank B. "A Cruise along the Blockade." *Soldier and Sailor Historical Society of Rhode Island Personal Narrative of Events in the War of the Rebellion.* Vol. 12, 2nd series, Providence, R.I.: Bangs William, 1881.

Carse, Robert. *Hilton Head Island in the Civil War.* Columbia, S.C.: State Printing, 1961.

Castel, Albert. *Tom Taylor's Civil War.* Lawrence: University Press of Kansas, 2000.

Chance, Frank, Paul Chance, and David Topper. *Tangled Machinery and Charred Relics.* Orangeburg, S.C.: Sun Printing, 1985.

Coggins, Jack. *Arms and Equipment of the Civil War.* Garden City, N.Y.: Doubleday, 1962.

Colquit, Adrian B. "Georgia's Thermopylae." *Savannah Morning News,* 20 April 1930.

Cooke, R. Jervis. *Sand and Grit: The Story of Fort McAllister: A Confederate Earthwork on the Great Ogeechee River, Genesis Point.* Washington, D.C.: U.S. Department of the Interior, National Park Service, 1938.

Cox, J. D. "The March to the Sea: Franklin and Nashville." *Campaigns of the Civil War.* Vol. 10. New York: Scribner's Sons, 1886.

Davies, Yerby. Letter to *National Tribune,* 20 February 1913. Microfilm copies available from University of Toledo Library, Toledo, Ohio.

Davis, William C. *The Image of War.* Vol. 2. Garden City, N.Y.: Doubleday, 1982.

Degman, Charles. Letter. *National Tribune,* 20 June 1907.

Donald, David Herbert, ed. *Gone for a Soldier, the Civil War Memoirs of Private Alfred Bellard.* Boston: Little, Brown, 1975.

Durham, Roger S. *The Blues in Gray: The Civil War Journal of William Daniel Dixon and the Republican Blues Daybook.* Knoxville: University of Tennessee Press, 2000.

Epps, Robert. "Born to Lose." *Savannah Morning Press, Sunday Magazine,* 11 January 1959.

Ericsson, John. "The Early Monitors." In *Battles and Leaders of the Civil War,* 30–31. Vol. 4. Reprint, New York: Thomas Yoseloff, 1956.

Gamble, Thomas. *The Gamble Collection.* Scrapbook Collection, Savannah Public Library, Savannah, Ga. One book on Fort McAllister and one on the McAllister Family.

————. "The McAllisters, Leaders in Three Great States." *Savannah Morning News,* 5 October 1930.

Genealogical Committee. *The 1860 Census of Chatham County Georgia.* Easley, S.C.: Southern Historical Press, 1979.

Genealogies of Old Philadelphia Families, vol. 3. N.p.: North American Publishing, 1909.

Gibson, John M. *Those 163 Days.* New York: Coward-McCann, 1961.

Gillmore, Quincy A. "Siege and Capture of Fort Pulaski." In *Battles and Leaders of the Civil War,* 1–12. Vol. 2. Reprint, New York: Thomas Yoseloff, 1956.

Glatthaar, Joseph T. *The March to the Sea and Beyond.* New York: New York University Press, 1986.

Greene, S. Dana. "In the 'Monitor' Turret." In *Battles and Leaders of the Civil War,* 719–20. Reprint, New York: Thomas Yoseloff, 1956.

Harden, William. *A History of Savannah and South Georgia.* Vol. 2. Chicago and New York: Lewis, 1913.

———. *Recollections of a Long and Satisfactory Life.* Savannah, Ga., 1934.

———. "Recollections of a Private in the Signal Corps, January 1863–April 1865." Address, Confederate Veterans Association, Confederate Veterans Association of Savannah, Georgia Historical Society, Savannah, Georgia, 3 November 1896.

Hayes, John D., ed. *Samuel Francis Du Pont, a Selection from His Civil War Letters.* 3 vols. Ithaca, N.Y.: Cornell University Press, 1969.

Hazen, William B. "General Hazen's Memoirs." *National Tribune,* 29 October 1914.

Henderson, Lillian, ed. *Roster of Confederate Soldiers of Georgia.* 6 vols. Hapeville, Ga.: Longino and Porter, 1955–58.

Hermann, Isaac. *Memoirs of a Veteran.* Atlanta: Byrd Printing, 1911.

Hill, Jim Dan, ed. *The Civil War Sketchbook of Charles Ellery Stedman, Surgeon, United States Navy.* San Rafael, Calif.: Presidio, 1976.

Hitchcock, Henry. *Marching to the Sea with Sherman.* New Haven, Conn.: Yale University Press, 1927.

Horner, J. S. Letter to the editor. *National Tribune,* 11 July 1907.

Howard, Oliver O. "General Howard's Memoirs." *National Tribune,* 30 January 1896.

Hughes, N. C., Jr. "Sherman at Savannah." *Georgia Historical Quarterly* 47 (March 1963): 43–63.

Jones, Charles C., Jr. "Chickamauga Address." *Speeches Given to Confederate Survivors Association, April 1866, 1888, 1890, 1896.* Savannah: Georgia Historical Society, 1900, 10–15.

———. *Historical Sketch of the Chatham Artillery during the Confederate Struggle for Independence.* Albany, N.Y.: Joel Munsell, 1867.

———. *The Siege of Savannah in December 1864 and the Confederate Operations in Georgia and the Third Military District of South Carolina during General Sherman's March from Atlanta to the Sea.* Albany, N.Y.: Joel Munsell, 1874.

Julian, Allen P. "Historic Fort McAllister." *Georgia Magazine,* June–July 1960.

Lane, Mills B. "Ford at Way's, Georgia." *Savannah Morning News,* 20 April 1940.

———. *War Is Hell.* Savannah, Ga.: Beehive, 1974.

Lattimore, Ralston B. *Fort Pulaski National Monument, Georgia.* Washington, D.C.: GPO, 1954.

Lawrence, Alexander A. *A Present for Mr. Lincoln. The Story of Savannah from Secession to Sherman.* Macon, Ga.: Ardivan, 1961.

———. *Storm over Savannah.* Athens: University of Georgia Press, 1951.

Lewis, Lloyd. *Sherman—Fighting Prophet.* New York: Harcourt, Brace, 1932.

Long, E. B. *The Civil War Day by Day, An Almanac 1861–1865.* Garden City, N.Y.: Doubleday, 1971.

McGraw-Hill Encyclopedia of World Biography. Vol. 4. New York: McGraw-Hill Book, 1973.

Monroe, Haskell. "Men without Law: Federal Raiding in Liberty County, Georgia." *Georgia Historical Quarterly* 44 ():154–71.

Myers, Robert Manson. *The Children of Pride.* New Haven, Conn.: Yale University Press, 1972.

Nichols, George Ward. *The Story of the Great March: From the Diary of a Staff Officer.* New York: Harper & Brothers, 1866.

Official Records of the Union and Confederate Armies in the War of the Rebellion. Washington, D.C.: GPO, 1893.

Official Records of the Union and Confederate Navies in the War of the Rebellion. Washington, D.C.: GPO, 1897.

Osbon, Bradley S. *Harpers Weekly,* 2 March 1863 and 28 March 1863.

―――. *New York Herald,* 13 February 1863, 28 March 1863.

Pepper, George W. *Personal Recollections of Sherman's Campaign in Georgia and the Carolinas.* Zanesville, Ohio: Hugh Dunn, 1866.

Perry, Milton F. *Infernal Machines.* Baton Rouge: University of Louisiana Press, 1965.

Ripley, Warren. *Artillery and Ammunition of the Civil War.* New York: Van Nostrand Reinhold, 1970.

Robinson, William Morrison. *The Confederate Privateers.* New Haven, Conn.: Yale University Press, 1928.

Rodgers, C. R. P. "Du Pont's Attack on Charleston." In *Battles and Leaders of the Civil War,* 32–47. Vol. 4. Reprint, New York: Thomas Yoseloff, 1956.

Saunier, Joseph A. *History of the 47th Ohio Volunteer Infantry.* Hillsboro, Ohio: Press of the Lyle Printing, 1903.

Scaife, William R. *The March to the Sea.* Atlanta, Ga.: Washington Printing, 1989.

Sheftall, John M. *Sunbury on the Medway.* Atlanta: Georgia Department of Natural Resources, 1971.

Sherman, William T. *Memoirs of General William T. Sherman, Written by Himself.* 2 vols. New York: Scribner's Sons, 1875.

―――. *Official Account of His Great March through Georgia and the Carolinas.* New York: Bunce and Huntington, 1865.

Soley, James R. "Minor Operations of the South Atlantic Squadron under Du Pont." In *Battles and Leaders of the Civil War,* 27–30. Vol. 4. Reprint, New York: Thomas Yoseloff, 1956.

Sterns, Philip Van Doren. *The Confederate Navy, a Pictorial History.* Garden City, N.Y.: Doubleday, 1962.

―――. *The Story of the 55th Regiment Illinois Volunteer Infantry in the Civil War.* Clinton, Mass.: Coulter, 1887.

Swiggart, Carolyn Clay. *Shades of Gray.* Darien, Conn.: Two Bytes, 1999.

Waage, Charles W. "Ossabaw Island, Ga. A Chapter from the Experiences of the 47th N.Y." *National Tribune,* 25 July 1907.

Will, Charles G. "Captain John Groce." Private collection, Karl R. Eby.

Wyant, W. K. "Fort McAllister's Defense among Bravest of All Wars." *Savannah Morning News,* 29 November 1937.

INDEX

ABOUT THE AUTHOR

ROGER S. DURHAM is the director of the U.S. Army Heritage Museum in Carlisle Barracks, Pennsylvania. Durham is a graduate of the University of Wisconsin and Georgia Southern University. His other books include *High Seas and Yankee Gunboats: A Blockade-Running Adventure from the Diary of James Dickson* and *Fort McAllister.*